POJO'S UNOFFICIAL

BIG BOOK of Pokémon®

INCLUDES POKÉMON GO!

20TH ANNIVERSARY SPECIAL EDITION

Angel Pelaez

Bob Baker & Jigglypuff, 2000

Jason Klaczynski, 2013

Andrew "aroramage" Cornell

Scott Gerhardt

Amy & Anna Gill, 1999

Bill Gill, a.k.a "Pojo", 2005

CREDITS

This book is not authorized, sponsored, endorsed, or licensed by Nintendo of America Inc. The trademarks POKéMON, POKéMON GO, and GOTTA CATCH 'EM ALL are owned by Nintendo of America Inc. and other company names and/or trademarks mentioned in this book are the property of their respective companies and are used for identification purposes only.

Editor in Chief: Bill Gill, a.k.a "Pojo"

Creative Director & Graphic Designer: Phil Deppen

Graphic Designer: Jake Ziech

Publishing Director: Bob Baker

Writers: Bob Baker, Anna Gill, Joseph "Otaku" Lee, Andrew Cornell, Jason Klaczynski, Angel Pelaez, Scott Gerhardt

Cover Deign: Preston Pisellini

From Pojo

Something for Everybody!

The Pokémon Franchise has something for everybody. What started as a video game for Nintendo's Game Boy back in 1996 has evolved like a Pokémon into so much more.

We put together our first *Big Book of Pokémon* with Triumph Books way back in February of 2000. That book covered only four years of Pokémon history, and we filled its 336 pages to the brim! We loaded it up with information on Video Games, the Trading Card Game, Toys and Anime.

Since then, the Busy Beedrills at Pojo.com have continued to bring you a wealth of Pokémon knowledge for 16 more years, and we're still going.

Now we're back working with Triumph Books on another *Big Book of Pokémon*. Only now we have 20 years of Pokémon History to work with. Where does one start? We could easily fill a 26 Volume Encyclopedia Set with Pokémon information to share with you. We knew we had to try to cover Pokémon History, Pokémon Video Games, the Pokémon Trading Card Game, the Pokémon Anime, and even Pokémon Go! We've done our best to focus on only the important things.

First, we kick things off with a Pokémon Timeline. It's a fantastic walk down Memory Lane. We tried to show you every single thing that happened in the Pokémon History over the last 20 years.

We cover Video Games - We have a detailed look at what we think are the 10 Best Pokémon Video Games of all-time. Then we also have a Top 10 List of the very best Pokémon for the Pokémon RPG's. We rank the Top 10 Pokémon by Type (fire, water, etc). That's a review of 180 different Pokémon right there!

We cover the Trading Card Games - We review the Top 100 Pokémon Cards every printed. There are over 9,000 English Pokémon cards in print. We narrow things down to the Best 100. We also break down the Top 5 Pokémon Cards

from every expansion. There are 69 expansions, so that's another whopping 345 Pokémon Cards reviewed for you. And we don't stop there. We rank the Top 25 Most Valuable English Pokémon Cards. And we also have a few pages on Pokémon Jargon, so you know how to talk Pokémon!

We cover the Anime – The Anime has been going strong for 19 years! There have been hundreds and hundreds of recurring characters on the show. So we put together an Alphabetical Reference of every human character that has appeared two or more times over 19 Seasons of Pokémon.

And we Cover Pokémon Go! – Pokémon Go has been sweeping the globe, and we have 20 Tips & Tricks to help you understand the game and become a Pokémaster!

We crammed a lot into this book, and we recruited many experts in the Pokémon field to write for you, so this book rocks like Tyranitar!

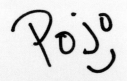

Our first BIG BOOK!

P.S. Feel free to contact us at www.pojo.com if you have questions or want to share something with us.

CONTENTS

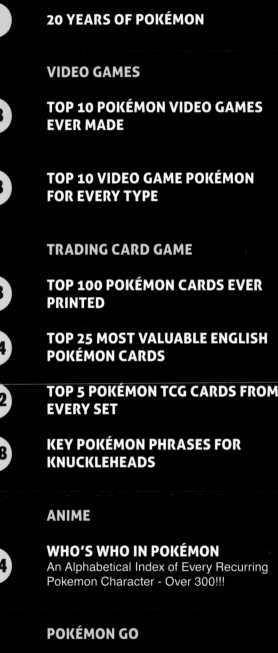

TIMELINE

8   **20 YEARS OF POKÉMON**

VIDEO GAMES

48   **TOP 10 POKÉMON VIDEO GAMES EVER MADE**

68   **TOP 10 VIDEO GAME POKÉMON FOR EVERY TYPE**

TRADING CARD GAME

88   **TOP 100 POKÉMON CARDS EVER PRINTED**

114   **TOP 25 MOST VALUABLE ENGLISH POKÉMON CARDS**

122   **TOP 5 POKÉMON TCG CARDS FROM EVERY SET**

158   **KEY POKÉMON PHRASES FOR KNUCKLEHEADS**

ANIME

164   **WHO'S WHO IN POKÉMON**
An Alphabetical Index of Every Recurring Pokemon Character - Over 300!!!

POKÉMON GO

188   **20 TIPS & TRICKS FOR GO FANATICS!**

20 YEARS OF

FEBRUARY, 1996
POCKET MONSTERS RED & GREEN IN JAPAN

In February 1996, the Pocket Monsters Red & Green video games were released in Japan. They introduced the concept of collecting, trading and battling with Pocket Monsters. Thousands of people lined up in Japan to buy the games, which instantly sold out. These games eventually sold more than 10 million copies in Japan. Pokémon Blue was released in the summer of 1996 and that game was mail-order only. The games appear to be simple children's games, but they are actually very deep Role-Playing Games (RPG's). The games feature a ton of strategy and a dynamic storyline.

1996

OCTOBER 1996
POKÉMON TCG DEBUTS IN JAPAN

Eight months later, thanks to the success of the Game Boy games, the Pocket Monsters Trading Card Game (TCG) was released. The Pocket Monsters TCG turned into a craze in Japan. TCGs were still a relatively new phenomenon in the world. Magic the Gathering debuted in 1993 and was easily the most popular TCG at the time. Magic the Gathering had a pretty strong teenager/young adult following. But common folk didn't even know that TCGs existed. Pocket Monsters / Pokemon really changed that.

The Japanese "Pocket Monsters" franchise name was changed to "Pokémon" in the United States due to copyright/trademark laws. There was already a media franchise in the U.S. named "Monsters in My Pocket".

POKéMON

BY BILL "POJO" GILL

Pojo breaks out the Wayback Machine and has a look back at the most important releases in Pokémon history over the last 20 years.

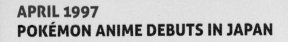

1997

APRIL 1997
POKéMON ANIME DEBUTS IN JAPAN

There have been many successful anime over the years, including: Dragon Ball Z; Naruto; Fullmetal Alchemist; Attack on Titan; Inuyasha; Yu Yu Hakusho; Yu-Gi-Oh!; Sailor Moon; and even Speed Racer! Pokémon is right up there with the most successful of all time. At the time we wrote this book, Pokémon was entering its 19th Season, and there are no signs of Pokémon slowing down.

The series follows the adventures of Satoshi and his Pocket Monsters. In North America, Satoshi is called Ash Ketchum, and Pocket Monsters are called Pokémon.

There have been over 900 episodes, 19 movies and dozens of TV specials based on the original game series.

The writers try to tie the anime in with the video games as much as possible. Ash will visit new Pokémon Regions (countries) at about the same time they are introduced in the new video games. The stories progress very much like a soap opera, with each episode building off previous episodes.

20 YEARS OF POKéMON

JULY 18, 1998
POCKET MONSTERS MOVIE – MEWTWO STRIKES BACK DEBUTS IN JAPAN

This first Pokemon movie introduces Mew and Mewtwo in the Anime franchise for the first time. All movies in Japan get a theatrical release. Only a few of the films were released into theaters in the U.S., most debut on cable television or go directly to DVD.

1998

SEPTEMBER 5, 1998
POKéMON ANIME DEBUTS IN NORTH AMERICA

North America is introduced to Ash Ketchum and Pikachu for the first time. The show essentially takes the base plot of the video games and converts it into 83 half-hour episodes. The first season sees Ash getting Pikachu, befriending Brock and Misty and defeating the Eight Gym Leaders from the Indigo League. Team Rocket (Jesse, James and Meowth) are introduced as evildoers who Ash has to contend with for many years to come.

SEPTEMBER 28, 1998
POKÉMON RED AND POKÉMON BLUE

The Pokémon Red and Blue Role Playing Games (RPGs) were released simultaneously in North America. These are essentially the English remakes of the Pokémon Red and Green video that were released in Japan in 1996. You are a trainer trying to catch the variety of pocket monsters (Pokémon) that appear in the game. Once caught, Pokémon can be added to your party and trained to assist you. The longer you train Pokémon, the more attacks they learn, and the stronger they become. There are a total of 150 Pokémon to catch, but only 139 are available on Red, and 139 are available on Blue. In order to "Catch 'Em All" you need to use a Game Link Cable and exchange captured Pokémon with friends. Traded Pokémon actually level up faster, so it's beneficial to trade your Pokémon.

These games have sold more than 11 million copies in the U.S., and more than 31 million copies worldwide. New, factory-sealed, unopened boxes of these games currently sell for over $400 on eBay.

NOVEMBER, 1998
POKÉMON PIKACHU

The Pokémon Pikachu was also known as The Pocket Pikachu. It was an upscale step counter! Pocket Pikachu was a digital virtual pet that you kept on your belt or in your pocket.

20 YEARS OF POKÉMON

JUNE 16, 1999
JUNGLE

The 2nd Pokémon TCG expansion is released. Introduced strong cards like Scyther, Mr. Mime and Wigglytuff.

JANUARY, 1999
POKÉMON TCG DEBUTS IN NORTH AMERICA

The Pokémon Trading Card Game hit North America in January and it took the U.S. by storm! Many kids simply collected the cards like baseball cards because they liked the video games or loved the anime. But soon, people realized that a beautifully designed beast of a game lived inside. The game is still going strong 20 years later. There have been over 70 expansions since the first base set.

JUNE 30, 1999
POKÉMON SNAP

The premise of this game is that you roll through various Pokémon environments in a cart on a track, and take photographs of Pokémon for Professor Oak. We know it sounds lame, but this game is a ton of fun and extremely addictive.

1999

JUNE 28, 1999
POKÉMON PINBALL

Pokémon Pinball is a Pokémon based Pinball game. Besides playing a typical pinball game, another goal is to "Catch 'em All". The original 150 Pokémon are available for capture during gameplay. This was one of the first games available for the new Game Boy Color at the time.

APRIL 26, 1999
SUPER SMASH BROS.

One of the best fighting games for the N64. The game features Pikachu and Jigglypuff as playable characters. New, sealed, unopened boxes of SSB games currently sell for over $300 on eBay.

SEPTEMBER 1999
POKÉMON ANIME SEASON 2

Adventures on the Orange Islands – 36 episodes. Professor Oak sends Ash to Valencia Island to help Professor Ivy. Ash meets and travels with Tracey Sketchit. Ash gathers badges to qualify for the Orange League Tournament.

OCTOBER 1, 1999
POKÉMON YELLOW

Pokémon Yellow was inspired by the anime. It is essentially an updated version of the original Red & Blue games, with a few more fun changes. You are forced to take Pikachu as your starting Pokémon. Pikachu follows you around on your adventure outside of his Poké Ball, just like in the anime. Jesse and James also appear in this version.

NOVEMBER 1999
ELECTRONIC I CHOOSE
YOU PIKACHU PLUSH

Many popular Pokémon Plush have been available for the last 20 years. This is one of the more memorable ones. Pikachu is about 10 inches tall. He moves, lights up and talks when you squeeze his paws. This guy can currently fetch up to $100 on eBay in a new, unopened box.

NOVEMBER 8, 1999
BURGER KING PROMOTIONAL TOYS

These Pokémon Toys came with Kids Meals in late 1999. I'm guessing a lot of kids got stuffed on BK Chicken Tenders for two months because these toys were a hot item! McDonalds has also carried Pokémon Toys and cards inside of Happy Meals. But this BK promotion was the first.

OCTOBER 10, 1999
POKÉMON FOSSIL

This is the 3rd Pokémon TCG expansion. Introduced strong cards like Ditto, Muk, Magmar and Articuno.

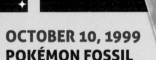

1999
POKÉMON MASTER TRAINER
BOARD GAME

This was the first of many board games based on the Pokémon theme. It was produced by Milton Bradly and Hasbro. The object of the game is capture Pokémon in the Kanto region. Unopened boxes of this game can currently fetch over $125 on eBay. Even open boxes can sell for almost $100! **Collector Tip:** Keep your eyes open for Pokémon Monopoly from 1999 as well, especially the one with Pewter Pokémon Movers.

NOVEMBER 10, 1999
POKÉMON THE FIRST MOVIE

The First Pokémon is released in the United States. The movie was an instant commercial success, debuting at number one on the U.S. box office charts and making $10,096,848 on its Wednesday opening day. It held the record for being the animated feature with the highest-grossing weekend in November. Worldwide, the film made $163,644,662, making it the highest-grossing anime film in the United States and the fourth highest-grossing animated film based on a television show worldwide. It was also the highest-grossing film based on a video game at the time.

20 YEARS OF POKéMON

FEBRUARY 24, 2000
BASE SET 2 TCG

This set had no new cards. The popularity of Pokémon made old cards tough to obtain. Wizards of the Coast made this set so older cards were easier to collect.

APRIL 10, 2000
POKéMON TRADING CARD GAME FOR GAME BOY COLOR

This is a video game adaption of the Pokémon TCG. The game features cards from Base Set, Jungle and Fossil. In the game you play a young boy who must travel around the game world interacting with other characters and challenging them to TCG duels. As you defeat other players, you win more cards that can help make your deck even better. It is an excellent adaption of the TCG.

JULY 21, 2000
POKéMON THE MOVIE 2000

The Legendary Pokémon Lugia makes its first appearance. This second Pokemon film made over $130 million dollars at the box office. The film also features the Lengedary Birds – Articuno, Moltres and Zapdos.

2000

APRIL 24, 2000
TEAM ROCKET TCG

This is the first set to include Dark Pokémon, with Dark Raichu as the first-ever secret card.

AUGUST 14, 2000
GYM HEROES TCG

This set first introduced Gym Leader's Pokémon and Stadium cards.

FEBRUARY 29, 2000
POKéMON STADIUM

Players are treated to Pokémon in 3D. There really is no RPG element to this game. The main catch here is that the game allows players to transfer their Red/Blue/Yellow Pokemon into the N64 Stadium using a Game Boy Transfer Pak. Once you've done that, you enter tournaments in Pokémon Stadium. The graphics are pretty good.

SEPTEMBER 25, 2000
POKéMON PUZZLE LEAGUE

Pokémon Puzzle League is a puzzle game that falls into the Tetris-Bejeweled genres. Blocks of various colors rise from the floor, and your task is to get rid of them. The Pokémon aspect to the game is merely thematic. The game is fun and addicting, but it's not really a Pokémon Game in our opinion.

OCTOBER 14, 2000
POKÉMON SEASON 3

The Johto Journeys — 41 episodes. Ash and his friends venture into the Johto region. Ash discovers many new Pokémon from the Gold & Silver Generation. Ash battles the first four leaders of the Johto League.

NOVEMBER 2000
HEY YOU, PIKACHU!

The game package includes the game cartridge, a Voice Recognition Unit and a Microphone. This was a very early attempt by Nintendo to include Voice Recognition into a game. You try to talk Pikachu through daily tasks, but most of the time he seems to ignore and do whatever he wants.

OCTOBER 16, 2000
POCKET PIKACHU COLOR

This one communicates with Pokémon Gold, Silver, and Crystal using the Mystery Gift function. The user can send watts accumulated by walking, which are then converted into items. Unlike the original Pokémon Pikachu, the user does not have to nurture Pikachu.

OCTOBER 16, 2000
GYM CHALLENGE TCG

The second part of the Gym Sets. Brought us cards for Koga and Giovanni.

DECEMBER 16, 2000
NEO GENESIS TCG

This expansion features Pokémon from the Johto region for the first time. Also introduced are Baby Pokémon and two new types: Darkness and Metal.

OCTOBER 2000
POKÉMON GOLD & SILVER

Pokémon Gold and Pokémon Silver leads players into the Johto region for the first time. These are the first sequels to Red & Blue and introduce Generation II Pokémon. A total of 100 new Pokémon were introduced into the Pokémon World here. The games also mark the introduction of two new types of Pokémon: Dark type and Steel type. New, factory-sealed, unopened boxes of these games sell for about $200 on eBay

DECEMBER 2000
POKÉMON PUZZLE CHALLENGE

This is essentially a re-release of the N64 Pokémon Puzzle League game, but on the Game Boy Color. Pokémon Puzzle Challenge is a puzzle game that falls into the Tetris-Bejeweled genres. Blocks of various colors rise from the floor, and your task is get rid of them.

20 YEARS OF POKÉMON

MARCH 28, 2001
POKÉMON STADIUM 2

This game is essentially a re-release of Pokémon Stadium, except now you can input your Gold & Silver Pokémon using your Transfer Pak. This game is for the Pokémon enthusiast who enjoys the battling aspect of the Pokémon Gold & Silver games, and wants more dueling action. Combat hasn't really changed from Stadium 1. The graphics are again great, and now you can play with 250 Pokémon instead of 150. There are also a few mini games inside for when battling gets a bit boring.

JUNE 1, 2001
NEO DISCOVERY TCG

Brought us powerful cards like Tyrogue and Unown C.

2001

APRIL 6, 2001
POKÉMON 3: THE MOVIE – SPELL OF UNOWN

This was the first Pokémon film to premiere in an IMAX theater. This film made over $68 million at the box office. The movie features the legendary Pokémon Entei.

JULY 29, 2001
POKÉMON CRYSTAL

Pokémon Crystal is a follow-up, sister-type game to the successful Gold & Silver Games with some enhancements. For the first time in a Pokémon game, you can play as a female character! Also, Suicine appears in various areas of the Johto region.

AUGUST 18, 2001
POKÉMON SEASON 4

Johto League Champions – 52 episodes. Ash continues his adventures in the Johto Region with Misty and Brock and further progresses with battling all the gym leaders in the Johto League. The gang runs into old friends such as Pokémon photographer Todd Snap, performing Pokémon trainer Duplica, and Pokémon breeder and beautician Suzie. They also run into baseball loving Casey again.

SEPTEMBER 21, 2001
NEO REVELATION TCG

Shining Pokémon make their debut, but these were mostly for collectors.

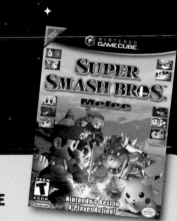

DECEMBER 2, 2001
SUPER SMASH BROS. MELEE

This was the first game on the new GameCube system to feature Pokémon, and man did folks love this game! IGN readers chose this as the 2001 Game of the Year. We believe this is the best-selling GameCube Game of all-time. The game features all the characters from the N64 SSB and adds many more. There are 25 playable characters. Mewtwo and Pichu were added as playable Pokémon in addition to Jigglypuff and Pikachu. New, unopened copies of this game can fetch over $200 on eBay.

FEBRUARY 28, 2002
NEO DESTINY TCG

Dark Pokémon return bringing in strong cards like Dark Gengar and Dark Tyranitar.

2002

MAY 24, 2002
LEGENDARY COLLECTION TCG

The 2nd reprint set. Includes strong cards from Base Set, Jungle, Fossil and Team Rocket.

SEPTEMBER 14, 2005
POKÉMON SEASON 5

Master Quest — 65 episodes.
Ash heads to the Whirl Islands and enters the Whirlpool cup. Ash battles Misty in the semi-finals. Ash then heads back to Olivine City to battle Claire and Jasmine to finish up his Johto League badges.

OCTOBER 11, 2002
POKÉMON 4EVER
– CELEBI: VOICE OF THE FOREST

This fourth Pokémon movie is the last to receive a theatrical release in the United States. All the Pokémon movies in Japan still receive a theatrical release. The film features time travel and the legendary Pokémon Celebi.

SEPTEMBER 15, 2002
EXPEDITION BASE SET TCG

The set began the e-Card series where cards had a dot code that the Nintendo e-Reader could scan for lore, minigames, and the like. Packs went down to nine cards but now holo-rares would replace a common and not the normal rare.

20 YEARS OF POKÉMON

MAY 12, 2003
SKYRIDGE TCG

This was the final set released by Wizards of the Coast (WOTC) as Nintendo took back their license.

JANUARY 15, 2003
AQUAPOLIS TCG

Crystal Pokémon make their debut, but these again were mostly for collectors.

MAY 16, 2003
POKÉMON HEROES: LATIOS AND LATIAS

This is the 5th Pokémon Movie. Pokémon Heroes focuses on Ash, Misty and Brock, traveling to Alto Mare, a city like Venice, Italy. There they must work with the Legendary Pokémon Latios and Latias to save the city and the world.

2003

MARCH 19, 2003
POKÉMON RUBY AND POKÉMON SAPPHIRE

Pokémon Ruby and Sapphire are the third installments of the Pokémon series of RPGs. Fans waited patiently for 2-1/2 years for brand new Pokémon RPG adventures, with gameplay similar to Red & Blue. Ruby and Sapphire introduced over 135 new Pokémon and brought us what are considered "Generation III" Pokémon. Ruby and Sapphire leads players into the Hoeen region and were the first Pokémon Games for the brand new Game Boy Advance (GBA). The GBA brought a larger screen, more pixels, and 32-bit power to the Nintendo's handheld lineup. So playing Pokémon on this portable system was more beautiful than before. We believe these were the bestselling games of all time for the GBA.

JUNE 18, 2003
EX RUBY & SAPPHIRE TCG

This was the first set released by Nintendo, not WOTC. The set introduced Generation III Pokémon into the TCG. This set also introduced EX Pokémon into the TCG for the first time.

AUGUST 25, 2003
POKÉMON PINBALL: RUBY AND SAPPHIRE

This is a sequel to Pokémon Pinball for the Game Boy Color. This is actually better than a makeover of the original Pokémon Pinball, and most players and reviewers loved this game. The pinball tables have nice layouts. There are over 200 Pokémon to catch during game play. And there are bonus stages to catch the rarer Pokémon.

SEPTEMBER 17, 2003
EX SANDSTORM TCG

This set brought in better EX cards, including Gardevoir EX.

DECEMBER 1, 2003
POKÉMON CHANNEL

This is a simple game along the lines of *Hey You, Pikachu!* This is technically geared for young children. You basically help Professor Oak by watching a new TV Channel – you guessed it – The Pokémon Channel. The entire storyline is based on watching TV with Pikachu. The game is basically a bunch of little distractions that will keep kids busy for a while.

NOVEMBER 1, 2003
POKÉMON SEASON 6

Advanced — 40 episodes. Ash and friends head into the Hoenn Region for the first time. Ash gains new companions in May, a new Pokémon trainer who is just beginning her journey, and her brother, Max. May and Max are the children of the Petalburg City Gym Leader, Norman. Ash's old friend Brock eventually catches up with Ash again to rejoin the group as well. Ash earns 3 badges, and may decides to become a Pokémon Coordinator.

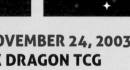

NOVEMBER 24, 2003
EX DRAGON TCG

This set brought us some Dragon Type Pokémon for the first time. Here they are all colorless Pokémon. Dragons become an Official Type in the TCG in 2012 with B&W Dragon's Exalted.

20 YEARS OF POKÉMON

MARCH 15, 2004
EX TEAM MAGMA VS TEAM AQUA TCG

It is the first expansion to feature dual-type Pokémon. In addition to the usual Type for the Pokémon, they were also Darkness. Many cards in this set fueled the 2004 World Championship Deck.

JUNE 1, 2004
POKÉMON: JIRACHI WISH MAKER

The sixth Pokémon movie debuts on DVD. The movie features Ash, Brock, Max and May. The movie also features Team Magma as the evil-doers, and the Legendary Pokémon Jirachi and Groudon.

JUNE 14, 2004
EX HIDDEN LEGENDS TCG

This set gave us strong cards like Ancient Technical Machine (Rock) and Steven's Advice.

2004

MARCH 22, 2004
POKÉMON COLOSSEUM

Pokémon Colosseum is essentially an upgrade of the Pokémon Stadium Games for Generation III Pokémon. Unlike the previous Stadium games, the game actually features a story mode. There is more here to do than simply battle. The story is kind of lame, but it's better than the non-story you got in the Stadium Games. The RPG aspect only gives you a dozen or so hours of gameplay, but you can battle endlessly with your Stadium team. The battles and Pokémon look great here.

JULY 11, 2004
POKÉMON BOX

This is not a game. This is an organizer for the Pokémon you've caught while playing Ruby & Sapphire (and later Fire Red and Leaf Green … See next review). This is targeted at diehard Pokémon Fans. It was only $20 and it included a memory card, GameCube Disc and a GBA cable. All in all, not bad at the time.

SEPTEMBER 9, 2004
POKÉMON FIRERED AND POKÉMON LEAFGREEN

Remakes of the original Red and Blue games, with simple facelifts to take advantage of the newer GBA technology. These updated games allowed players to trade for Generation I and II Pokémon with the newer Generation III Pokémon in Ruby and Sapphire. Players could now play as a male or female. Pokémon have natures, genders and can hold items. Team Rocket appears more. A new region exists as well to catch Generation II Pokémon. Pokémon can also breed.

SEPTEMBER 11, 2004
POKÉMON SEASON 7

Advanced Challenge — 52 episodes
Ash and the gang continue their journey through the Hoenn region, where Ash and May continue following their dreams of becoming a great Pokémon trainer and coordinator. Throughout the season, Ash has the opportunity to win three more gym badges, including a rematch with Norman at the Petalburg City Gym, and May gains three more Pokémon contest ribbons. Ash and Brock are also reunited with Misty for a few episodes, as she has been invited to a Togepi festival.

AUGUST 30, 2004
EX FIRERED & LEAFGREEN TCG

A set of cards based on the Game Boy Advance remakes of the first Pokémon Games.

NOVEMBER 8, 2004
EX TEAM ROCKET RETURNS

It is the first expansion to feature Pokémon Star. We also see the return of "Dark" and "Rocket's" Pokémon. Dark Dragonite is a powerful beast here.

20 YEARS OF POKéMON

JANUARY 22, 2005
POKéMON: DESTINY DEOXYS

The seventh Pokémon movie premieres on Kids' WB. The network received their best ratings in two years with the premiere of the movie. This is the first film without a short at the beginning. The extra running time started going into the plot of the actual movies. The film features the legendary Pokémon Deoxys and Rayquaza. Ash is accompanied by May, Max and Brock again.

MAY 1, 2005
POKéMON EMERALD

Pokémon Emerald is a follow-up / sister-game to the Ruby and Sapphire Game Boy Advance games, with a few enhancements and changes. The most notable changes are where and how you caught certain Pokémon. Kyogre and Groudon are caught in different places now. Puzzles are changed. Double Battles happen more frequently. The Eighth Gym has a different Gym Leader. And the Battle Frontier replaces the Battle Tower.

2005

MAY 9, 2005
EX EMERALD TCG

A set released to promote the new Emerald game on the Game Boy Advance. This set featured special holographic basic Energy cards often known as "Matrix Energy" due to their design. They were in high demand.

FEBRUARY 14, 2005
EX DEOXYS TCG

The set brought us Jirachi (Wishing Star) which had a huge impact on competitive decks.

MARCH 13, 2005
POKéMON DASH

The first Pokémon game for the Nintendo DS. You are basically controlling Pikachu in a foot racing game by showing him where to go using the DS Stylus. It's a pretty bad game that was simply designed to show off the new DS technology. There's not a whole lot here for most Pokémon fans.

This book is not sponsored, endorsed by, or otherwise affiliated with any companies or the products featured in the book. This is not an official publication.

OCTOBER 3, 2005
POKÉMON XD: GALE OF DARKNESS

This is direct follow up to Pokémon Colosseum. The events in this story take place 5 years after the events in Colosseum.

Gale of Darkness has a longer single player campaign than Colosseum, and allows the player to actually capture some wild Pokémon and transfer them to their handhelds. The Pokémon that folks want to catch here is a Shadow Lugia that appears at the very end of the game. Almost all of the battles here are double battles. The Pokémon look pretty good on the GameCube, and the single-player story mode will take you about 25 hours.

AUGUST 22, 2005
EX UNSEEN FORCES TCG

Unown make their return! Lugia EX and Steelix EX are powerful cards released in this set.

SEPTEMBER 17, 2005
POKÉMON SEASON 8

Advanced Battle — 54 Episodes. Ash finally earns the last two badges needed to qualify for the Hoenn League Championship. Meanwhile, May's final Hoenn Contest comes around, and she comes dangerously close to not earning her last ribbon as she becomes distracted when her opponent in the contest sees her as a romantic rival.

OCTOBER 31, 2005
EX DELTA SPECIES

This set introduced Delta Species Pokémon, plus Holon's Pokémon that could be used as Energy cards.

20 YEARS OF POKéMON

FEBRUARY 13, 2006
EX LEGEND MAKER TCG

React Energy debuts here. Mew-ex is a powerful card from this set.

MAY 3, 2006
EX HOLON PHANTOMS TCG

This was first set to bring us δ Delta Species Pokémon. Raichu δ and Exeggutor δ took advantage of δ Delta Species support to form a strong deck that spread damage with ease.

AUGUST 30, 2006
EX CRYSTAL GUARDIANS

Delta Species Pokémon-EX make their debut. This set also had some strong trainers like: Windstorm, Cessation Crystal, Castaway and Crystal Beach.

2006

MARCH 6, 2006
POKéMON TROZEI

A Pokémon Puzzler that isn't half bad. It looks like a simple "match-three" type puzzle game. But actually, typical Pokémon strength and weaknesses must be accounted for. And if you weren't keeping up with Generation III Pokémon, you were at a bit of a disadvantage. The goal is to fill your Pokédex by battling and capturing wild Pokémon. You do that by matching 3 or more Pokémon and sending them into combat. If the Pokémon your battling is weak to the 3 monsters you match, you do more damage.

SEPTEMBER 8, 2006
POKéMON SEASON 9

Battle Frontier — 47 episodes. Ash begins his adventures in the Battle Frontier. Even though the territory is familiar to both Ash and Brock, they are faced with many new discoveries in their home region of Kanto. May hears of more contest opportunities in the Kanto region, she decides to continue her journey with Ash, Brock and her younger brother Max in order to obtain more contest ribbons.

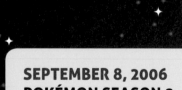

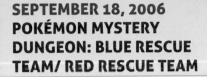

SEPTEMBER 18, 2006
POKÉMON MYSTERY DUNGEON: BLUE RESCUE TEAM/ RED RESCUE TEAM

These are essentially the same games for different systems. Blue is for the DS, and Red is for the GBA. You are a human who has been turned into a Pokémon, and thrown into a crazy Pokémon World fraught with disasters. You assemble a Rescue Team and help out other Pokémon in danger. The game becomes a typical dungeon crawler that gets old and repetitive rather quickly.

OCTOBER 30, 2006
POKÉMON RANGER

Pokémon Ranger introduced a new way to catch Pokémon. It's a little reminiscent to the true Pokémon RPGs, but takes things in a new and different direction. Instead of being a Pokémon Trainer, you now play a Pokémon Ranger. Rangers use Pokémon to help maintain the peace in the Pokémon World. You tame and capture Pokémon by drawing circles around them on the Touch Screen. If you can draw a complete circle around the Pokémon, you wrangle it, and the Pokémon will tag along with you. This isn't quite as good as the classic Pokémon RPG, but it's a decent change if you want to try something a little different.

SEPTEMBER 19, 2006
POKÉMON: LUCARIO AND THE MYSTERY OF MEW

The eighth Pokémon movie actually made its U.S. debut at Comic-Con in San Diego, California. This was also the last film to be dubbed by 4Kids Entertainment, who had been dubbing Pokémon from the start of the television series in 1998. All future Pokémon episodes and films would be dubbed by The Pokémon Company. This time around, it's Pikachu who disappears. Ash and gang must work with Lucario and Mew to find and save Pikachu.

NOVEMBER 8, 2006
EX DRAGON FRONTIERS TCG

Two new mechanics are introduced with this set: Imprison Markers and Shock-wave markers. Rayquaza-ex δ was a strong Pokémon card in this set.

FEBRUARY 14, 2007
EX POWER KEEPERS TCG

This is the final set released as part of the EX. This was the first time since Team Rocket that some cards were designed outside of Japan.

APRIL 22, 2007
POKéMON DIAMOND AND POKéMON PEARL

Diamond and Pearl (D&P) are the fifth installments of the Pokémon series of RPGs. Pokémon D&P introduced over 100 new Pokémon and brought us what are considered "Generation IV" Pokémon.

Pokémon D&P leads players into the Sinnoh region and were the first true Pokémon RPG Games for the Nintendo DS. The DS (Dual Screen) brought a touch screen and Wi-Fi capabilities into the Pokémon World. Worldwide battles and trading were now possible thanks to Wi-Fi. Friend Codes allowed you to find trusted friends online. A real-time clock feature allowed you to capture specific Pokémon that were only available at certain times of the day. Pokémon contests became more elaborate thanks to the touch screen. Graphics again took another step forward, with more details in the Pokémon World. Buildings were rendered in 3D.

2007

MARCH 23, 2007
POKéMON RANGER AND THE TEMPLE OF THE SEA

This is the ninth Pokémon movie and it debuted on DVD. The film features a new English Voice Cast since 4Kids Entertainment is no longer involved. This is the last film to feature May and Max as main characters in the scrics. Ash and the gang work with new characters to protect Manaphy – The Prince of the Sea.

MAY 23, 2007
DIAMOND & PEARL TCG

This set includes Pokémon from the Sinnoh region (Generation IV) for the first time.

JUNE 2007
POKéMON SEASON 10

Diamond and Pearl — 52 episodes. Ash and Pikachu visit Sinnoh for the first time. Ash meets and travels with Dawn. Dawn is a Pokémon Trainer, learning to become a Pokémon Coordinator. Ash and friends participate in many different Pokémon contests, and Ash battles many different Gym leaders and eventually gets involved in the Hearthome City Pokémon Tag-Team battle tournament.

JUNE 25, 2007
POKÉMON BATTLE REVOLUTION

Pokémon Battle Revolution is essentially an upgrade of the old Pokémon Stadium Games for Generation IV Pokémon. It's also the first Pokémon game to appear on the Wii. You can import Pokémon easily from your Diamond and Pearl games. The graphics and fights looked wonderful. And thanks to the Wii's internet capability, you are able to duel friends and even other live trainers at random. The downfall with Battle Revolution is that for some reason Nintendo didn't include the fun single player RPG campaign that folks came to love in Pokémon Colosseum and Gale of Darkness.

OCTOBER 1, 2007
POKÉMON TRADING FIGURE GAME

This collectible miniatures game (like HeroClix) only lasted a couple of years. I'm not sure anyone ever played this game, but sculpts of the figures are beautiful and wonderful to collect. You can find some of the Pokémon figures on eBay for about $5 each, but rarer figures can cost 10 times that price.

AUGUST 22, 2007
D&P MYSTERIOUS TREASURES TCG

This set gave us the Gen IV Pokémon which Evolved from Fossil cards. Some Pokémon had "Held Items" which were an added effect printed on that Pokémon's card.

NOVEMBER 7, 2007
D&P SECRET WONDERS TCG

Secret Wonders birthed a potent deck with its Gardevoir and Gallade.

20 YEARS OF POKÉMON

FEBRUARY 13, 2008
D&P GREAT ENCOUNTERS TCG

Diamond & Pearl Great Encounters is a set that lacks a proper Japanese counterpart. It was created to fill a gap. This set lined up TCG set releases to coincide better with Japan's sets.

MARCH 9, 2008
SUPER SMASH BROS. BRAWL

Super Smash Bros. Brawl (SSBB) is the third installment of the hugely popular Smash Bros. fighting series franchise. This is the eighth best-selling game of all time on the Wii. The game features most the characters from the previous games, and included a few more. Playable Pokémon include: Pikachu, Jigglypuff, Pokémon Trainer and Lucario. This Wii version allowed for 4 players to play local Co-op. One the main draws of this new game was that for the first time you could battle other people online! You could share "friend codes" and battle your buddies anywhere in the world. Simply a great game.

2008

FEBRUARY 24, 2008
POKÉMON: THE RISE OF DARKRAI

This is the 10th Pokémon movie, and is actually the first part in a trilogy of Diamond and Pearl films. The movie introduces the Legendary Pokemon Dialga and Palkia. Ash, Brock, Dawn, and Pikachu visit the town of Alamos, which is dominated by two lofty towers that represent space and time. Ash and the gang must help stop the battle of Dialga and Palkia to stop the space-time fabric from tearing!

APRIL 20, 2008
POKÉMON MYSTERY DUNGEON EXPLORERS OF DARKNESS / EXPLORERS OF TIME

This is the 2nd installment of Nintendo's attempt at a Pokémon Dungeon Crawler. Mystery Dungeons are randomly generated dungeons that the player fights through. The player has turn-based attacks with Pokemon inside the dungeon. Sixteen Pokémon are playable in this version, including several Generation IV Pokémon. You assemble a team of 4 Pokémon and get to work. Some folks really love these Mystery Dungeon games, others find them boring and repetitive.

APRIL 2008
POKÉMON SEASON 11

DP Battle Dimension — 52 episodes. Ash & Brock continue their journey though the Sinnoh region. Dawn tags along again facing many challenges as a Pokémon Coordinator. Team Galactic is introduced as the new evildoers that Ash has to contend with.

AUGUST 20, 2008
D&P LEGENDS AWAKENED TCG

Shortly after this set released, the Standard Format shifted to Diamond & Pearl and later sets (DP-On). Unlike in the past, this time the format was worldwide and even Japan followed it.

MAY 21, 2008
D&P MAJESTIC DAWN TCG

This set brought us power cards like Unown Q, Call Energy, Empoleon and Scizor.

NOVEMBER 5, 2008
D&P STORMFRONT TCG

Stormfront introduces Shiny Pokémon to the Diamond & Pearl Series. Future rule changes would put Sableye in a deck that could win on the first turn.

JUNE 9, 2008
MY POKÉMON RANCH

This is a WiiWare game. WiiWare titles are downloaded via the Internet from Nintendo's Online Store. This is a somewhat weird game. You are "Wii Mii" rancher running a Pokémon Ranch. You upload all your Pokémon from Diamond and Pearl onto the ranch. Then your ranch essentially becomes a farm for all your Pokémon and Mii's to interact with each other. The best use of your ranch is to use it as storage for your army of Pokémon. The game gets old rather quickly as there is not much to do here.

NOVEMBER 10, 2008
POKÉMON RANGER:
SHADOWS OF ALMIA

This action-adventure game is a sequel to Pokémon Ranger. This time you are in the Region of Alma. The game features Pokémon from Generation I-IV. Capturing Pokémon is a little easier this time around. Captured Pokémon join your team and help you solve puzzles within the game. This isn't quite as good as the classic Pokémon RPG, but isn't a bad change if you want to try something a little different.

20 YEARS OF POKÉMON

FEBRUARY 11, 2009
PLATINUM TCG

This expansion introduces Pokémon SP and the Lost Zone.

MARCH 22, 2009
POKÉMON PLATINUM

Pokémon Platinum is a follow-up, sister-type game to the Pearl and Diamond games, with quite a few enhancements and changes. The most notable changes are 59 more Pokémon; more Legendary Pokémon are available for capture; a new Distortion World; and a new Villa for you to place your valuables. There are also improved graphics and more characters to interact with. Some buildings have different layouts, with different puzzles. Gym Leaders may have different Pokémon as well.

MAY 20, 2009
RISING RIVALS TCG

More Pokémon SP and r they can be Pokémon Gl Pokémon E4. "GL" stand for Gym Leader while "E stands for Elite Four. The cards have an image of t face of the correct Gym Leader or Elite Four to o that Pokémon.

2009

FEBRUARY 13, 2009
POKÉMON: GIRATINA
AND THE SKY WARRIOR

The 11th Pokémon movie is the second of the Diamond & Pearl trilogy of films. Ash and friends are trying to help the Pokemon Shaymin return to its friends, but instead get caught up in a struggle over the fate of the Reverse World. An evil-doer is trying to harness the power of the Legendary Pokémon Giratina. This a convoluted storyline that finishes in the next film.

MAY 9, 2009
POKÉMON SEASON 12

DP Galactic Battles — 53 episodes. Ash, Dawn, Brock and Max continue their journey through the Sinnoh region. Ash squares off with Paul. Ash has to also contend with Team Galactic who continue their evil plans.

OCTOBER 2009
POKÉMON MYSTERY DUNGEON: EXPLORERS OF SKY

This is a sister game to the Explorer of Time / Explorers of Darkness games we reviewed earlier. This time around, there are new starting Pokémon. New buildings and shops have been added. A new location called Shaymin Village unlocks after you defeat the game. Players now only lose half their money if they're defeated in a dungeon. Some of the Pokémon in the game have been changed as well. If you haven't played a Mystery Dungeon game before, and really want to test the game play, this is a pretty good place to start.

NOVEMBER 20
POKÉMON: ARCEUS AND THE JEWEL OF LIFE

This the 12th Pokémon movie, and it completes the Diamond and Pearl trilogy of films. The English dub premiered on Cartoon Network. This movie actually contains a prequel to the trilogy, explaining how Arceus is causing the disturbance between Palkia and Dialga, which is causing the rift in space and time. Ash must help save the world, the Reverse World, space and time. Are you confused yet? Well, the trilogy of films is difficult to explain but a joy to watch. Rent them or pick them up on DVD.

NOVEMBER 4, 2009
ARCEUS TCG

Each Arceus in this set had a rule printed on it stating you could have as many cards with the name "Arceus" in your deck as you wished. The 60 card deck count still applied though.

NOVEMBER 16, 2009
POKÉMON RUMBLE

Another Wiiware title. This was a new type of Pokémon Game from Nintendo. This is strictly an action game. You start off as a low level Pokémon and battle other Pokémon. You learn more moves and recruit more Pokémon as you play. Gameplay is essentially real-time-melee, smash-your-opponent type battles. This game supports up to four players simultaneously. Players can play Co-op battles, and competitive battles. If you have ever played the "Gauntlet" series of video games, this has a similar feel when playing the Co-op version. This can be some mindless fun for folks, but it can also become old and repetitive fairly soon.

AUGUST 19, 2009
SUPREME VICTORS TCG

This set brought us two more kinds of Pokémon SP. We now have Pokémon C and Pokémon FB. The "C" is for Champion while "FB" is for Frontier Brain.

20 YEARS OF POKÉMON

FEBRUARY 10, 2010
HEARTGOLD & SOULSILVER TCG

This set introduced Pokémon LEGEND cards and focused on Generation I and II Pokémon.

MAY 12, 2010
HS UNLEASHED TCG

This set introduced Pokémon Prime cards.

2010

MARCH 14, 2010
POKÉMON HEARTGOLD AND POKÉMON SOULSILVER

Pokémon HeartGold and Pokémon SoulSilver are released for Nintendo DS on March 14.

JUNE 5 2010
POKÉMON SEASON 13

DP Sinnoh League Victors — 34 episodes. Having disposed of Team Galactic, Ash and Dawn focus on their goals of qualifying for the Sinnoh League Championship and the Grand Festival. Brock considers becoming a Pokémon Doctor.

AUGUST 18, 2010
HS UNDAUNTED

This set brought more Pokémon Prime and Pokémon LEGEND. Pokémon Prime become a major force.

NOVEMBER 1, 2010
POKÉPARK WII:
PIKACHU'S ADVENTURE

This is a single player action-adventure game for children. This time, you are playing as Pikachu. The goal here is to save the Poképark by finding shards of the Sky Prism. These shards are hidden throughout the zones in the park. To find the shards, the game puts you through a variety of mini-games similar to what you would find in a Mario Party game. The game really takes advantage of the Wiimote's Motion Controls. A very cute but very simple game.

OCTOBER 4, 2010
POKÉMON RANGER:
GUARDIAN SIGNS

This action-adventure game is a sequel to Pokémon Ranger: Shadows of Almia. Action takes place in the Region of Oblivia. Gameplay is similar to the previous titles. The bad guys this time are the Pokémon Pinchers and they are trying to capture some Legendary Pokémon. You can team up with 3 other players to do some missions simultaneously using local Wi-Fi. Many people think this is the best Ranger game in the series, and a good place to start if you haven't played a Ranger title.

NOVEMBER 2, 2010
HS TRIUMPHANT TCG

The final set in the HS series and the last with Pokémon Prime and Pokémon LEGEND. Unlike the other HS sets, this one has many Gen IV Pokémon because it was used to promote a film that had Gen IV Pokémon.

20 YEARS OF POKÉMON

FEBRUARY 5, 2011
POKÉMON—ZOROARK: MASTER OF ILLUSIONS

The 13th Pokémon movie aired first on Cartoon Network before heading to home video. Ash, Dawn and Brock travel to Crown City to watch the Pokémon Baccer World Cup. Strange things start happening. Celebi flies by. The Legendary Dogs are running through the streets. Ash and the gang must work with Zoroark to stop the madness!

FEBRUARY 12, 2011
POKÉMON SEASON 14

Black & White — 48 episodes. Ash begins a new quest in the Unova region. Ash meets and travels with new friends Iris and Cilan who are Pokémon Trainers as well. Ash also befriends Trip, a Pokémon photographer, and Bianca, another trainer. Team Rocket (Jesse, James & Meowth) returns to cause trouble along the way.

JUNE 7, 2011
POKÉDEX 3D

At the time of release, this Pokédex App was free. The Nintendo 3DS was released in February 2011, and this app showed some of the power of the new 3DS. The app had stats on 150 Pokémon from Black and White. You could rotate the Pokémon in 3D, hear their cries, and watch them moving. You were able to download three new Pokémon each day, and send captured downloaded Pokémon to friends.

2011

FEBRUARY 9, 2011
CALL OF LEGENDS TCG

This expansion included the Lost World Stadium card, which provided a new way to win the game.

APRIL 25, 2011
BLACK & WHITE TCG

This first expansion of the Black & White Series was comprised entirely of newly discovered Pokémon from the Unova region.

MARCH 6, 2011
POKÉMON BLACK VERSION AND POKÉMON WHITE

Black and White are the fifth installments of the Pokémon series of RPGs. Black and White introduced over 150 new Pokémon and brought us what are considered "Generation V" Pokémon.

Pokémon Black and White leads players into the Unova region. Game advances include new Pokémon moves; new Pokémon Abilities; new villains in Team Plasma; the introduction of Seasons of the Year; and the introduction of Triple Battles and Rotation Battles. Gameplay is similar to original Red and Blue turn-based RPG games. The new 150 Pokémon species brought the total to around 650 Pokemon at the time of release. These games will provide well over 40 hours of gameplay to beat the game, not including all the side quests. Highly recommended!

AUGUST 31, 2011
BW EMERGING POWERS TCG

The expansion contains 26 newly discovered Pokémon from the Unova region. Many good Trainers debuted in this set, like Pokémon Catcher, Max Potion & Crushing Hammer.

DECEMBER 3, 2011
POKÉMON THE MOVIE: WHITE —VICTINI AND ZEKROM
&
DECEMBER 10, 2011
POKÉMON THE MOVIE: BLACK —VICTINI AND RESHIRAM

These films actually received a limited theatrical release in America before heading to Cartoon Network three months later, and eventually home video. The film plots are almost identical; the only differences revolve around the Pokémon that appear. Each version has its own set of Pokémon and there are some subtle differences. For example in White, Damon recruits the help of Reshiram, while in Black he convinces Zekrom to help him, but they do exactly the same thing.

In this outing, Ash and his friends Iris and Cilan have made their way to Eindoak Town, where the three trainers decide to compete in the town's annual battle competition. The characters end up on a floating castle. And of course Ash must save the day. He is depicted as the "chosen one". He does get some unexpected help from the mythical Pokémon Victini.

AUGUST 2011
THE POKÉMON TRADING CARD GAME ONLINE LAUNCHES FOR PC AND MAC

The Pokémon TCG Online still exists today. It is improved and updated continuously. It is a "Free to Download - Free to Play" version of the paper TCG. The game started off a little rough around the edges, but bugs have been ironed out over the years. There are great tutorials here to learn the game. You will start off with some free cards and free decks to get you going. You can always play for free and earn some card rewards for you deck. The single player campaign is actually pretty good. Like many other online TCGs (Magic: the Gathering, Hearthstone, etc.), the game can cost you a few dollars if you want to invest in more cards and enter tournaments. A nice feature is that can also redeem codes from specially marked TCG Products to unlock online boosters, theme decks and Promo Cards. The value is pretty good if you're really into the TCG.

OCTOBER 2011
POKÉMON RUMBLE BLAST

This is the first true Pokémon game for the 3DS. This is a sequel to the Pokémon Rumble WiiWare game we reviewed earlier. This is an action game, where you control a Toy Pokémon with the circle pad and use a single button to attack. You unlock other button attacks as you play. You can collect over 600 Pokémon. This is a simple, cute, fun, action-packed dungeon crawler type game. Your loot is Pokémon and more moves for your Pokémon. The WiiWare game was sort of a beta for this much improved version of the game.

NOVEMBER 16, 2011
B&W NOBLE VICTORIES TCG

This set brought us the Support Card "N" which would become a staple in many decks for years to come.

20 YEARS OF POKéMON

FEBRUARY 8, 2012
B&W NEXT DESTINIES TCG: BW

Next Destinies is the first set to officially introduce the powerful Pokemon-EX into the game! Not only were Pokemon bigger than ever before, they were more powerful too.

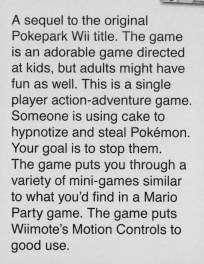

FEBRUARY 27, 2012
POKéPARK 2: WONDERS BEYOND

A sequel to the original Pokepark Wii title. The game is an adorable game directed at kids, but adults might have fun as well. This is a single player action-adventure game. Someone is using cake to hypnotize and steal Pokémon. Your goal is to stop them. The game puts you through a variety of mini-games similar to what you'd find in a Mario Party game. The game puts Wiimote's Motion Controls to good use.

MAY 9, 2012
B&W DARK EXPLORERS TCG

Dark Explorers provided a bunch of powerful cards for Dark decks and lead the way for Darkrai-EX to become a great leader!

AUGUST 15, 2012
B&W DRAGONS EXALTED

This set officially introduced Dragon-type Pokémon to the TCG. Rayquaza EX is a powerful card here!

2012

FEBRUARY 18, 2012
POKéMON SEASON 15

BW Rival Destinies — 49 episodes. Ash, Iris and Cilan continue exploring in the Unova region. Ash, Iris and Trip decide to compete in the Pokémon World Tournament Junior Cup. Team Rocket is still causing trouble.

JUNE 2012
POKéMON CONQUEST

A new twist in the Pokémon franchise. Pokémon Conquest is a tactical, turn-based, strategy game that is very similar to the Fire Emblem series.

In this game, you play a feudal Japanese Warlord (based on real Japanese historical characters). You recruit Pokémon to be your warriors as you do battle in a chess-like setting. This game requires you to use your brain. It's not mindless action whatsoever. You have to know the tactical movement of characters across the grid, and which Pokémon attributes will provide your best opportunity for attacks. Pokémon level as you complete missions. This is a really good spin-off of the Pokémon franchise. If you like Fire Emblem games, you'll like this game. If you haven't tried a tactical game, this is a great place to wet your feet.

NOVEMBER 7, 2012
B&W BOUNDARIES CROSSED TCG

Blastoise makes a powerful splash here with his Deluge attack. The ACE SPEC game mechanic is introduced here. This allowed for powerful cards to be printed, but they were limited to one card per deck.

OCTOBER 7, 2012
POKÉMON BLACK 2 AND POKÉMON WHITE 2

These two games are actually sequels rather than remakes. The story here takes place two years after Black and White. The Unova region has changed. The towns have changed. The characters have changed. The Pokémon to capture have changed. The gyms have changed. There is now a World Tournament where the Gym Leaders from Johto, Hoenn, Kanto, Sinnoh and Unova can be battled. This sequel is excellent and highly recommended for all Pokémon RPG Fans!

DECEMBER 8, 2012
POKÉMON THE MOVIE: KYUREM VS. THE SWORD OF JUSTICE

The 15th Pokémon movie, debuts on December 8th on Cartoon Network. Ash, Iris and Cilan, are on a train when Ash spots an injured Keldeo. As Ash tries to get off, the train gets attacked by the Legendary Kyurem. Ash has to help solve another mystery. This movie has a lot of Pokémon doing battle, and many other legendary Pokémon get involved in the storyline.

OCTOBER 7, 2012
POKÉMON DREAM RADAR

This is another strange Pokémon spinoff. You use the Camera on your 3DS to walk around your house and use the 3DS system as a radar. Dream Clouds will appear partially blocking your view on the screen. You clear the dream clouds off your screen like a First Person Shooter. Occasionally the cleared Dream Clouds will reveal Pokémon to capture. If you are playing Black and White 2, you can transfer these captured Pokémon into your game. This is simply a silly diversion for the cost of about $3 from the eShop.

NOVEMBER 2012
POKÉDEX 3D PRO

This is an update/upgrade of the Pokédex 3D that was available previously on Nintendo's eShop. The original only had 150 Pokémon from the Unova Region. This new version has the majority of the 650 Pokémon available. Each Pokémon has 3D modeling. The Pokémon look great. Each Pokémon page is packed full of information including: evolutions; heights; weights; move-sets; attacks; etc. There are Pokémon quizzes. The old one was free. This new version will set you back about $15.

20 YEARS OF POKÉMON

FEBRUARY 2, 2013
POKÉMON SEASON 16

BW Adventures in Unova and Beyond — 45 episodes. Ash competes in the Unova League Championship. Ash meets a boy named "N" who joins Ash's party along with Iris and Cilan. Ash's gang has to contend with Team Plasma during their travels.

MARCH 24, 2013
POKÉMON MYSTERY DUNGEON: GATES TO INFINITY

This is another installment of Nintendo's Pokémon Dungeon Crawler series. You can recruit any Pokémon you have defeated into your party. Nearly all of the Pokémon that existed at the time of release are available in the game. Many people didn't think this game was as good as previous Mystery Dungeons.

2013

FEBRUARY 6, 2013
B&W PLASMA STORM TCG

This marks the Pokémon TCG debut of the villainous Team Plasma. Plasma cards featured a blue border instead of the typical yellow border.

MAY 8, 2013
B&W PLASMA FREEZE

The Plasma trend continues with strong cards like Team Plasma Ball.

FEBRUARY 2013
POKÉMON TV MOBILE APP

The Pokémon TV app launches for iPad, iPhone, iPod touch, and Android devices.

AUGUST 14, 2013
B&W PLASMA BLAST TCG

The last Plasma set. This set actually brought in cards to counteract some of the strong Plasma cards that were introduced in earlier sets.

NOVEMBER 8, 2013
B&W LEGENDARY TREASURES TCG

Legendary Treasures was mostly a reprint set, featuring many of the biggest cards in the Black & White era.

AUGUST 29, 2013
POKÉMON RUMBLE U

This was the first true Pokémon game for the Wii U. This is a sequel to the Pokémon Rumble Blast game we discussed earlier. This is an action game, where you control a Toy Pokémon and use a single button to attack. You unlock other button attacks and collect Pokémon to use as you play. This game is downloaded from the Nintendo eShop. This is basically Rumble Blast "light".

OCTOBER 19, 2013
POKÉMON THE MOVIE: GENESECT AND THE LEGEND AWAKENED

This 16th Pokémon movie debuted in the U.S. on Cartoon Network, and then was released on DVD in time for the holidays. This movie takes place in New York City. A plethora of Genesect Pokémon begin building a giant cocoon that threatens the city's power supply. Mewtwo is back and comes to the aid of Ash, Iris and Cilan.

OCTOBER 12, 2013
POKÉMON X AND POKÉMON Y

Pokémon X and Y are the sixth installments of the Pokémon series of RPGs. Pokémon X and Y are the first in the RPG series to take advantage of the 3D modeling of the 3DS. These games introduce over 70 new Pokémon and bring us what are considered "Generation VI" Pokémon. This brought the total Pokémon in the Pokeworld to 721.

Pokémon X and Y leads players into the Kalos region. Gameplay is somewhat similar to original Red and Blue turn-based RPG games. The biggest feature this time around is Mega Evolutions (a temporary state some Pokémon experience during battle that increases their stats and abilities). For the first time, players are also able to choose their skin tone and hair color at the start of the game. Fairy-type Pokémon are introduced. Super Training features mini-games that help build the stats of your Pokémon. You should own at least one of these titles!

NOVEMBER 15, 2013
POKÉMON ORIGINS

The four-part special Pokémon Origins premieres on Pokémon TV on November 15.

20 YEARS OF POKéMON

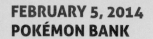

FEBRUARY 5, 2014
POKéMON BANK

The bank is optional online cloud storage of all your Pokémon. The Pokémon Bank runs about $6 per year and is compatible with X, Y, Omega Ruby, Alpha Sapphire, Sun and Moon. The Pokémon Bank is also compatible with the virtual eShop versions of Red, Blue and Yellow. The bank will let you store up to 3000 Pokémon! A good idea from Nintendo.

JANUARY 18, 2014
POKéMON SEASON 17

XY — 48 episodes. Ash and Pikachu begin their travels in the Kalos region. Ash makes new friends in Clemont, an inventor, and his little sister Bonnie. They are soon joined by Serena, a Pokémon Performer in training. Team Rocket continues to cause trouble under new orders from Giovanni.

AUGUST 13, 2014
XY FURIOUS FISTS TCG

This set gave Fighting decks a ton of support cards like Fighting Stadium and Strong Energy. Seismitoad EX is the beast here!

2014

MAY 7, 2014
XY FLASHFIRE TCG

This set brought in many cards that made Evolution Decks more powerful. Also introduced the "Lysandre" Trainer card that could switch one of your opponent's Benched Pokémon with his or her Active Pokémon.

FEBRUARY 5, 2014
XY TCG

This is the first expansion to feature Fairy-type Pokémon and Mega Evolution Pokémon.

MARCH 20, 2014
POKéMON BATTLE TROZEI

This is a sequel to the original Pokémon Trozei that was released in 2006, and is available online from the Nintendo eShop. At the time of this review, the price of this game is only $8. That's a great price for this puzzler.

OCTOBER 24, 2014
POKÉMON ART ACADEMY

This is an educational art game for the 3DS. The game teaches you how to draw a variety of Pokémon characters on your 3DS as you advance through the lesson plan. You learn to sketch and paint your Pokémon in 2D. The lessons are really well done. The stylus and touch screen work great here. And you can actually make some beautiful images on the 3DS. If you want to learn how to draw some Pokémon, then you can't go wrong with this beauty of a game.

NOVEMBER 5, 2014
XY PHANTOM FORCES TCG

This set featured Team Flare and Pokémon Spirit Link cards. Lysandre's Trump Card and Battle Compressor are introduced in this set.

NOVEMBER 8, 2014
POKÉMON THE MOVIE: DIANCIE
AND THE COCOON OF DESTRUCTION

This 17th Pokémon movie premiered on Cartoon Network. The Pokémon Diancie enlists the help of Ash, Serena, Clemont and Bonnie to protect and restore the Heart Diamond. There are many villains in this movie including Team Rocket. Ash has to find Xerneas for help, but Yveltal stands in his way.

OCTOBER 2014
CAMP POKÉMON

This a free download for iPhones & iPads. This is a children's application with several Pokémon mini games inside. Camp Pokémon seems to be designed to hook kids on the Pokémon theme, and prepare them for the real RPG adventures they'll really want to play (and pay for) when they get older. There's not too much here for the older crowd.

NOVEMBER 21, 2014
POKÉMON OMEGA RUBY
AND ALPHA SAPPHIRE

Remakes of the original Ruby and Sapphire (R&S) games. The main storyline is essentially the same. Graphics have obviously been upgraded and look great on the 3DS. Also, more animations have been given to the major characters in the game. These new animations give the game more of a movie-type quality over the originals.

There is an improved PokeNav Plus on the bottom screen of the 3DS. The AreaNav shows your movements in real time, and locations of trainers who want rematches. The DexNav displays all the Pokémon available near your current location. The Battle Resort replaces the Battle Tower from the originals. Some of the small towns from the original have grown into big cities. Also, Mirage Islands randomly appear on the map, where you can catch Legendary Pokémon. There are also some Mega Evolutions that weren't in the original games, as well as "Cosplay" Pikachu.

20 YEARS OF POKÉMON

FEBRUARY 4, 2015
XY PRIMAL CLASH

This set introduced the new Ancient Traits mechanic. This set also introduced Primal Reversion Pokémon. Wailord-EX broke the HP record with 250 HP.

FEBRUARY 7, 2015
POKÉMON SEASON 18

XY Kalos Quest — 45 episodes. Ash and his friends continue their journey through the Kalos region. Ash earns a few more badges. Serena continues to pursue her goal of becoming a Pokémon Performer.

MAY 6, 2015
XY ROARING SKIES TCG

This set had a big focus on Colorless Pokémon with strong cards like Shaymin-EX and M Rayquaza-EX.

2015

AUGUST 12, 2015
ANCIENT ORIGINS TCG

It features the first appearance of the Mythical Pokémon Hoopa. Forest of Giant Plants led to a resurgence of Grass Decks.

FEBRUARY 18, 2015
POKÉMON SHUFFLE

Shuffle is very similar to the Pokémon Trozei games we reviewed earlier. Shuffle is Free to Play on all devices (3DS, IOS and Android), but Nintendo hopes you'll spend more money while owning it. There is only a limited amount of time you can play during the day for free. If you want to play more than the free limit allowed each day, then you have to pay some of your hard-earned money.

APRIL 8, 2015
POKÉMON RUMBLE WORLD

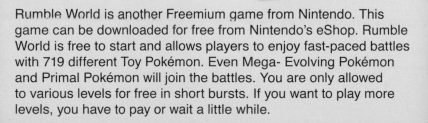

Rumble World is another Freemium game from Nintendo. This game can be downloaded for free from Nintendo's eShop. Rumble World is free to start and allows players to enjoy fast-paced battles with 719 different Toy Pokémon. Even Mega- Evolving Pokémon and Primal Pokémon will join the battles. You are only allowed to various levels for free in short bursts. If you want to play more levels, you have to pay or wait a little while.

SEPTEMBER 2015
POKÉMON SHUFFLE MOBILE

Pokémon Shuffle Mobile is released for iPad, iPhone, and Android devices.

DECEMBER 19, 2015
HOOPA AND THE
CLASH OF AGES

This 18th Pokémon movie debuted on Cartoon Network. Ash and his friends Serena, Clement and Bonnie travel to the desert and encounter a legendary Pokémon named Hoopa. It has a dark side that looks just like a genie and is imprisoned in a bottle. Once the dark Hoopa escapes, he recruits six legendary Pokemon to help with his dirty work. Ash has to also summon some legendary Pokemon to fight back. There are a lot of Legendary Pokémon doing battle in this movie! This storyline seems lifted straight out of One Thousand and One Arabian Nights.

NOVEMBER 4, 2015
BREAKTHROUGH TCG

This set introduced Pokémon BREAK and Stadium cards with two different effects.

NOVEMBER 2015
POKÉMON SUPER MYSTERY DUNGEON

Another installment of Nintendo's Pokémon Dungeon Crawler series. Just like the original, you wake up as a Pokémon. You are a human who is turned into one of 20 different Pokémon and try to discover why. You assemble a team of Pokémon and go dungeon crawling. You can recruit any Pokémon you have defeated into your party. All of the 700+ Pokémon that exist are available in the game!

This game starts off a little slow but is one of the better games in the Mystery Dungeon series. The tutorial is great. The graphics are improved. More than four Pokémon can enter the dungeon with you. The story is good. All in all, if you haven't played a Mystery Dungeon game before, this is a great place to start.

DECEMBER 3, 2015
POKÉMON PICROSS (3DS)

Another Freemium game. Mario Picross was released in 1995, and is a pretty good logic puzzler. Your deductions reveal images if you solve the puzzle correctly. Pokémon Picross reveals Pokémon images. This game is actually pretty good if you like working your brain.

20 YEARS OF POKéMON

FEBRUARY 3, 2016
POKéMON TCG: XY BREAKPOINT

This set brought us more powerful Pokémon BREAK and Pokémon-EX. Also featured a lot of water support.

MARCH 2016
POKéMON POKKEN TOURNAMENT

Pokken is something new for the Pokémon franchise. This is an Arcade Style Fighting game for the Wii U. This game plays similar to other popular Arena fighters like Dragon Ball Z, Naruto, Tekken, SoulCalibur, etc. The game is a collaboration between Nintendo and some of the great minds behind Tekken and SoulCalibur. One major difference is that this game is not strictly a 2D fighter. At times the camera angle switches from 2D to a shifting 3D camera angle.

The graphics and art style are gorgeous in High Definition. The game and controls are simple to learn, and fairly intuitive. There is a fun single player mode, as well multiplayer modes. This single player mode starts off easily with a nice tutorial and ramps up the difficulty over time. Online multiplayer is good as well, with ranked battles. If you like Super Smash Bros. action, then you probably want to give this game a try.

2016

FEBRUARY 20, 2016
POKéMON SEASON 19

XYZ. This season is currently airing on television in the U.S. The gang has begun their journey to Snowbelle City for Ash's final gym match before qualifying for the Kalos league. Along the way, Bonnie finds a friend in a little green creature whom she names Squishy, but not even Professor Sycamore knows what it is! Team Rocket also have their eye on Squishy.

FEBRUARY 27, 2016
POKéMON RED / BLUE / YELLOW FOR THE 3DS

Released as part of the Pokemon 20th-anniversary event. These games are downloaded from Nintendo's eShop for only $10 each. These games are basically re-releases of the original games, not remakes. Pokemon Red, Blue and Yellow all come exactly how they were made back in the day. You can also transfer captured Pokemon to your Pokebank. A must have if you've never played the original games.

FEBRUARY 22, 2016
GENERATIONS TCG

Another reprint set that appears exclusively in bundles. Strong cards include Jolteon-EX and Revitalizer.

JULY 8, 2016
POKÉMON GO

This is a fantastic free App for Smart Phone users. Pokémon Go uses your phone's GPS to detect where you are in the world. Pokémon can appear randomly around you at any time. There are fixed locations in the world that act as Pokémon Gyms and Pokéstops. You can load up on supplies at Pokéstops and battle at gyms. The game uses Generation I Pokémon and is a ton of fun!

NOVEMBER 18, 2016
POKÉMON SUN & POKÉMON MOON

These games will be out in the Fall of 2016. They introduce new Pokémon from the Alola region. A new Battle Format called Battle Royal is also presented, which allows four players to battle one another at the same time in a furious melee.

AUGUST 3, 2016
STEAM SIEGE

This set is not out yet at the time we wrote this book, and we've only seen a few Promo cards up this point.

2016
POKÉMON THE MOVIE: VOLCANION AND THE EXQUISITE MAGEARNA

This 19th Pokémon film hasn't been released yet, but a movie trailer has. Ash and Volcanion somehow get invisibly linked together through the powers of a mysterious belt. They must learn to work together to stop a corrupt minister. Serena, Clement, Bonnie and Team Rocket also appear.

MAY 4, 2016
FATES COLLIDE XY

This set brings Zygarde and BREAK Evolutions of Basic Pokémon to the TCG.

THE TOP 10 POKÉmon VIDEO GAMES OF ALL TIME

By Bill "Pojo" Gill

When it comes to making Top 10 Lists, usually there is some form of judgment being used by the author. In this case of the "Top 10 Pokemon Video Games of All Time", I had to ask myself questions like:

- Should I make this Pokémon Top 10 List based on sales figures? *That would put Red & Blue way above the rest.*
- Should I include all games that contain Pokémon? *Like Super Smash Bros.*
- Should I include remakes of existing games? *Like Fire Red and Omega Ruby.*

There have been about 80 video games that feature Pokémon that are in our Pokémon Timeline Article earlier in the book. For this Top 10 List, I'm taking a couple of liberties:

- I am not going to figure sales statistics into my ratings. Just because a game sold like hotcakes doesn't necessarily make it a Top 10 game.
- I am excluding games that do not have "Pokémon" in the title. The Super Smash Bros. games are some of the best games ever created, but I'm excluding them from our Top 10 List.
- I am merging all remakes together. I am going to consider Pokémon Red and Pokémon FireRed to be the same game, since Pokémon FireRed it is essentially a facelift of Pokémon Red, and both feature Generation I Pokémon.

In creating this Top 10 List, I did surf the Internet and I read a lot of Pokémon Game Reviews, Metacritic Scores and Top 10 Lists. I also weighed heavily my own enjoyment when I played these games.

I'm sure your personal Top 10 List might be a lot different. But I think these are all games you should at least play through once if you haven't tried them. Let's start the countdown!

#10

POKÉMON PINBALL
RUBY AND SAPPHIRE

Release Date: August 2003
Platform: Game Boy Advance
Worldwide Sales: 1.37 million

This is a sequel to "Pokémon Pinball" for the Game Boy Color (which had sold over 5 million copies). This is a fantastic Pokémon themed Pinball game. Besides playing a traditional pinball game, another goal is to "Catch 'em All". The original 150 Pokémon are available for capture during gameplay, along with 50 more Generation II Pokémon. This was one of the first games available on the Game Boy Advance, and the graphics looked great. This is actually better than a simple makeover of the original Pokémon Pinball, and most players and professional reviewers loved this game.

The left button on the D-pad is used to control the left flipper, while the A-button is used to control the right flipper. The shoulder buttons were used to shake the table. The giant silver balls from real pinball machines are replaced with Pokéballs in this version.

There are two different pinball tables to choose from. One is based on Ruby, and the other is based on Sapphire. Both the pinball tables have nice layouts. The feel of the game is great. You almost get lost in the feeling that you're actually playing a real pinball machine. Hitting bumpers reveals Pokémon that are available for capture. You have to hit the Pokémon 3 times to capture it. You can evolve your Pokémon in the same fashion. There are even bonus areas that allow you to capture stronger Pokémon.

Save points are fantastic, and it's an easy game to pick-up and play for a little while, put it down, and return back to it.

I highly recommend this game if you have a system to play it on. You can find it for about $10 at GameStop these days. Game Boy Advance games can be played on the following systems: Game Boy Advance; Game Boy Advance SP; Game Boy micro; Nintendo GameCube Game Boy Player; and Nintendo DS. This game is also available for download on the Wii U, but I don't think it plays as well on the big screen.

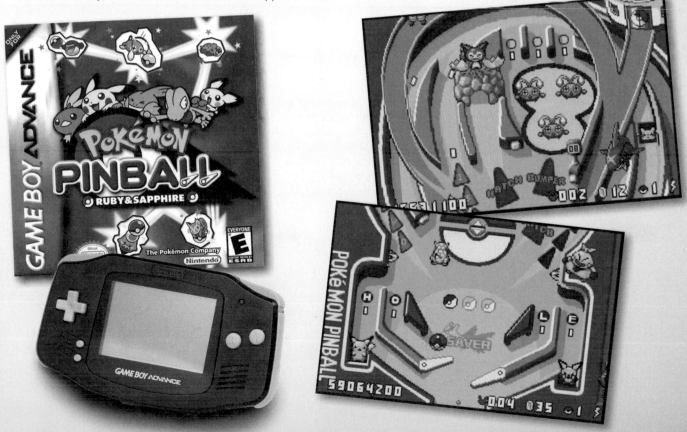

LUGIA used SHADOW BLAST!

#9

POKÉMON XD: GALE OF DARKNESS

Release Date: October 2005
Platform: GameCube
Worldwide Sales: 1.25 million

This was the 2nd Pokémon RPG (Role Playing Game) to appear on a home console. It is a direct follow up to Pokémon Colosseum which was a pretty decent game in its own right. The events in this story take place in the Orre region 5 years after the events in Colosseum.

Gale of Darkness and Colosseum are essentially bulked up Pokémon Stadium games with a bit of RPG action built into them. The RPG elements are not as good as the standard Pokémon handheld RPG's, but they are a very welcome addition to the simple battles of Pokémon Stadium. Gale of Darkness has a longer single player campaign than Colosseum, and allows the player to actually capture some wild Pokémon to trade to your handheld games. Some new Shadow Moves were introduced in this game, which were much better than the single Shadow Rush move used by all the Shadow Pokémon in Colosseum.

The storyline is pretty good. The bad guys are a criminal syndicate known as Cipher. They are creating Shadow Pokémon (whose hearts have been shut artificially) and using them as a plot for world domination. It's your job to stop them. You try to capture Shadow Pokémon and cure them (purify them). The maps and puzzles are well designed.

Improvement over previous games include:

- The ability to save your progress anywhere.

- The "Purify Chamber" is way easier to use than in the previous game. The Purify Chamber is used to purify Shadow Pokémon. Purified Pokémon can then learn moves they might not normally learn.

- There are also Pokéspots in this game that allow you to catch wild Level 10 Pokémon as well, though it's a bit tedious.

The Pokémon that folks really want to catch here is a Shadow Lugia that appears at the very end of the game. All Pokémon caught here can then be transferred to any of your Generation III games (Ruby, Sapphire, Emerald, FireRed, LeafGreen).

Almost all the battles here are double battles, where you and your opponent have two Pokémon in play at the same time. Pokémon look great on the GameCube, and the single-player story mode will take you about 25 hours.

We highly recommend this game and Pokémon Colosseum if you haven't tried them yet, and if you have a system to play them on. You can find these two games for about $25-$30 at GameStop or eBay these days. GameCube games can be played on the GameCube and the Wii.

#8

POKéMON CONQUEST

Player
I have formed a link with Tepig!

Release Date: June 2012
Platform: Nintendo DS
Worldwide Sales: 1.04 million

Yes, this is #8 on our list, and I'm guessing many of you readers have never heard of it. This game takes Pokémon into an entirely new direction for the franchise. Pokémon Conquest is a tactical, turn-based, strategy game that is very similar to Fire Emblem, Final Fantasy Tactics, Banner Saga, etc. It's essentially Fire Emblem with Charizard! There are nearly 200 Pokémon at your disposal, including Pokémon from Generation I through V.

In this game you play a Feudal Japanese Warlord (based on real Japanese historical characters). You recruit Pokémon to be your warriors as you do battle in a chess-like setting. Battles are 6-on-6 turn-based action on a wide variety of battlefields. This game really requires you to use your brain. It's not mindless action whatsoever. You have to know the tactical movement of characters across the grid, and which Pokémon attributes will provide your best opportunity for attacks. Pokémon will level up as you complete battles. When you win a battle, you take control of the new castle, recruit Warriors from that kingdom, and gain access to new Pokémon.

The art is fantastic. The battle animations are well done. The game is very deep for young players, but gives you a wonderful tutorial along the way. It's a great game for the older Pokémon crowd.

This is a really good spin-off of the Pokémon franchise. If you like Fire Emblem games, you'll love this game. If you haven't tried a tactical game, this is a great place to wet your feet.

One of the downsides from this game these days is that Nintendo has retired the Wi-Fi service for older games. Online features are no longer available, but the game still provides hours of entertainment.

We highly recommend this game! It's a sleeper, and it's tough to put down! The game is in fairly high demand. It has a cult following, and many people are still finding out about it. A used copy will set you back about $30 on eBay or GameStop.

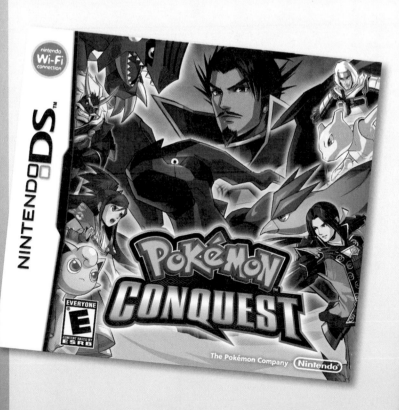

Shingen

Hahaha! You?! Challenging me to a battle?! Oh, very amusing! Very amusing indeed!

How's the Pose?
It's scratching its tummy.
1000pts!

#7

POKÉMON SNAP

KANGASKHAN

Release Date: June 1999
Platform: Nintendo 64
Worldwide Sales: 3.6 million

Wow! It's been over 15 years since this game was released. That has to make some of you feel old!

Pokémon Snap fits into the "Rail Shooter" category of games. In a Rail Shooter, the player does not have control of the path the character takes from beginning to end. It's as if you are playing the game while riding on a very slow roller coaster. Even though this falls into the Rail Shooter gaming category, there are no guns here! The shooting you are doing is being done with an old school, handheld camera!

You play as Pokémon photographer Todd Snap. The premise of this game is that you roll through various Pokémon environments in a cart on a track, and take photographs of Pokémon for Professor Oak. We know it sounds lame, but it's a ton of fun and extremely addictive. After each Rail Ride, Professor Oak will give you grades on your photos. You keep trying to photograph all the Pokémon and get better shots on each pass. You have some items at your disposal to interact with the Pokémon environment while riding along, like a flute, apples and Pester Balls. During each pass (rail ride), you only have enough film in your camera for 60 photographs. Someone get Todd Snap a bigger memory card!

There are seven environment levels and 63 Pokémon in the game. The levels include a beach, tunnel, cave, volcano, river, valley and a rainbow cloud. You are rewarded more for getting larger photos, centered photos and cool action shots. Do you dare wake a Snorlax for a better picture? Can you lure a Pikachu onto a surfboard for a picture? Can you get Scyther out of the bushes for an action shot? This a fun game, and a nice change from the typical Pokémon RPG.

Most fans and critics gave this favorable reviews. It sold well. Yet there's never been a sequel. I'm baffled. This game seems perfect for a remake on Wii U. You could use that sweet Wii U controller as your old school camera as you ride the rails.

If you have never tried it, and you still own a Nintendo 64, then you should really get it. Used copies of Snap can be found on eBay for less than $10. New, unopened, sealed copies of Snap will fetch over $100 on eBay. The game could be purchased on the Wii through virtual console, but it doesn't have the feel of the original.

#6

POKÉMON DIAMOND, PEARL AND PLATINUM

(Generation IV)

Release Date: April 2007 (D&P), March 2009 (Platinum)
Platform: Nintendo DS
Worldwide Sales: 26 million (All 3 combined)

Pokémon Diamond and Pearl were the fifth installments of the Pokémon series of RPG's. Pokémon Diamond and Pearl introduced over 100 new Pokémon and brought us what is considered "Generation IV" Pokémon. Platinum showed up on the scene two years later with a few tweaks and updates, and is essentially a sister game to Diamond and Pearl.

Pokémon Diamond and Pearl leads players into the Sinnoh region and were the first true Pokémon RPG Games for the Nintendo DS. The DS (Dual Screen) brought a touch screen and Wi-Fi capabilities into the Pokémon World. The DS was backwards compatible with the Game Boy Advance as well, which was pretty sweet for Pokémon players. Worldwide battles and trading were now possible thanks to Wi-Fi. Friend Codes allowed you to find trusted friends online. A real-time clock feature allowed you to capture specific Pokémon that were only available at certain times of the day. Pokémon contests became more elaborate thanks to the touch screen. Graphics again took a huge step forward on the DS, which brought more details in the Pokémon World. Buildings were now rendered in 3D. The color palette was also improved.

Gameplay is similar to most of the other Pokémon RPG's. You are a trainer trying to catch the variety of Pokémon that appear in the game. Once caught, Pokémon can be added to your party and trained to assist you. The longer you train a Pokémon, the more attacks they learn, and the stronger they become. The Pokémon Watch shows up for the first time here.

Pokémon Platinum is a follow-up game to the Pearl and Diamond games, with quite a few enhancements and changes. The most notable changes are: 59 more Pokémon; more Legendary Pokémon available for capture; a new Distortion World; and a new Villa for you to place your valuables. There are also improved graphics and more characters to interact with. Some buildings have different layouts, with different puzzles. Gym Leaders may have different Pokémon as well.

The 160 new Pokémon species in these 3 games brought the total to around 550 at the time. Like other Pokémon games, not all Pokémon are available in a single cartridge. In order to "Catch 'Em All" you need to trade with other players. This game will provide well over 40 hours of gameplay to beat the game, not including all the side quests. Highly recommended!

These games have not been remade yet, so the only way to play these games is to buy the originals. These old DS games will still play on the newer 3DS technology. Game cartridges can be found for as little as $12 on eBay. If you want the original case, expect to pay closer to $30. New, unopened, sealed copies of these games will fetch over $100 on eBay.

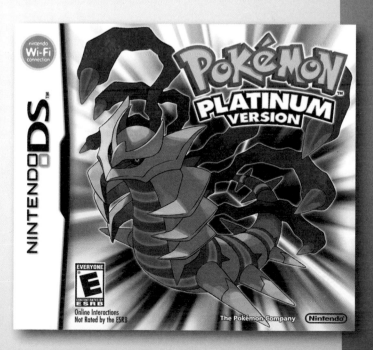

Pojo Note: *As we mentioned in our Pokemon Conquest review previously, In May of 2014, Nintendo terminated all online services for DS and Wii games. This has affected the following Pokemon games: Pokemon Diamond/Pearl/Platinum; Pokemon HeartGold and SoulSilver; Pokemon Black/White/Black 2/White 2; Pokemon Battle Revolution; Pokemon: Mystery Dungeon: Explorers of Time, Explorers of Darkness, and Explorers of Sky; My Pokemon Ranch; Pokemon Ranger: Guardian Signs; Pokemon Ranger: Shadows of Almia; and Pokemon Conquest.*

#5 POKÉMON RUBY, SAPPHIRE, OMEGA RUBY AND ALPHA SAPPHIRE
(Generation III)

Release Dates: March 2003 (Ruby & Sapphire), November 2014 (Omega Ruby and Alpha Sapphire)
Platform: Game Boy Advance
Worldwide Sales: 26 million (all 4 combined)

Okay, here is where I start taking some extra liberties in my game rankings. Some of you may think I'm cheating by combining these games that are 11 years apart into one group, but you can't deny the overall gaming experience is the same. The main storyline is essentially the same in all four games, and the same Pokémon are prominent in all these games. Pokémon Ruby and Sapphire were the third installments of the Pokémon series of RPG's. Pokémon Ruby and Sapphire introduced over 135 new Pokémon and brought us what are considered "Generation III" Pokémon.

Pokémon Ruby and Sapphire lead players into the Hoeen region and were the first Pokémon Games for the brand new Game Boy Advance (GBA) at the time. The GBA brought a larger screen, more pixels, and 32-bit power to the Nintendo's handheld lineup. So playing Pokémon on this portable system was more beautiful than before. We believe these were the bestselling games of all time for the GBA.

Mega Evolution is a phenomenon that has long been shrouded in mystery

Ruby and Sapphire introduced new types of Poké Balls, Pokémon Contests, Double Battles and Ribbons. Gameplay is similar to other Pokémon RPG's. You are a trainer trying to catch the variety of Pokémon that appear in the game. Once caught, Pokémon can be added to your party and trained to assist you. The longer you train a Pokémon, the more attacks they learn, and the stronger they become. These games feature 100 new Pokémon species, plus the 151 Generation I Pokémon. Team Magma and Team Aqua are crime syndicates that you must defeat along the way.

Omega Ruby and Alpha Sapphire were made available for the Nintendo 3DS system in 2014. It had been over 10 years since the release of the original Pokémon Ruby and Sapphire. Nintendo figured it was time for an upgrade, and to give a new generation of Pokemon players a chance to play these older games. Ruby and Sapphire were originally released on the GameBoy Advance, so these games received a very nice facelift.

What changed in Omega Ruby and Alpha Sapphire? The main storyline is essentially the same. Pokémon Omega Ruby and Alpha Sapphire still lead players into the Hoeen region again where you are trying to become a Pokémon Master. Graphics have obviously been upgraded and look great on the 3DS. Also, more animations have been given to the major characters in the game. These new animations give the game more of a movie-type quality over the originals.

There is an improved PokeNav Plus on the bottom screen of the 3DS. The AreaNav shows your movements in real time, and locations of trainers that want rematches. The DexNav displays all the Pokémon available near your current location. The Battle Resort replaces The Battle Tower from the originals. The Battle Resort is an island near the Elite Four that is great for battling, and home to Move Tutors where Pokémon can learn new moves. Some of the small towns from the original have grown into big cities. Also, Mirage Islands randomly appear on the map, where you can catch Legendary Pokémon. There are also some Mega Evolutions that weren't in the original games.

Another strange addition here are "Cosplay" Pikachu that you can obtain. These are female Pikachu that can be dressed in human clothing.

If you haven't played any of these games, then Omega Ruby and Alpha Sapphire are the games here that should be added to your play list. These are great games if you missed Ruby and Sapphire, or if you want to replay the game again with some significant changes. The only reason to go back and get the original Ruby and Sapphire games is collectibility and based on what systems you currently own. The old, used cartridges can be found for about $12 on eBay. We've seen new, unopened, sealed copies of Ruby and Sapphire fetch as much as $200 on eBay.

#4

POKÉMON BLACK, WHITE, BLACK 2 AND WHITE 2

(Generation V)

Release Date: March 2011 (B&W) and October 2012 (B&W2)
Platform: Nintendo DS
Worldwide Sales: 15.27 million

Yeah … I know … I'm sort of cheating here … but let me explain …. for those of you who don't know, Black and White 2 are not remakes of Black and White. They are actually sequels! So they are different games … er … sort of. Anyway, I think they should be played as a package, thus I'm ranking them as a package. Let me try to explain even more.

Pokémon Black & White were the fifth installments of the Pokémon series of RPG's. Pokémon Black & White introduced over 150 new Pokémon and brought us what is considered "Generation V" Pokémon.

Pokémon Black & White leads players into the Unova region. And the villains this time around are Team Plasma. The storyline follows the similar Pokémon formula you've grown to love, but are maybe getting tired of. These weren't the first Pokémon games on the Nintendo DS, so there weren't that many new system features. But there were many game advances including: new Pokémon moves; new Pokémon Abilities; new villains in Team Plasma; the introduction of Seasons of the Year; and the introduction of Triple Battles and Rotation Battles.

Gameplay is similar to the other turn-based Pokémon RPG games. The new 150 new Pokémon species in Black and White brought the total to around 650 Pokemon at the time of release. Black and White will take about 40 hours to beat.

Pokémon Black 2 and White 2: Then about 1.5 years after the first release, Black 2 and White 2 hit the streets. And these two games are actually sequels rather than remakes. The story here takes place 2 years after Black and White. The Unova region has changed. The towns have changed. The characters have changed. The Pokémon to capture have changed. The gyms have changed. There is now a World Tournament where the Gym Leaders from Johto, Hoenn, Kanto, Sinnoh and Unova can be battled.

There's a new feature in the Pokédex – The Habitat List – which allows you to track monsters you've encountered and caught previously. This makes it easier to "Catch 'Em All".

These games also introduce a new feature called "Join Avenue". This is a new building that starts off empty, and you become the owner. Over time, you meet folks and invite them to visit. Some will open shops where you can buy berries, potions, candy, etc.

So, all in all, any Pokéfan should play both of these games. When played back to back, the game flow and storyline are great.

It's super effective!

Salamence Lv. 50
HP

#3

POKÉMON X & Y

(Generation VI)

Release Date: October 2013
Platform: Nintendo 3DS
Worldwide Sales: 13.70 million

A wild Pikachu appeared!

Pokemon X & Y are the sixth installments of the Pokémon series of RPG's. Pokémon X & Y are the first in the RPG series to take advantage of the 3D modeling of the 3DS. These games introduce over 70 new Pokémon and bring us what is considered "Generation VI" Pokémon. This brought the total Pokémon in the Pokeworld to 721.

Pokémon X & White leads players into the Kalos region. Gameplay is similar to previous turn-based Pokémon RPG games. But, your goal is not to "Catch 'em All" this time around. Your goal is to discover the mystery behind "Mega Evolutions" of Pokémon. Mega Evolutions are a temporary state some Pokémon experience during battle that increases stats and abilities. Mega Evolutions can only be used once per battle, and not every Pokémon has a Mega Evolutionary Form.

The graphics on the 3DS are phenomenal. The entire Pokémon World is rendered in beautiful 3D. The animation has an anime type quality now. Characters, Pokémon and your environment are no longer pixelated. The battle scenes are reminiscent of Pokémon Colosseum. Each Pokémon move has its own animation.

At the beginning of the game you are able to choose more options for your starting character than ever before, including skin tone, hair color and clothing styles and fashion accessories. Also, Fairy-type Pokémon have been introduced, changing the Rock, Paper, Scissors Pokémon Chart slightly again. Super Training features mini-games that help build the stats of your Pokémon.

There is now a "Player Search System" that allows fans to trade safely and easily with online friends and strangers. There is also a Wonder Trade feature that allows players to make blind trades with anyone in the world.

After five generations of Pokémon, Game Freak has gotten just about everything right this time. These games will provide well over 40 hours of gameplay to beat the game, not including all the side quests. This is a great place to start for newer players. Older players should definitely get this newer title if they've missed it.

#2

POKÉMON RED, BLUE, YELLOW, FIRERED AND LEAFGREEN

(Generation I)

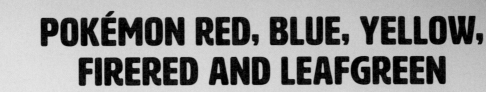

Release Date: September 1998 (Red & Blue), October 1999 (Yellow), September 2004 (FireRed and LeafGreen)

Platforms: Game Boy, Game Boy Color, and Game Boy Advance respectively

Worldwide Sales: 57 million (All five games combined)

Coming in at #2 are the Generation I Pokémon Games.

Pokémon Red & Blue: Pokémon Red and Blue were released simultaneously in North America in 1998. They are the granddaddies of all Pokémon games. The games appear to be simple, but they are actually very deep. The games feature a ton of strategy, and originally these games featured a dynamic storyline for the 8-bit world.

You are a trainer trying to catch the variety of pocket monsters (Pokémon) that appear in the Kanto region. Once caught, Pokémon can be added to your party and trained to assist you. The longer you train Pokémon, the more attacks they learn, and the stronger they become. There are a total of 150 Pokémon to catch, but only 139 were available on Red, and 139 were available on Blue. In 1998, in order to "Catch 'Em All" you needed to use a Game Link Cable and exchange captured Pokémon with friends. Traded Pokémon actually level up faster, so it was beneficial to trade your Pokémon.

The ultimate goal of these games is to become Pokémon League Champion by defeating the eight Gym Leaders, and then defeating the Elite Four.

The strategy of this game is knowing how to battle properly. There are 15 types of Pokémon, and each has a strength and weakness (almost like a giant version of Rock – Paper – Scissors). Fire Pokémon are weak against Water Pokemon. Flying Pokémon are weak against Bug Pokémon, etc. You can change Pokémon to your advantage, but you also lose an attack phase if you do.

Pokémon Yellow: This is an enhanced version of Pokémon Red and Blue. A Special Edition Yellow Pokémon themed Game Boy Color was also released at the same time as this game. Pokémon Yellow was inspired by the Pokémon anime.

Yellow is essentially an updated version of the original Red and Blue games, with a few fun changes. You are forced to take Pikachu as your starting Pokémon. Pikachu follows you around on your adventure outside of his Poké Ball just like in the anime. Jesse and James appear in this version of the game. The Gym Leaders have different teams based on the anime. Thirteen Pokémon are still unattainable in this version unless you trade for them.

Pojo Note: *New, Factory-Sealed, Unopened boxes of the original Red & Blue games sell for over $400 on eBay. A nice collectible for those who have one!*

Pokémon FireRed and LeafGreen: These were remakes of the original Red and Blue games, with simple facelifts to take advantage of the newer GBA technology at the time. Players could now play as a male or female. Pokémon have natures, genders and can hold items. Team Rocket appears more. A new region exists as well to catch some Generation II Pokémon. Pokémon can also breed.

I really believe that every Pokémon Fan should play some version of Red, Blue or Yellow. You should see how it all started. Luckily, in 2016, Nintendo re-released the original versions of Red, Blue and Yellow as digital downloads for the 3DS in their original 8 bit, black and white, pixelated glory! And Nintendo is only charging $9.99 to download these games! Nintendo also released a Pokemon 20th Anniversary Edition of the New 3DS in 2016 with Red and Blue pre-installed.

POJO'S UNOFFICIAL BIG BOOK OF POKÉMON

#1

POKÉMON GOLD, SILVER, CRYSTAL, HEARTGOLD AND SOULSILVER

(Generation II)

U.S. Release Date: October 2000 (Gold and Silver), July 2001 (Crystal), and March 2010 (HeartGold and SoulSilver)
Platform: Game Boy Color and DS
Worldwide Sales: 41 million (All five games combined)

Pokémon Gold and Silver: Gold and Silver were the first two true Pokémon RPG's since Red and Blue. Pokémon Gold and Silver introduced over 100 new Pokémon and brought us what are considered "Generation II" Pokémon.

What was great about these games is that Red & Blue were a phenomenon and fans wanted more. We were hoping for a game equal to the previous title, but Gold and Silver surpassed our expectations! These games were simply awesome at the time. Pokémon Gold and Silver lead players into the Johto region and introduced two new types of Pokémon: Dark type and Steel type. These games featured 100 new Pokémon species, plus the original 151 Generation I Pokémon. Gold and Silver featured backward compatibility at the time with Red, Blue and Yellow as well. The introduction of the day/night cycle created a style of play. Some Pokémon could only be caught at certain times of the day. Pokémon could hold items, and there was also breeding.

Also, the game didn't end this time when you beat the Elite Four. After your victory, you continued to explore the world and could do battle with the original Gym Leaders from the Kanto Region (Red and Blue). This all added up to one fantastic experience, making it #1 on our list.

New, Factory-Sealed, Unopened boxes of these games sell for about $200 on eBay

Pokémon Crystal: Crystal is a follow-up, sister-type game to Gold & Silver Game Boy Color games, with several enhancements. The most notable change is that for the first time in the Pokémon RPG's, players have the option to play as a female character in the game. Some of the puzzles in Gold & Silver were changed. You could also connect Crystal to your Pokémon Pikachu pedometer and earn mystery gifts based on your steps. Unlike Gold & Silver, the Pokémon Suicine appears in various areas of the Johto Region. You need to capture Suicine before you can unlock other phases of the game. Other small graphic improvements were made as well.

Pokémon HeartGold and SoulSilver (HGSS): HGSS are remakes of the Original Pokémon Gold and Silver games, with facelifts to take advantage of the new DS technology of 2010. Gold and Silver were already 10 years old at the time these newer remakes were released. The big change is the introduction of the Pokéwalker. The Pokéwalker was an enhanced Pokémon pedometer you could wear on your belt or pants. People were encouraged to walk/exercise to generate steps. The steps allowed you to capture Pokémon on your Pokéwalker. The Pokéwalker had wireless capability and you could transfer the Pokemon you captured back into the main games. Many rare Pokémon were caught this way, including Elekid, Dratini, Spiritomb and Pikachu (holding rare berries).

Other changes from the Original Gold & Silver? Obviously there were some great graphic improvements. There are new Pokémon. Gyms were revamped. The main storyline received some minor changes. More Legendary Pokémon were available. And there were some new Rivals. You also had the ability to have a Pokémon follow you around, much like Pikachu in Pokémon Yellow. Luckily HG&SS can still be played on the new 3DS systems. Six years later, these game are still in high demand! Loose cartridges will still cost you about $35 on eBay. If you want the original case, expect to pay closer to $50. If you want the box with game, case and Pokéwalker, expect to pay close to $100!

THE TOP 10 VIDEO GAME POKÉMON

For Every Type:
Bug, Dark, Dragon, Electric, Fairy, Fire, Fighting, Flying, Ghost, Grass, Ground, Ice, Normal, Poison, Psychic, Rock, Steel, Water.

By Angel Pelaez

It's been 20 years and more than 720 creatures since we all first met Pokémon, and, since then, many of us can say that it has had some influence on our present lives. I know that's my case.

We've all had our favorite Pokémon over the years: It may be because we won the Pokémon league with them; got to see them in 3D for the first time on Pokémon Stadium; they were super rare like the surfing Pikachu; they looked awesome as a shiny; or got them on a trade with that special someone. Truth is, all of our Pokémon tell the story of our lives in some way. And that's why I'll be forever thankful for the Pokémon Bank, so we can keep on using almost every one of our old Pokémon.

But as time passed and things changed, so did the game itself evolve. It is far more complex to battle effectively in a world where competition is global. And we face a terrible truth: our favorites may not be the very best for the job anymore.

Fear not, because time after time we've seen the enormous potential of each Pokémon; however small or weak it may seem, it can be aided by a great team to support and help it and the creativity and skill of its trainer.

So yeah, while our team may not always be expected to win a world championship, there are more than enough Pokémon out there to be effective in battle and respect your uniqueness and taste in Pokémon.

Of course, part of the fun is to breed and train them to get in perfect shape. It is a long process; I won't deny that. But that gets you more invested and mindful of your own strategy and potential weaknesses. So it is a process of learning. That's half of the battle you will face later on. I wouldn't suggest skipping it.

And how am I defining "the very best" in this piece? They are a mix of competitive powerhouses, all-time fan favorites and creative strategies applied with some of these monsters. Remember there are more than 720 of them. I'll just talk very briefly about 180 of them. We could, of course, write an entire book based on strategy and team building, but not this time.

So here you go: 180 of the very best Pokémon to play competitively, giving you a lot of options to build your own team and still having fun. Oh yeah! And winning of course.

Both types and Pokémon are in strict alphabetical order.

Top 10
BUG Pokémon

1. Beedrill

It may not be a very competitive Pokémon, but having a mega evolution allowed Beedrill to have very good attack and speed stats. Moves like U-Turn and Knock-Off are essential to get out of tough situations and can make an important difference in double or triple battles.

2. Galvantula

It may have a lot of weaknesses due to its type combination, but it is a power to be reckoned with if you let it prepare the ground. You'll want to use Sticky web right away, followed by attacks like Thunder as its ability Compound Eyes give Galvantula an important boost on accuracy.

3. Genesect

This one's a lot of fun to use. Download is a really interesting ability that can give Genesect a huge boost to its already high Attack and Special attack stats. On top of that, moves with STAB like U-Turn can even be a one-hit defeat in late game. Choice Scarf is the answer to its relatively poor speed.

4. Heracross

Even without mega evolving, Heracross is one aggressive sweeper with access to moves like Mega Horn and Close Combat. Both abilities Moxie and Guts elevate further its sweeping capabilities. This is one Pokémon you can use to deal a great amount of damage if used properly. Just don't let it out against a Flying Pokémon.

5. Ninjask

This one is really fast and you should take advantage of it using Baton Pass to get that boost to a sweeper (having Speed Boost as your ability, of course). It is kind of fragile and probably won't do much damage by itself, but it is a great support if you are setting up something that requires a good boost of speed.

6. Pinsir

This one became even better with a mega evolution. Especially since its ability, Aerilate, turns all of its normal type attacks into flying type and gives them a healthy 30% boost. So Quick Attack and Return become interesting attack options along Swords Dance for extra power.

7. Scizor

He may look like a really offensive Pokémon, but he needs some setting up before he can start sweeping. Fortunately, he can learn Swords Dance to boost its attack and speed. Roost is another fantastic move to use in case things go south.

8. Scolipede

Another awesome Bug type with Speed Boost? Yes, please. Scolipede can open a battle and set up spikes or toxic spikes and then attack a couple times so the rest of your team can start dealing some damage. Equip Focus Sash for some extra juice and make it count.

9. Volcarona

Its high Special Attack becomes even better after using the one move you don't want to miss on this Pokémon: Quiver Dance. You can pretty much start boosting and sweeping with powerful moves at your disposal such as Fire Blast of Hidden Power. This may be hard to breed and evolve for some, but it is totally worth it.

10. Yanmega

This is one bug with a lot of potential, but also a very fragile one. Its defenses aren't the best so you need to be careful on its timing on battle. Hit, let Speed Boost do its thing and get out with U-Turn. Rinse and repeat.

Top 10
DARK Pokémon

1. Absol

Its mega evolution is one to fear, really. Did you know the ability Magic Bounce prevents the effect of moves such as Thunder Wave? He can also boost its impressive Attack via Swords Dance and then decimate the enemy team with moves like Sucker Punch or Knock Off.

2. Darkrai

He has an awesome Speed stat and an even better Special Attack, so you want to take advantage of that. Boost with Nasty Plot and even equip something like a Life Orb and witness all those faints. This one does not have good defenses so get out if you see another sweeper in front of you.

3. Houndoom

Another great Pokémon that becomes even better thanks to mega evolution, Houndoom is not the first choice for many trainers, but having access to moves like Nasty Plot or Will-O-Whisp makes Houndoom a well-balanced choice for either offense or disruption. Don't forget to take advantage of STAB moves like Fire Blast and Dark Pulse.

4. Hydreigon

Yes, it may look intimidating and have a very good Special Attack stat. But Hydreigon still needs an extra boost (provided by Life Orb) to become a Pokémon capable of breaking almost anything. Remember to teach Roost to it, you will be thankful for the extra HP later in battle.

5. Krookodile

This is what I like to call a "hit and runner". You can equip Choice Band to it, pick a move according to the situation and then get out of the field. Intimidate is also a good ability to have in case your opponent likes to switch a lot.

6. Sharpedo

This is a very interesting Pokémon. You don't want to mega evolve right away as you may find a couple turns to let Speed Boost work its magic and then mega evolve and take advantage of its ability Strong Jaw with moves like Crunch. Its defenses are bad, so be extra careful of your timing.

7. Umbreon

Who doesn't love this Eeveelution? I know I do (especially on shiny colors). Umbreon is not a Pokémon you want to use to attack, but one that can heal your team with Heal Bell and Wish. It probably won't see a lot of action but can become a vital part of your team in the long run without a doubt.

8. Weavile

I don't really like the move Ice Shard on many of my Pokémon, but I consider it a vital part of my Weavile strategy. It has a great Attack stat as well so you might want to start taking advantage of that and use moves like Poison Jab or Pursuit for an extra (nasty) surprise on switching Pokémon.

9. Yveltal

This one is practically a god among Pokémon. Great Attack, Special Attack and HP. A great ability that boosts all dark type moves and Oblivion Wing; its signature move is capable of stealing some of your opponent's HP. There's not much more to say. If you have one, train it and bring it to battle.

10. Zoroark

He has a very good selection of available moves and a fantastic confusions Ability (Illusion), but unfortunately its stats aren't the best. It is a fragile Pokémon that's rarely used on competitive ecosystems. Do you want to use it because you like it a lot like I do? Fine, equip Choice Specs and sweep as much as you can. And try to protect it if you are fighting in double battles.

1. Dialga

This one has incredible stats and a move pool that allows it to sweep and also shuffle. Use Toxic to force a switch or Roar to keep it interesting and eliminate potential threads with brute force via Draco Meteor or Flash Cannon. Equip Leftovers and stay on the field for a good amount of time.

2. Dragonite

You gotta love Dragonite. He has been with us for a very long time and in all these years it just continues to deliver. Thanks to an amazing Ability (Multiscale) allowing him to cut 50% of the damage, you have full HP and a wide variety of moves at your disposal. Want more? Try Dragon Dance and sweep away!

3. Flygon

Maybe one day we'll have a Mega Flygon? Meanwhile, you know Flygon is a very good support Pokémon thanks to moves like Defog, Toxic and U-turn. Add Roost and keep on stalling. Levitate makes it immune to Ground attacks, so just be careful of those burn and poison status conditions.

4. Garchomp

Awesome for Sandstorm teams if mega evolved, but still great if you want to switch that Mega Stone for a Rocky Helmet in combination with the Rough Skin ability. Your opponent may be forced to switch a physical sweeper giving you the chance to boost or set some Stealth Rocks on the field.

5. Goodra

A great Special Defense makes Goodra your special tank. It can resist a lot of punishment while dealing some with moves like Outrage or Power Whip. Sap Sipper is a very good Ability as well, making Goodra immune to Grass type moves and boosting its attack if hit by one. It happens very often, believe me on this one.

6. Haxorus

This is another dragon that becomes great if Dragon Dance is applied a couple times. It is kind of fragile to STAB Ice and Dragon type moves so act fast, boost whenever you see the chance and hit hard. I've seen some Haxorus with Taunt as well, just to add a little surprise factor to the mix.

7. Palkia

Don't want to boost yourself before attacking? Palkia will become a favorite of yours. Equip a Life Orb and start using Special Rend, Thunder and even Fire Blast and start sweeping. It's defenses and speed are not great for a legendary, so just keep attacking for as long as you can and hopefully you can take a couple foes with you.

8. Rayquaza

I have to say I'm really scared of Mega Rayquaza. It has a great ability, access to very powerful moves as Dragon Ascent, and really over the top Attack and Special Attack stats. It has been banned from many competitions and will probably still be one of the most devastating Pokémon even in the new generation. Have it? Use it.

9. Salamence

Salamence wasn't the first option for many trainers until we learned it was capable of mega evolving. Now it has become a very powerful physical sweeper that is capable of defeating entire teams thanks to its ability Aerilate, and moves like Dragon Dance, Roost and Double-Edge.

10. Zygarde

There is still much we don't know about Zygarde, but we do know it is a very cool-looking Pokémon with great defenses and access to standard powerful moves as Earthquake and Dragon Tail. Will it become even better on Pokémon Sun/Moon? Definitely YES.

1. Ampharos

Upon evolution, Ampharos becomes not only fabulous but also a dragon type. Meaning he can now use Dragon Pulse in a much more devastating way. It can also self heal with Rest or get out of trouble with Volt Switch, so it is relatively safe to learn and dominate Mega Ampharos.

2. Eelektross

It is a hard Pokémon to master because of its poor Speed. But Eelektross can deal a decent amount of damage with special attacks like Giga Drain, Thunderbolt and even Flamethrower. Don't think you will be hitting first with this one, think you will be hitting the hardest.

3. Electivire

This is a pretty straight forward physical sweeper: do the best you can do with its great Attack stat and use a variety of moves for different encounters such as Ice Punch or Wild Charge. Use Motor Drive as its ability and make it immune to other Electric type attacks.

4. Jolteon

Your instinct may tell you to use this Pokémon's speed for offensive purposes. Truth is you'll be making a wiser decision teaching it Substitute, Wish, Thunderbolt and some attack you find fitting for the job. You will be switching him a lot, but you will also be helping the rest of your team get the upper hand on a tough battle.

5. Luxray

Intimidate is a great ability for an easy-to-use sweeper like this one, as you will be affecting the opposing team without doing anything but attacking. Equip Choice Band and select your moves carefully for better results. Some good choices are Wild Charge, Ice Fang and Volt Switch.

6. Manectric

This one earns a beastly Speed stat after mega evolving. Use that to your advantage and take the lead with moves like Flamethrower, Thunderbolt and Hidden Power. Volt Switch is a great way to get out of trouble with style.

7. Raikou

I love the idea of an Electric type capable of learning Calm Mind. Try to use it a couple times, equip Leftovers for more time in battle and start attacking with Thunderbolt (Thunder is too risky), Hidden Power, Shadow Ball or Extrasensory. Don't like Calm Mind? Try switching your equipped item to Choice Specs and sweep away.

8. Rotom

This is one of the most versatile Pokémon out there. It can transform and get another Type among Flying, Ice, Fire, Water and Grass. As well as moves that support these changes. It is still a great ghost type however, having access to moves like Will-O-Wisp and Pain Split.

9. Thundurus

Both forms of this Pokémon are great in a way. For this list I'll have to go with its base form. Prankster is a great ability to have if you are using Thunder Wave. But you can also teach it Nasty Plot and get rid of your opponent's team with moves like Focus Blast or Thunderbolt.

10. Zekrom

It has a scary Attack stat that's even better if you decide to use Hone Claws. Bolt Strike, Dragon Claw and some other move like Outrage (for desperate situations) will become really effective weapons against most Pokémon. Unless they are faster, in which case you'll want to equip a Choice Scarf.

1. Azumarill

It's type combination is just fantastic. And Azumarill is one of the best Pokémon to use if you love Belly Drum like me. Play Rough, Waterfall and Aqua Jet are great attack choices, but this also means Azumarill is very predictable, so be careful.

2. Diancie

Its mega evolution is amazing thanks to great offensive stats and the Magic Bounce ability. It is also capable of boosting itself thanks to moves like Rock Polish and Calm Mind. But be careful of its bad speed stat before evolution.

3. Florges

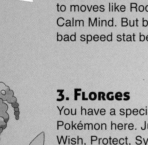
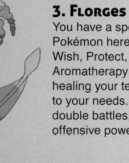

You have a special defensive Pokémon here. Just use Wish, Protect, Synthesis and Aromatherapy and keep on healing your team according to your needs. Better used on double battles, as you have zero offensive power with this one.

4. Gardevoir

Being immune to Dragon type attacks is by itself a huge perk for Gardevoir. Add its great ability, Pixilate, and turn moves like Hyper Voice into powerful devastation for many Pokémon in front of this one. Lots of fun to use.

5. Granbull

One of the most offensive fairies out there, Granbull is a great sweeper with moves like Earthquake and Play Rough. It can also play a support role with moves like Heal Bell. Too bad its Speed is simply awful.

6. Klefki

Thanks to its ability, Prankster, you can send a Thunder Wave of Spikes and have it become a priority move. So this one is a great lead for many battles. It can probably work decently as an offensive option, but it's better used as support in double battles.

7. Mawile

Take advantage of that high enough Attack stat, and when mega evolved start using STAB moves like Iron Head or Play Rough. It has enough defenses to resist some serious hits, but Leftovers is a good item to be held by Mega Mawile.

8. Sylveon

Great Special Attack and Special Defense. This one also has Pixilate as its ability and that makes this little fairy even more scary. Equip Choice Specs, hit hard with moves like Hyper Voice and then get it out of battle before it's too late.

9. Togekiss

Great defenses on this one. If you want to attack then I'd recommend moves like Nasty Plot. You want to have Serene Grace as your ability of course, and try to flinch with Air Slash.

10. Xerneas

The King of fairies is not only fabulous; it also packs serious heat. If you manage to use Geomancy the right way, you can easily take on entire teams with powerful moves ranging from Moonblast to Focus Blast.

Top 10 FIRE Pokémon

1. Arcanine

He may not be used a lot but this one has the cool factor we all want on our teams, right? Start by intimidating upon switch, and sweep away with moves like Flare Blitz and Extreme Speed.

2. Chandelure

This would be a great Special Sweeper if it wasn't for its very poor HP. So be extra careful of attacks like Pursuit. Choice Specs is a good item to be held as it may give Chandelure enough power to One-Hit KO the correct Pokémon, then switch and repeat.

3. Charizard

Decisions, decisions… Mega evolve it into X or Y? Both are great! Mega Charizard X Is one powerful dragon capable of boosting itself with Dragon Claw. Mega Charizard Y with Blaze ability and the Fire Blast/ Solar Beam combo is amazingly satisfying. So, maybe try both? There's no wrong answer here.

4. Delphox

This one is great but needs the extra power only a Life Orb can provide. Plus, it is a really interesting type combination with STAB moves like Psychic and Fire Blast. And you could use Calm Mind a couple of times as well for even more power.

5. Entei

I like how Intimidate works as an ability in the game, and Entei can force some switches with it. Guess one of them correctly and you could burn them with Sacred Fire. So it's a little bit of mental work but totally worth it.

6. Ho-Oh

If you can train one with the Regenerator ability and then teach it Recover, you have a very durable and powerful Pokémon. This one can also use Sacred Fire with a high chance of burning your enemy, so use it. Brave Bird is also a great move for tough situations.

7. Magmortar

Not used often in competitive environments. But hey, still one of the best looking fire types in my opinion. This one is really easy to use special sweeper. And it can learn a variety of moves like Thunderbolt and Focus Blast.

8. Reshiram

Another sweeper with godly stats. Blue Flare and Draco Meteor are not only cool looking moves but really effective when used by Reshiram. Equip Life Orb for extra damage.

9. Torkoal

Do you need a Pokémon able to use Rapid Speed and love fire types? Then this is your turtle! It may not be very impressive but Shell Smash is a move that can quickly turn the tables when using Torkoal.

10. Typhlosion

This is probably the least used of the fire starters. But still a cool addition to your team thanks to powerful moves like Eruption and Focus Blast. Be sure to raise its Special Attack with Choice Specs.

1. Blaziken

This is one of my favorite Pokémon of all time. And it's even better after mega evolving. The Speed Boost ability goes well with Protect and/or Swords Dance. I just complete the set with moves like Aerial Ace, Low Kick or Flare Blitz.

2. Breloom

Who hasn't faced a well-trained Breloom with Spore that practically wrecks a complete team? I know I have! And I have also been on the other side of the wrecking. Bullet Seed, Focus Punch and Mach Punch are battle changers. Breloom can make use of these moves fantastically.

3. Chesnaught

Spike Shield is kind of a signature move for Chesnaught and you can extend its lifespan by using Spikes, Leech Seed and a STAB move like Drain Punch. May not sound like much, but it is a pretty exasperating Pokémon to face.

4. Conkeldurr

Having Iron Fist as its ability allows him to enjoy a 20% boost on punching-moves. So think about Mach Punch, Drain Punch and elemental punches and you are on your way to a very aggressive Pokémon.

5. Gallade

Mega evolve it so you can benefit from much better Attack and Speed stats. Then try to get a Sword Dance or two and sweep away. I like Close Combat and Zen Headbutt for this one.

6. Hitmonlee

Not as competitive as others but still a great physical attacker. High Jump Kick and Mach Punch are well rounded moves for Hitmonlee. It can even learn Rapid Spin for some versatility,

7. Infernape

The fiery monkey is a great Life Orb user and an easy to use physical sweeper. Close Combat and Flare Blitz are common choices, but you can be a little bit more creative and use Grass Knot or Hidden Power.

8. Machamp

The No Guard ability prevents this Pokémon from missing an attack. So Dynamic Punch and Stone Edge are pretty cool options for this one. It is a high risk Pokémon due to its non-ideal stats, but a very rewarding Pokémon nonetheless.

9. Pangoro

I love the Scrappy ability as you will be able to hit Ghost types with Fighting and Normal moves. Take advantage of this and surprise unaware opponents with Superpower or Knock Off. Equipping Choice Band for extra damage is a relatively safe bet for Pangoro.

10. Toxicroak

Afraid of fairies? Toxicroak can help you overcome that fear thanks to its good type combination and great Attack. Equip Black Sludge on this one and have Gunk Shot ready for a good switch prediction.

Top 10 FLYING Pokémon

1. Aerodactyl

Not as good of an option as your mega evolution, but still capable of holding its own. Use Hone Claws and sweep with standard powerful moves like Earthquake or Stone Edge. An alternative strategy consists on using moves like Stealth Rock and Toxic to deal some indirect damage.

2. Articuno

Yes, it is really weak against Rock Types, but it can manage them by using a Substitute/Roost combo. Its Special Defense is also very good and its speed can be boosted with Agility. So think about what you can do with these tools. Life Orb gives Articuno that much needed extra juice.

3. Braviary

It may not be as aggressive as other birds, but it can fix that using Substitute, then Bulk Up a couple times and Roost when needed. If all goes well, you'll have a highly powerful bird on the field in just a couple of turns.

4. Gliscor

This is a hard to read Pokémon as you can use it offensively with Swords Dance, or start using moves like Toxic, Roost and Taunt to disrupt your opponent's strategy. So you may want to try both strategies and see what works best for you.

5. Hawlucha

Unburden is a great ability to use that boosts Speed after using or losing the held item. So equip a berry according to your needs and start unleashing Hawluchas' full potential. You can even boost with Swords Dance as well.

6. Landorus

Both forms are good but I find myself using the standard one more. Sheer Force and Life Orb give Landorus a huge power boost for moves like Earth Power and Knock Off. Be aware however of its weak defenses.

7. Pidgeot

Just Mega Evolve it and use Hurricane and U-Turn as needed. Most teams aren't quite sure what to do against Mega Pidgeot so capitalize on that. You can also use Roost if you find yourself in a tough situation.

8. Staraptor

This is one really aggressive bird! Close Combat, Brave Bird and Double Edge may be considered "last resort" moves, but the Reckless ability may help you take 2-3 Pokémon out before fainting. Want more? Equip Choice Band.

9. Talonflame

The Gale Wings ability makes Talonflame the king of Brave Birds (if there is even such a thing). But you can also surprise your opponent with moves like Taunt or Will-O-Wisp when they are expecting a full offensive from you.

10. Zapdos

It is a very powerful Pokémon, but it is also capable of getting out of trouble via Volt Switch or recover with Roost. There are not a lot of move options here but some choices like Toxic or Defog are really interesting and effective.

1. Aegislash

It has always been a great wall and we are not going to change something that works. King's Shield, Toxic and Pursuit will all (hopefully) work out for you just fine. Equip Leftovers on this one.

2. Banette

Mega evolve and prepare to use Destiny Bond a lot with this one thanks to its Prankster ability. Will-O-Wisp and Knock Off are other great move choices for a competitive Mega Banette.

3. Cofagrigus

This is a really slow Pokémon but that doesn't mean it's bad. You can use Trick Room to give it the upper hand. You can then burn your opponent with Will-O-Wisp, boost yourself with Nasty Plot or get some health back with Pain Split. It's just so much fun using it.

4. Dusknoir

Great defenses let you use Dusknoir without much fear of a one hit KO. In fact, it is a really simple Pokemon to use. Use moves like Shadow Sneak, Will-O-Wisp and Sucker Punch and that's pretty much it. Choice Band or Life Orb are suggested for extra power.

5. Froslass

This is a great game opener having Taunt and Spikes at its disposal. You can play some mind tricks as well predicting good Destiny Bonds. It is fast enough, but its weak defenses mean you probably will lose Froslass pretty early in battle. Equip Focus Sash in case you get a bad matchup.

6. Gengar

This is another one of my favorites. Levitate ability before mega evolution keeps it safe from Earthquake. But it is after mega evolving that Gengar gets Shadow Tag and a great potential for trapping and getting rid of your opponent's monsters with high Speed and Special Attack. You can also try Destiny Bond on this one.

7. Giratina

Its original form is the one I prefer due to its defensive potential. Equip Leftovers and you should be able to resist some heavy hits from almost any type Pokémon. Complement this with Toxic, Roar and Rest and you will have one of the most durable Pokémon out there. Just don't let it fight against Fairy types.

8. Jellicent

This is a tricky one to use as you want to make a good switch prediction and get it in at the right time. It is a defensive Pokémon, although not with the best defenses. So try to destabilize your opponent's strategy with moves like Will-O-Wisp and Taunt. Better if used in doubles.

9. Mismagius

It doesn't have a lot of HP or Defense, so you need to set up the game for Mismagius if you want to use it effectively. Moves like Nasty Plot, Destiny Bond and Will-O-Wisp are to force switching and start boosting. Equip Leftover to make your life a little bit easier while using Mismagius.

10. Sableye

Getting Magic Bounce and that huge defensive boost after mega evolving makes this one a tough Pokémon to beat. It is just a great defensive wall against many things your opponent can think of. Use Knock Off and Toxic when you get the chance and then Recover your way to victory.

1. Celebi

Believe it or not, Celebi is a great Baton Pass user as it has two different ways to boost: Swords Dance and Nasty Plot. It can take some of the opponent's HP via Giga Drain and can also use Recover to gain longevity. Unfortunately, its stats are not the best, so a strong Bug attack can finish your strategy way too soon.

2. Gourgeist

Remember to train the biggest one you can find as it has better stats. Frisk is a cool ability allowing you to find out what the other Pokémon are holding. It can learn two recovery moves: Leech Seed and Synthesis, so you should be able to hold for some time while hitting with a STAB move like Seed Bomb.

3. Leafeon

Good Attack and Defense stats make Leafeon a decent physical sweeper with moves like Leaf Blade and Return. You can also use other moves like Knock Off, but it's poor Speed makes it hard to use if not supported in some way.

4. Ludicolo

Do you want a Rain Dance Sweeper? This is probably the one you're looking for. Swift Swim makes Ludicolo really fast and a Life Orb gives extra power to already good moves like Surf, Giga Drain or Ice Beam.

5. Roserade

Natural Cure is a great ability to have on Roserade because you want him for the long run. Hit once with something like Sludge Bomb or Giga Drain and then switch quickly. You can also set Spikes or Toxic Spikes as an alternative setup.

6. Sceptile

Mega evolve and then use its great Special Attack and Speed stats with moves like Leaf Storm, Dragon Pulse or Focus Blast. Be careful however of faster Pokémon because Mega Sceptile's Defense stats are not great.

7. Shaymin

Its Sky form is great because of Serene Grave and its good use of Air Slash. It is often used as support with moves like Healing Wish. It's not a great sweeper, but can be a pretty resistant one.

8. Torterra

I love using Torterra! It is a pretty solid sweeper thanks to Rock Polish and crushing moves like Wood Hammer and Stone Edge. If you can make Torterra faster, you will have a great time with this one.

9. Venusaur

After mega evolving, it is a pretty balanced option as your Grass type Pokémon. There's not much strategy to this one: hit with STAB moves like Giga Drain and Sludge Bomb and use Synthesis to regain some HP when needed.

10. Virizion

Great Special Defense and a pretty interesting Type combination. You can boost yourself with Swords Dance followed by Close Combat or Leaf Blade. It's a pretty straight forward sweeper, so you should give it a chance if you are just starting on the competitive stage.

1. Camerupt

Mega Camerupt has a lot of Type resistances. Unfortunately, its Speed is really bad. So you will have to endure a couple of hits or try to get Trick Room into the field. After this, it's all about the sweeping.

2. Donphan

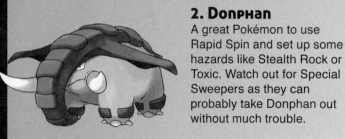

A great Pokémon to use Rapid Spin and set up some hazards like Stealth Rock or Toxic. Watch out for Special Sweepers as they can probably take Donphan out without much trouble.

3. Dugtrio

Its Arena Trap ability is great to take out some slower sweepers, but unfortunately Dugtrio is kind of fragile as well. That's why you should probably equip Focus Sash, hit hard with moves like Earthquake or Stone Edge and then get out.

4. Excadrill

Ideal for Sandstorm teams because of the Sand Rush ability. After that you can start attacking without fear. Iron Head and Earthquake are great moves specially with Life Orb equipped.

5. Golurk

This one is great because of its Type combination. It is immune to Volt Switch and can hit hard with its monstrous Attack with STAB moves like Shadow Punch and Earthquake. Be careful though, it is pretty slow.

6. Groudon

It's probably the most used Pokémon right now, and with good reason. It's Primal evolution (or reversion) and Desolate Land ability give huge power to moves like Earthquake and Lava Plume. Stealth Rock is also a great move option for this one.

7. Hippowdon

One of the best Physical walls nowadays. It can use disruptive moves like Toxic and Whirlwind and can take a lot of heat in doubles while setting up a sand storm. Equip Leftovers for extra durability.

8. Quagsire

Unaware is a great ability to have as it ignores boosts and debuffs, and it is also a really bulky Pokémon. I like using moves like Encore and Scald on this one. It is also a great Pokémon to teach Recover.

9. Sandslash

Another great Pokémon to have if you are running Sand Storm. Rapid Spin and Knock Off are great to mess with your opponent's head, and Swords Dance can make it even better if you find the chance to boost safely.

10. Swampert

A great Pokémon for rain teams and immune to Electric attacks. It's boosted Speed and STAB moves like Waterfall and Earthquake turn Mega Swampert into a natural choice for a sweeper on a Rain Dance team.

1. Abomasnow
This is a really dangerous sweeper and pretty easy to use. Mega Evolve and make the most out of its great attack with moves like Ice Shard or Giga Drain. Be extra careful when facing a Fire type.

2. Avalugg
It is a great wall capable of also giving you the upper hand with moves like Rapid Spin, Roar and Recover. Equip Leftovers for maximum duration, but be careful as Ice Types are fragile against common moves like Close Combat or Fire Blast.

3. Cloyster
This is another great Shell Smash user. Go on and equip Focus Sash. After that, attack with moves like Icicle Spear and Hydro Pump. Finally go out with a bang using Explosion.

4. Glaceon
The only problem with Glaceon is that it can learn a poor variety of moves. You are restricted to just a couple of good setups and that makes Glaceon really predictable. Ice Beam, Hidden Power and Shadow Ball are decent attack options.

5. Glalie
After mega evolving, Refrigerate, turns all Normal type attacks into Ice and boosts them by 30%, so if you are thinking about teaching Double Edge to Glalie you are on the right track. Return and Explosion are other good options to take out tough foes on single or double battles.

6. Kyurem
Pick your favorite among its Black or White versions as they are far more useful. Both forms are really offensive and have huge attack potential. White learns Fusion Flare and Black learns fusion Bolt.

7. Lapras
There's not much strategy to Lapras. Just have the right moves like Ice Beam, Freeze Dry or Surf and proceed to sweep. You may want to equip Choice Specs for extra damage.

8. Mamoswine
Pretty good attack stats but low Speed and defenses. You want to be sure you can get out Mamoswine safely before anything else. Equipped with a Life Orb, you can do quite good damage with moves like Ice Shard and Earthquake.

9. Regice
Look at that huge Special Defense! Go ahead and make this your tank. Equipping Leftovers and moves like Thunder Wave and Protect, you can extend its life by a lot. That is, of course, as long as you don't face a good physical sweeper.

10. Walrein
It's a really defensive Pokémon, but can also work as a good support for your team with access to moves like Roar, Toxic, Encore and Protect. It's kind of slow however, so be careful of Pokémon able to outspeed it.

Top 10
NORMAL Pokémon

1. Arceus

The god of Pokémon can be any type it wants, but this time we are focusing on its normal form. Its huge overall stats, ability to boost itself by Swords Dance and moves like Extreme Speed and Shadow Claw will most likely do a lot of damage. Be very careful of being affected by status conditions.

2. Blissey

It feels like Blissey was created for the sole purpose of supporting teams. As such, we are going to do exactly that. It's great HP and decent Special Defense allow us to use moves like Soft Boiled, Heal Bell, Protect, Wish or Toxic without fear, so long as a physical sweeper is not on the field. Great with Leftovers equipped, of course.

3. Ditto

Believe it or not, Ditto has a place on the competitive scene as a late-game sweeper. Whenever it switches in, you become almost an identical copy or the Pokémon in front of you (except for things like boosts). So get in with a Choice Scarf so you can outspeed your opponent, hit hard and get out. You can do this 2-3 times in a single battle if you are confident enough.

4. Kangaskhan

Its Parental Bond ability after evolving makes Kangaskhan one of the greatest offensive Pokémon in the game. Even moves like Fake Out will do massive damage. Not to mention other STAB moves like Return or Double Edge.

5. Miltank

You've known this is a dangerous monster since the Gold/SIlver era. It has a very good Speed stat for a physical tank and, as such, you should focus on indirect damage and disruptive attacks like Toxic and Thunder Wave. Heal Bell and Milk Drink are obvious attack choices as well.

6. Porygon-Z

It has moves that are rarely used on a competitive stage. I just love having that luck factor with moves like Tri Attack on Porygon-Z. It is also capable of boosting itself with Nasty Plot and/or a Life Orb equipped.

7. Regigigas

Having Slow Start as its ability is a challenge, yes, but Regigigas has good enough defenses to hold for 5 turns (especially in doubles). It can also help itself with moves like Substitute, Thunder Wave and Knock Off. This makes it a really resistant support.

8. Slaking

This is another challenging Pokémon but also a very rewarding one. It can learn a lot of moves so you can have a counter for almost anything you find in your way. Some suggestions are Double Edge, Earthquake and Giga Impact.

9. Snorlax

Rest and Sleep Talk along with equipped Leftovers are a safe bet for one of the most recognizable Pokémon ever. You can also boost via Curse and try to paralyze via Body Slam.

10. Zangoose

Be a kamikaze and equip Poison Orb as its ability. Toxic Boost will give some extra power to Zangoose. Act fast because it will faint quickly. You can use moves like Facade and Close Combat.

1. Arbok
Better used with Black Sludge equipped. It may not have very good stats but can boost with Coil and attack with STAB moves like Gunk Shot. If you can protect it in doubles, it can be a very interesting choice for your team.

6. Nidoking
It hits hard, but can hit even harder thanks to Life Orb, which is the most obvious choice for a held item. It also has access to a wide variety of moves, so you will want to be unpredictable with this one. Want some suggestions? Try Earth Power, Ice Beam and Flamethrower.

2. Crobat
This is another of my all-time favorites and, even if it's a pretty fragile choice, I like using it offensively. Equip Choice Band and attack according to your needs with moves like U-Turn, Brave Bird and Cross Poison. Then get out of there before you take damage.

7. Skuntank
With a decent HP stat you can open a game with this one and use Taunt or Pursuit and then hit with Poison Jab or Sucker Punch. There is a way you can use it as a special attacker with moves like Dark Pulse and Fire Blast.

3. Dragalge
A poisonous dragon is a pretty cool concept isn't it? Dragalge can set up Toxic Spikes and then attack with STAB moves like Draco Meteor and Sludge Wave. Equip Black Sludge for extra durability.

8. Swalot
There is not a lot of moves Swalot can learn, but that makes it simpler for you to choose right? Sludge Bomb, Giga Drain and Earthquake are obvious choices for this one. Return can also be an interesting choice.

4. Drapion
Boost with Swords Dance, disrupt with Knock Off (especially useful in a good switch prediction), and attack with moves like Poison Jab. Taunt and Toxic Spikes are also good choices for some variety.

9. Tentacruel
This one can set up some Toxic Spikes and get rid of annoying things with Rapid Spin. Use Toxic as needed and keep a high HP with Black Sludge and mind your switches.

5. Muk
There's not much strategy for this one. Try to hit hard with Choice Band and attack with Gunk Shot or Focus Punch. If you know the end is near, go out with a bang using Explosion.

10. Weezing
Immune to Ground attacks thanks to Levitate, and with high enough defenses, you'll want to use this one as a physical defensive Pokémon. Moves like Pain Split can keep you alive long enough to burn some Pokémon with Will-O-Wisp and defend yourself with Sludge Bomb.

Top 10
PSYCHIC Pokémon

1. Alakazam
It gets a very good boost of Special Attack and Speed after mega evolving, so a boost is not that needed. Hit hard with Psychic, Focus Blast and Shadow Ball. Easy to use and get used to, so this one is a safe bet if you're starting on the competitive stage.

2. Deoxys
Normal form, attack form, defense form or speed form? I like to be aggressive, so let's go with attack and let's hit hard with Life Orb equipped. Use outrageous moves like Psycho Boost and Super Power. Extreme Speed is also suggested, just in case.

3. Espeon
Magic Bounce is an awesome ability for good switches. And you can switch Choice Specs to give more punch to moves like Psychic, Dazzling Gleam and Shadow Ball.

4. Jirachi
Moves like Iron Head and U-Turn are great if you have Choice Scarf equipped. Unfortunately, there's not much more Jirachi can do as an attack option. But he can support decently with Toxic, Wish and Protect.

5. Latios
Even before having a mega evolution, we all knew Calm Mind was practically a must-use move for Latios. It is still the case! Mega evolve, boost and sweep away with Draco Meteor or Psychic.

6. Medicham
Pure Power is a scary ability and Mega Medicham can really get a good use of it with moves like High Jump Kick and Zen Headbutt. Throw some elemental punches in the mix and you have a really well rounded physical sweeper.

7. Metagross
One of the best mega evolutions out there thanks to its already awesome Attack stats and the Tough Claws ability. Meteor Mash, Mach Punch and Hammer Arm are natural choices for this one. It is as easy to use as it is devastating.

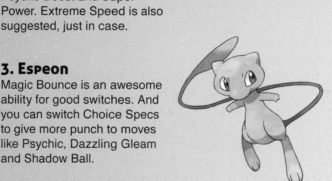

8. Mew
Mew gets a sure spot on this list because of its awesome versatility. It can learn every TM and HM in the game and a totally neutral spread among its stats. You can inflict status conditions, support, disrupt or attack with this one. I won't even suggest some moves for this one. My only advice: have fun being creative with Mew.

9. Mewtwo
Both mega evolutions are awesome so why not try both? Mega Mewtwo X is awesome with physical moves like Earthquake, Low Kick and Stone Edge. Mega Mewtwo Y excels with special moves like Focus Blast, Ice Beam and Fire Blast.

10. Slowbro
Mega Slowbro is a great defensive Pokémon with some offensive potential here and there. It can also boost with Calm Mind and disrupt with moves like Thunder Wave. Slack Off is also a great move to have on Slowbro whether you choose to mega evolve it or not.

1. Aggron

This is a great physical tank after evolving. You can screw up some of your opponent's intentions with moves like Thunder Wave and Stealth Rock. Heavy Slam is one awesome move for this one due to Aggron's weight.

2. Aurorus

Refrigerate could be a very good ability to have if only Aurorus would have better moves to choose from. Blizzard, Freeze-Dry and Earth Power are good moves for Aurorus, but be careful of faster Pokémon.

3. Golem

Thanks to its Sturdy ability it cannot be one-hit KO'd, so you can set up some Stealth Rocks on the field early in battle. Attack as much as you can and go out with a good Explosion when the time comes.

4. Kabutops

This is a solid physical sweeper with interesting STAB moves like Stone Edge and Waterfall. It is not as fast as it could be and its HP is really poor. But you can get ahead of your opponent with other moves like Aqua Jet if needed.

5. Rampardos

I love having Rampardos as my physical sweeper because he can automatically boost twice with Sheer Force and Life Orb without having to do it between turns. Hit hard with Zen Headbutt and Superpower, and you can even force some switches with brute force.

6. Regirock

It will resist most hits, so this one is ideal to open a game with Stealth Rock and Thunder Wave. Just focus on staying alive, predicting switches and attacking when convenient with Stone Edge and Earthquake.

7. Rhyperior

Solid Rock reduces the damage of super effective moves by 25%, so it's only natural to think of this as an outstanding tank with some help from Leftovers. Stealth Rock and Toxic are good disruptive options, while Rock Blast, Earthquake and some elemental punch can complete the move set.

8. Shuckle

How can something so small be so awesome? You will find a lot of these on the competitive stage, and it's because of its almost-godly defenses and access to awesome moves like Sticky Web and Stealth Rock. This Pokémon alone can win battles as soon as they start if your opponent gets too comfortable facing Shuckle.

9. Tyranitar

If you want to assemble a sand team, then Tyranitar must be your star Pokémon. It can support a lot of things with Sand Stream, but, more importantly, it can stand up for itself with gargantuan Attack and moves like Stone Edge or Pursuit.

10. Tyrantrum

It doesn't have the best stats, so you will probably want to boost it with Dragon Dance, followed by Dragon Claw or Outrage against Dragons. Equip Life Orb for better results.

1. Bisharp

Pretty straightforward physical sweeper but also a very effective one. Boost with Swords Dance and then use STAB moves like Iron Head and Sucker Punch. It is a very resistant Pokemon, so don't be too afraid if you get in front of other potential sweepers, unless you aren't boosted.

2. Empoleon

This is a great defensive option with the potential to do some indirect damage with moves like Roar, Toxic and Stealth Rock. Scald is a good STAB move option and other moves like Aerial Ace can complete the set nicely.

3. Ferrothorn

It would seem like Steel types are made to be durable support right? Ferrothorn is another great example of this. Awesome defenses and access to moves like Spikes and Leech Seed can give you the better hand on single or double battles.

4. Forretress

A great option if you are looking for a good Rapid Spin user. Complemented by some very useful moves ranging from Volt Switch to Spikes, Forretress can be an extremely useful Pokémon for different situations.

5. Heatran

Awesome type combination, awesome stats and awesome moves, that's what Heatran's all about. It can annoy with Taunt, Toxic or Protect and hold its own with Lava Plume, Earth Power and even Solar Beam.

6. Lucario

It doesn't necessarily need to boost after mega evolving but it has access to Swords Dance anyway. Watch its outstanding power with moves like Close Combat and Bullet Punch. Even better, of course.

7. Magnezone

A great option against Steel Type because of its ability Magnet Pull, which prevents these type of Pokémon from switching. Try to get Hidden Power Fire for this one, as it's a good combo. Thunderbolt and Flash Cannon are good for STAB Damage. Equip Choice Scarf preferably.

8. Registeel

Use it defensively, opening with Toxic or Thunder Wave and then let it live longer with Protect. You probably won't be doing much damage but you will be slowly marching towards victory. Registeel requires patience and Leftovers equipped.

9. Skarmory

Open the game with Skarmory and set up some Spikes. Then disrupt with Taunt or Whirlwind and heal whenever you need to with Roost and some Leftovers equipped. Great as a Defog user as well.

10. Steelix

As much as I would like to use this one offensively thanks to its Sand Force ability, we all know it has more efficient ways acting defensively. It can use Stealth Rock and Toxic, as well as STAB moves like Heavy Slam when needed.

Top 10 WATER Pokémon

1. Blastoise

Coolest mega evolution ever, and a really useful one as well. Go ahead and mega evolve it and get that sweet boost to moves like Aura Sphere or Dark Pulse. Complement with Scald and Rapid Speed if needed.

2. Feraligatr

It may not have the best offensive stats, but Feraligatr becomes really interesting thanks to its ability to learn Dragon Dance. So if you get the chance to boost once or twice, you can get a really strong Pokémon with moves like Crunch, Ice Punch and Waterfall.

3. Greninja

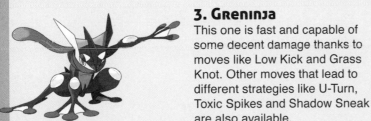

This one is fast and capable of some decent damage thanks to moves like Low Kick and Grass Knot. Other moves that lead to different strategies like U-Turn, Toxic Spikes and Shadow Sneak are also available.

4. Gyarados

Another Pokémon begging for a good boost via Dragon Dance. If you manage to pull it off, Mega Gyarados will be an unstoppable force in no time. Ice Fang and Earthquake are there to cover some weaknesses.

5. Kingdra

A great Pokémon to use if you have a rainy team because of its Swift Swim ability, but that will be pretty much the only boost it can get by itself. So better use what you've got and use high damage moves like Hydro Pump and Draco Meteor. It can get some extra power with Choice Specs.

6. Kyogre

It is still a really good special sweeper thanks to its Primordial Sea ability after mega evolving and access to Calm Mind. You know the rest: Thunder, Ice Beam and Origin Pulse as needed. Be aware you'll also have a very predictable Pokémon on your hands.

7. Milotic

It is a defensive Pokémon by nature, but it also has potential to do some damage with STAB moves live Scald and Recover. Toxic can also be used to expand its viability.

8. Starmie

This is another great Pokémon to teach Rapid Spin. It is pretty fast and can deal interesting damage with moves like Hydro Pump, Psychic and Hidden Power. In a tough spot? It can also learn Recover.

9. Suicune

Suicune doesn't have great stats for a legendary, but there's Calm Mind for that. Use Scald to hopefully burn something and a Rest/Sleep Talk combo could work wonderfully for you.

10. Vaporeon

Vaporean is great support with Water Absorb ability. You can use Protect and Scald, followed by Wish in case you need to heal (it will be enough thanks to its great HP stat). Use Roar or Baton Pass when in trouble. Better in doubles.

THE TOP 100 POKÉMON CARDS OF ALL TIME

By Jason Klaczynski
3-Time World Champion, 2015 U.S. National Champion

Playing the Pokémon TCG since its U.S. debut in 1998, I've had the pleasure of competing through every year of the game's history, and have seen every expansion the game has released. Over the following pages, I've compiled a list of what I believe to be the greatest 100 Pokémon cards of all time, relative to the formats they existed and competed in. When ranking cards, I assessed cards at their strongest point, but also gave consideration to cards that were strong across multiple years and formats.

POJO NOTE:
By my estimate, there are approximately 9,000 English Pokémon cards in print as of July 2016. Jason had to knock this down to the 100 Best Cards. That was no easy task! Great work here Jason!

100 Blaziken

(EX—Ruby & Sapphire, 2004)

Blaziken, alongside Ruby & Sapphire's Delcatty, dominated the 2003–2004 season, though it fell just short of capturing the World Championship title. Blaziken's Firestarter was used to fire up powerful attacks, like Rayquaza-ex's (EX—Dragon) Dragon Burst, and Blaziken ex's Volcanic Ash, which could hit any Pokémon for 100 damage.

99 Prism Energy

(Black & White—Next Destinies, 2012)

As if EX Pokémon weren't strong enough on their own, they debuted alongside Prism Energy, which provided the right type of Energy these strong Pokémon-EX— and any Basic Pokémon—needed. Hydreigon (Black & White—Dragons Exalted) decks showed off the card's strength, as they could use the same Prism Energy to provide Darkness Energy. This allows Hydreigon's Ability to transfer it between Pokémon, Fighting Energy to power up a Terrakion, and Grass Energy to activate Virizion-EX's Ability.

98 Pichu

(Neo Genesis, 2000)

Throughout the early years of the game, there were several cards aimed at countering Pokémon Powers, but one of the best came from the Neo Genesis expansion. Since Pichu was a Baby Pokémon, opponents needed to flip Heads before trying to attack it. This meant that with some luck, Pichu could survive turn after turn, spreading Zzzap damage until it knocked out several opposing Pokémon. To make it even more difficult to KO (Knock Out), players could attach a Focus Band to Pichu, making opponents need an additional flip to KO it!

97 Mr. Briney's Compassion

(EX—Dragon, 2003)

Unlike its modern-day reprint AZ, which forces you to discard cards attached to the Pokémon you return to your hand, Mr. Briney's Compassion returns Energy cards and Pokémon Tools to your hand, allowing you to preserve more of your cards. It not only allowed players to heal high HP Pokémon, but also re-use Pokémon Powers that were activated when playing a Pokémon from your hand.

96 Pow! Hand Extension

(EX—Team Rocket Returns, 2004)

Pow gave players two strong options: either switch your opponent's Active Pokémon with one of his or her Benched Pokémon, or move an Energy card from his or her Active Pokémon to a Benched one. The latter of these two is where Pow's tricks came in. By sending your opponent's Energy to the Bench, you could prevent a Pokémon from attacking or retreating, and strand it active. Another trick was to send Special Energy Cards that could only be attached to Evolved Pokémon to an opposing Basic Pokémon, which, by rule, resulted in the Energy card immediately being discarded.

95 Magnezone

(HeartGold SoulSilver—Triumphant, 2010)

Magnezone's Magnetic Draw allowed players to create powerful boards full of Evolved Pokémon, but it wasn't just Magnezone's Poké-Power that made it strong. Magnezone's Lost Burn attack could unleash huge amounts of damage, capable of one-hit KOing every Pokémon in the format. A common strategy with Magnezone was to play cards that lowered both players' hand size, such as Judge. Since Magnezone allowed you to draw back up to 6, such cards would hit the opponent harder than the Magnezone player.

94 Tropical Beach

(Black & White Promo, 2011)

Tropical Beach is unique in being the only World Championship promotional card to ever be used in competitive play. (It was even used in World Championship-winning decks!) It served as the foundation for evolution decks to get started on the first turn, helping players draw into their Evolved Pokémon (and Trainer cards like Rare Candy). By drawing up to 7, Tropical Beach often set up an explosive Turn 2 that could quickly overwhelm an opponent.

93 Double Rainbow Energy

(EX—Team Magma vs Team Aqua, 2004)

For years, Double Rainbow Energy permitted the use of attacks that would have simply been too expensive in terms of Energy to be competitively viable. Double Rainbow Energy not only allowed players to attack more quickly, but also splash multiple types of Pokémon into decks without having to worry about splitting their Energy cards.

92 Delcatty

(EX—Ruby & Sapphire, 2003)

The engine that powered the dominant Blaziken decks through the 2003–2004 season, Delcatty allowed players to draw massive hands to build powerful boards full of Evolved Pokémon. Pokémon like Magneton (EX—Dragon) could be used to recover the Energy cards Delcatty pitched away. Since it was reprinted four years later in the EX—Power Keepers expansion, it continued to see competitive play for many seasons.

91 Mew ex

(EX—Legend Maker, 2006)

Mew ex was integral to two of the strongest decks from 2006. The first was the World Championship-winning Mewtrick, which used Mew ex to repeatedly copy Manectric ex's Disconnect attack, preventing the opponent from playing crucial Trainer cards. The second was the less known "Mew Lock" deck, which used Mew to copy a variety of attacks that ultimately trapped an opposing Pokémon Active, and then switched to bench-damaging attacks to win the game. It wasn't just these two decks Mew was used in either; the card was as versatile as its Poké-Body suggests.

90 Level Ball

(Black & White—Next Destinies, 2012)

Since its release in 2012, every deck that has relied on Pokémon with 90 HP or less has received a huge boost in both speed and consistency from Level Ball. It uses its ability with the 90 HP Eelektrik to power up Pokemon with Lightning Energy cards from the discard pile. Or, Level Ball, in a blazingly field Vespiquen deck, can quickly search out low HP Pokemon to send to the discard pile to fuel Vespiquen's Bee Revenge Attack. This card does wonders in any deck where it fits.

89 Puzzle of Time

(XY—BREAKpoint, 2016)

Until Puzzle of Time was released, there were limited ways in the Standard format to recover key Stadium cards, or Special Energy Cards, such as Double Colorless Energy. However, since Puzzle of Time's recent debut, players have begun getting away with running as few as four Energy cards in their deck. The card gains strength from the fact that it can be fetched out by other Trainer cards, like Teammates, Trainers' Mail, and Korrina.

88 Yanmega

(HeartGold SoulSilver—Triumphant, 2010)

Arguably the greatest Prime Pokémon from the HeartGold SoulSilver era, Yanmega's strength stemmed from the wide variety of cards that allowed players to easily match their opponent's hand size, such as Supporter cards like Judge and Copycat, or card-drawing Abilities like Magnezone's (HeartGold SoulSilver—Triumphant) Magnetic Draw. 70 damage for no Energy is obviously great, but being able to pick off a benched Pokémon before it could evolve was a strong option, too.

87 Shaymin

(HeartGold SoulSilver—Unleashed, 2010)

Shaymin allowed all kinds of cool tricks in the 2010–2012 formats. The most notable was to fuel massive X Ball attacks from Mewtwo-EX, which did 20 damage for each Energy attached to both Active Pokémon. It also ruined many players' days by being part of the 3-card "ZPS" combo of Zekrom-Pachirisu-Shaymin. This strategy used Pachirisu's (HeartGold SoulSilver—Call of Legends) Ability to get three Energy in play, then moved it to Zekrom (Black & White) with Shaymin's Celebration Wind, and last, hit for 120 damage, all on the first turn of the game!

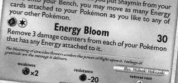

86 Archie's Ace in the Hole

(XY—Primal Clash, 2015)

The key Supporter card of the 2015 Masters Division World Championship-winning deck, Archie's Ace in the Hole allows for powerful Stage 2 Pokémon to hit the Bench on the first turn of the game. Blastoise was the focus of the World Championship-winning deck, but many players also paired Archie's with Empoleon (Black & White—Dark Explorers) as a way of both doing damage and drawing cards.

85 Maxie's Hidden Ball Trick

(XY—Primal Clash, 2015)

The Fighting version of Archie's Ace in the Hole, Maxie's has and continues to see play in both the Standard and Expanded formats, as there are several strong Fighting Pokémon it can restore to the Bench. The most powerful of these is Archeops, which once in play, prevents either player from evolving any of their Pokémon. In addition to Archeops, we also see strong attackers, like Gallade (XY—BREAKthrough) being paired with it.

84 Chaos Gym

(Gym Challenge, 2000)

The earliest years of the game were dominated by powerful Trainer cards, so you can imagine anything that had a chance at preventing your opponent from using their Trainers was very powerful, even it it affected both players. The best way to use Chaos Gym was to power up a strong Pokémon, then place Chaos Gym in play to protect it from Energy Removal and Super Energy Removal.

83 Pokémon Center

(Base Set, 1999)

Pokémon Center was a great healing card for high HP Pokémon, particularly ones that could attack for a single Energy card. However, its best use was pairing it with Base Set Alakazam, which could use its Ability to move damage counters to Pokémon without Energy cards. This allowed healing massive amounts of damage, without losing any Energy cards at all!

82 Forest of Giant Plants

(XY—Ancient Origins, 2015)

Being able to evolve on the first turn of the game is always strong, but given how powerful some of the evolved Grass-type Pokémon are, Forest of Giant Plants has become a popular card in today's Standard format. The most popular use of Forest of Giant Plants is getting a Turn 1 Vileplume (XY—Ancient Origins), which prevents players from playing Item cards. However, don't forget about Shiftry (Black & White—Next Destinies), which could allow easy wins on the first turn of the game. Forest of Giant plants made this card so strong that it had to be banned!

81 Strong Energy

(XY—Furious Fists, 2014)

Fighting Pokémon are known for having fast and heavy-hitting attacks, but Strong Energy took this to a new level. An extra 20 damage, especially when combined with other damage-raising cards, like Fighting Stadium & Muscle Band, allows Fighting Pokémon to hit for huge amounts of damage for low amounts of Energy. Take a Pokémon like Primal Groudon-EX, pair it with Strong Energy, and there's virtually nothing it's going to miss a KO on!

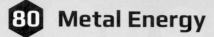

80 Metal Energy

(Neo Genesis, 2000)

The very first version of Metal Energy was unique in that a technicality allowed it to reduce self-damage from non-Metal Pokémon by 20. This meant Pokémon like Base Set's Chansey could stack Metal Energy cards to reduce their self-damage significantly, while still hitting the opponent's Pokémon for heavy amounts of damage. Several successful decks during the early 2000's relied on building "walls" of high-HP Pokémon, like Steelix (Neo Genesis), that were simply too tough to penetrate.

79 Oracle

(Skyridge, 2003)

Oracle's strength wasn't just that it placed two cards on top of your deck, but rather stemmed from the fact that it could be combined with cards that allowed you to immediately draw those two cards. Pair Oracle with Ruby & Sapphire Delcatty, or a Trainer card like Bill, and it becomes a double Computer Search, allowing decks to draw everything they need to set up.

78 Eelektrik

(Black & White—Noble Victories, 2011)

Easily searched out by Trainer cards like Level Ball, players could get out multiple Eelektrik, using its Dynamotor Ability to fuel massive attacks that could one-hit KO anything. Eelektrik was paired with a variety of powerful Pokémon over the years, such as Black & White Zekrom, Next Destinies Mewtwo-EX, and Dragons Exalted Rayquaza-EX. All of these strategies were strong enough to win tournaments.

77 Wigglytuff

(Jungle, 1999)

Among the first competitively viable Evolved Pokémon, Wigglytuff was strong for two reasons. The first was that Double Colorless Energy allowed it to attack for only two Energy cards, giving it a chance against Energy Removal and Super Energy Removal cards. The second was that it could use a full bench and a PlusPower to score one-hit KOs on the popular 70 HP Pokémon of the time.

76 Trevenant

(XY, 2014)

Trevenant saw competitive play as soon as it was released, as it was a Stage 1 version of Emerging Powers Gothitelle that itself had seen success. Trevenant became even stronger in recent years, as the Supporter card Wally (as well as a Phantump with an Ascension attack) allows players to evolve to Trevenant on the first turn of the game, quickly denying your opponent opportunities to play their key Item cards. Additionally, it gained a Trevenant BREAK card, giving it a stronger attack, and more HP.

75 Virizion-EX

(Black & White—Plasma Blast, 2013)

Paired alongside the Grass-type Genesect-EX (Black & White—Plasma Blast), which could unleash a massive 200-damage G-Booster attack, Virizion-EX took both 1st and 2nd in the Masters Division at the 2014 World Championships. Virizion-EX wasn't just used to power up Genesect-EX; its useful Verdant Wind Ability allowed it to be splashed into any decks that could run Grass Energy (or any Special Energy cards that provided Grass). This protected them from the powerful Hypnotoxic Laser Trainer that was used in many decks.

74 Hypnotoxic Laser

(Black & White—Plasma Storm, 2013)

Hypnotoxic Laser was strong enough by itself, but with Virbank City Gym, which increased poison damage from 10 to 30, its damage could further supplement powerful, fast attacks to quickly overwhelm opponents. As if this poison damage wasn't enough, Hypnotoxic Laser would also sometimes leave the Defending Pokémon asleep. You can be sure that many games were won and lost by a Hypnotoxic Laser sleep flip!

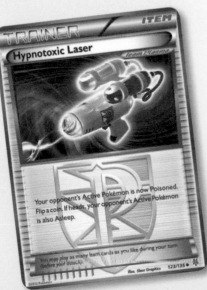

73 Rocket's Admin.

(EX—Team Rocket Returns, 2004)

Rocket's Admin. was great both early and late in games. In the beginning of the game, it gave you a fresh new hand of six cards. At the end of the game, it allowed you a chance to deprive your opponent of the key card he or she needed to beat you, reducing his or her hand to a mere 1 or 2 cards.

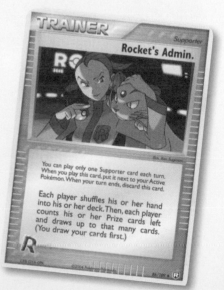

72 Junk Arm

(HeartGold SoulSilver—Triumphant, 2010)

Junk Arm was a strong card as soon as it was released, but became even stronger as other powerful Item cards were released in the Black & White expansions. The ability to repeatedly recycle Items like Pokémon Catcher allowed fast, aggressive decks to dominate in 2012, and the two-card discard it required was used to discard Energy cards, fueling Abilities & Trainers that recovered these Energy cards from the discard pile.

71 Mr. Mime

(Jungle, 1999)

Mr. Mime definitely threw a wrench at many popular decks during the earliest years of the game. If your deck didn't have a variety of ways to deal 20 or less damage, a single Mr. Mime could tear through your entire Bench untouched. Mr. Mime functioned as a great stalling Pokémon, but that's not saying its Meditate damage didn't add up.

70 Dusknoir

(Diamond & Pearl, 2007)

Dusknoir was so powerful during 2007 and 2008 that players would routinely limit their Bench size to 3 Pokémon, just for the small chance their opponent might surprise them by dropping a sudden Duskull plus Rare Candy & Dusknoir on them. It might seem like paranoia, but there was a reason for it: if you got caught with more than 3 Benched Pokémon, Dusknoir's Dark Palm would cost you your strongest Benched Pokémon, and probably the game.

69 Rocket's Zapdos

(Gym Challenge, 2000)

Rocket's Zapdos had all the attributes that strong Pokémon needed during the early years of the game: high HP, no Weakness, a Resistance to Fighting, and an attack that worked both with and against Super Energy Removal. To top it off, cards like Defender, Gold Berry and Metal Energy allowed you to heal or reduce the self-damage from Electroburn, making the card even stronger.

68 Accelgor

(Black & White—Dark Explorers, 2012)

One of the most annoying cards to play against. Properly built Accelgor decks could repeatedly chain Accelgor's Deck and Cover attack, while Gothitelle (Black & White—Emerging Powers) Trevenant (XY) could be promoted active to prevent the opponent from using Trainer cards like Switch to remove paralysis. To eliminate any chance the opponent had at breaking this cycle, some Accelgor decks even played Dusknoir (Black & White—Boundaries Crossed). It could move damage from the paralyzed Pokémon to the bench, stranding it active until enough damage was in play to wipe out the opponent's entire board in one turn.

67 Pokémon Collector

(HeartGold SoulSilver, 2010)

Pokémon Collector was maxed out in most decks during the 2010–2011 season, as most decks required a Turn 1 Pokémon Collector to get their key Basic Pokémon in play. In a game where one player played an Early Pokémon Collector, and the opponent did not, it was the player who played the Collector that would usually be victorious. If it were re-released today, you can be sure this powerful Supporter would still make its way into decks.

66 Max Potion

(Black & White—Emerging Powers, 2011)

Max Potion functions as a great way to heal high HP Pokémon, especially those that can attack for a single Energy, like Landorus-EX (Black & White—Boundaries Crossed). Max Potion can also be abused by pairing it with Energy-moving Abilities, like Aromatisse's (XY) Fairy Transfer, allowing you to completely heal a Pokémon, without losing any Energy.

65 Mewtwo-EX

(Black & White—Next Destinies, 2012)

When EX Pokémon were brought back into the game in 2012, the format changed, as these strong Basic Pokémon could use their powerful attacks to land easy one-hit KOs. The strongest of these new Pokémon-EX was Mewtwo-EX, which could be fueled by Double Colorless Energy and Eelektrik's Dynamotor Ability to hit for massive damage.

64 Bill

(Base Set, 1999)

Two cards, no drawback. Bill is a card that allowed decks to be fast and consistent through the earliest years of the game. As the game became even faster with the Gym expansions, Bill excelled even more. The only thing that stopped players from adding four Bill into every deck was being limited to 60 cards!

63 Dark Patch

(Black & White—Dark Explorers, 2012)

Dark Explorers, as the name suggests, unveiled several strong Dark-based Pokémon & Trainer cards. Dark Patch was one of these cards. Given that Ultra Ball and Professor Juniper existed to allow easy discarding of Darkness Energy, Dark Patch allowed players to quickly build powerful Darkness-type attackers, like Darkrai-EX. Making the card even stronger was the fact that the newly released Sabelye could use its Junk Hunt attack to recover Dark Patch cards from the discard pile.

62 Gold Berry

(Neo Genesis, 2000)

Until Gold Berry, healing 40 damage from one of your Pokémon meant you'd have to discard an Energy card, as Super Potion was your best bet. With Gold Berry, there was no drawback; it simply healed 40 damage in-between turns. Gold Berry was useful with any 50+ HP Pokémon, but especially great with higher HP Pokémon like Neo Genesis' 110 HP Steelix and Base Set Chansey, making them extremely difficult to KO.

61 Energy Gain

(Platinum, 2009)

Perhaps the strongest Item card in the huge arsenal SP decks have, Energy Gain allowed Pokémon-SP to launch their powerful attacks quickly. Making the card even stronger was the fact that it was easily accessible through the Cyrus's Conspiracy Supporter card.

60 Luxray GL LV.X

(Platinum—Rising Rivals, 2009)

Blazingly fast, Luxray GL LV.X could not only use Energy Gain to attack for a Single energy card, but also pick off a Pokémon right off the Bench with its Bright Look Ability. This might seem strong enough, but remember that as an SP Pokémon, Luxray GL LV.X benefitted from all the tricks and Trainers SP Pokémon were awarded.

59 Muscle Band

(XY, 2014)

It wasn't too many years before Muscle Band that PlusPower was still being used in competitive decks. Instead of adding only 10 damage and being immediately discarded, Muscle Band offered an attacking Pokémon an extra 20 damage, turn after turn. It should be no surprise that Muscle Band continues to see a lot of play today in competitive Pokémon.

58 Focus Band

(Neo Genesis, 2000)

No card in the history of the game created more game-changing (and game-deciding) flips than Focus Band. When two big Stage 2 attackers squared off in the game's first Modified format, whoever got the first big attack against the other's would usually be victorious—that is, unless the Pokémon being attacked had a Focus Band attached, in which case the tides could be turned by the flip of a coin. Another great use for Focus Band was attaching it to Baby Pokémon, making your opponent need not just one coin flip to KO it, but two.

57 Twins

(HeartGold SoulSilver—Triumphant, 2010)

Twins allowed slower decks to fall behind in prizes, then mount a comeback. Clever players would often search out another Twins, while intentionally staying one prize card behind the opponent. This allowed them to play Twins turn after turn, creating incredibly strong setups that would overpower the opponent.

56 Float Stone

(Black & White—Plasma Freeze, 2013)

Float Stone continues to be one of the strongest Pokémon Tool cards in the game. Think of it like a Switch, except that it can be used as many times as needed, and it can also be played on a Pokémon before you even need to retreat it. Perhaps the best use Float Stone ever had was to activate Garbodor's (Black & White—Dragons Exalted) Garbotoxin Ability, which simultaneously disabled all other Abilities, while also lowering Garbodor's retreat from three Energy to zero.

55 Lickitung

(Jungle, 1999)

Given how many draw cards were in decks during the earliest years of the game, it wasn't uncommon for a player to lose by running out of cards. Lickitung played right into this strategy, using its high HP and paralyzing Tongue Wrap attack to stall the opponent out, until his or her deck reached zero. With an impressive 90 HP, there was no easy counter to Lickitung!

54 Sableye

(Black & White—Dark Explorers, 2012)

Given the vast amount of strong Item cards that were printed in the Black & White expansions, Sableye's Junk Hunt could threaten a powerful Turn 2 on the first turn of the game. But that isn't to say Sableye was reserved for fast, aggressive decks. It also functioned great as a stalling Pokémon, allowing players to recycle Crushing Hammer to deplete the opponent's Energy cards.

53 Jirachi

(EX—Deoxys, 2005)

Jirachi was one of the greatest Pokémon for setting up a strong Turn 2, and functioned perfectly in decks based around Stage 1 Pokémon. The common strategy was to use Wishing Star on the first two turns of the game, then switch Jirachi into a different Basic Pokémon with the use of Swoop! Teleporter (EX—Team Rocket Returns), which then allowed it to immediately evolve and attack.

52 Medicham ex

(EX—Emerald, 2005)

It seemed like all decks in 2005 relied on one of two card-fetching Poké-Powers: Pidgeot's (EX—FireRed LeafGreen) Quick Search, or Magcargo's (EX—Deoxys) Smooth Over. Medicham shut both of these down, leaving decks helpless as its Pure Power attack slowly wiped out their bench. Artful placement of damage counters with Pure Power allowed the Medicham player to stay behind in prizes, using cards like Rocket's Admin. and Pow! Hand Extension to their fullest potential.

51 Dunsparce

(EX—Sandstorm, 2003)

One of the greatest starting Pokémon of all time, Dunsparce could not only search out three Basic Pokémon to your bench, but then also switch into a different Pokémon, such as Hidden Legends Jirachi, which could evolve your Pokémon for a one-Energy attack. Making Dunsparce even stronger was the fact that it could stall with a paralyzing attack when you were in a pinch.

50 Scoop Up

(Base Set, 1999)

Scoop Up was not just a great way to heal your Pokémon, but also functioned as a way to get your Active Pokémon back to safety when you found yourself in trouble. It was particularly useful in allowing Base Set Hitmonchan to elude the Fighting-resistant Pokémon that menaced it during the early years of the game.

49 Spiritomb

(Platinum—Arceus, 2009)

Spiritomb had two strong starting attributes combined into one. First, it could evolve your Pokémon—for no Energy, mind you. Second, it slowed your opponent down by disabling players from playing Item cards. As if that wasn't enough, Spiritomb resisted Colorless, and had no Weakness!

48 Call Energy

(Diamond & Pearl—Majestic Dawn, 2008)

Call Energy was a great addition into a variety of decks during 2008–2009, allowing players to get Baltoy down Turn 1, and evolve it into the card-drawing Claydol on Turn 2. It improved the consistency of decks, allowing them to skimp on Supporter cards that would otherwise have been needed to search out Basic Pokémon.

47 Keldeo-EX

(Black & White—Boundaries Crossed, 2012)

Keldeo-EX could be used in one of two ways. The first was as a powerful attacker, with Boundaries Crossed Blastoise's Deluge providing as many Water Energy cards as a player could draw. The second was as a defense against Special Conditions. Using cards like Float Stone to give Keldeo EX free retreat, a Keldeo EX plus Float Stone was like having a free retreat for every Pokémon you had in play.

46 Erika's Jigglypuff

(Gym Challenge, 2000)

If you played against this card, you almost certainly hated it, but there's no denying it was one of the greatest cards of all time. That's because Erika's Jigglypuff could use Double Colorless Energy, alongside several PlusPower cards, to hit for as much as 80 damage on the first turn. With few Basic Pokémon at the time having more than 80 HP, opening with only one Pokémon meant Erika's Jigglypuff could beat you before you even got a turn.

45 Recycle Energy

(Neo Genesis, 2000)

Energy cards were precious during the first years of the game, since they were so frequently discarded by Energy Removal and Super Energy Removal. Recycle Energy offered a solution to running out of Energy cards, while also pairing great with your own Super Energy Removal. Nearly every deck had room for a few of these.

44 Smeargle

(HeartGold SoulSilver—Undaunted, 2010)

Being able to play two Supporter cards in one turn allowed for explosive first turns. When the Black & White expansions unveiled some strong new Item cards, Smeargle became even more powerful, occasionally fueling 3-Energy attacks on the first turn. With two Smeargle, a player could even switch to their second Smeargle, and use an opponent's Supporter twice in a row!

43 Poké Turn

(Platinum, 2009)

Similar to Scoop Up, Poké Turn was one of the many reasons SP Pokémon were so strong in 2009 and 2010. It not only worked to heal Pokémon, but also as a way to re-use strong SP Abilities, like Crobat G's Flash Bite, or Luxray GL LV.X's Bright Look. Making the card even stronger was the fact that it could easily be searched by the Cyrus's Conspiracy Supporter card.

42 Holon's Castform

(EX—Holon Phantoms, 2006)

Though Holon's Castform is a Pokémon, its strength came from its ability to function as an easily searchable Energy card. It isn't just the fact that it provided two of any Energy card that made it good, but rather the fact that Supporter cards like Holon Mentor could fetch out three Basic Pokémon, making it possible to grab both Basic Pokémon and Energy with one card.

41 Chansey

(Base Set, 1999)

In the first year of the game, Chansey's high HP allowed it to function as a great stalling Pokémon. When Neo Genesis released Metal Energy and Gold Berry together in 2000, Chansey gained ways to reduce and heal its self-damage from Double Edge, becoming a solid attacker. Boasting incredible offense and defense, this strategy went on to win the 15+ Division tournament at the 2002 World Championships.

40 Yveltal EX

(XY, 2014)

Remember Mewtwo-EX's X Ball attack? Evil Ball was that, but even better. As if Yveltal-EX wasn't good enough, being Darkness-type allowed it to take advantage of the Dark Patch Trainer card, further boosting its massive Evil Ball attack. If your opponent had a way to KO your Yveltal-EX, you could play it safe, using Y Cyclone to prepare a fresh Yveltal-EX on the bench.

39 Crobat G

(Platinum, 2009)

Crobat G was yet another reason SP decks were so dominant in 2009 and 2010. Since Crobat G could be returned to its owner's hand with the Poké Turn Trainer card, it was possible to repeatedly use Flash Bite. While a KO might seem out of reach when it was 30 damage short, Crobat G and Poké Turn teamed up to turn seemingly unreachable KOs into a reality.

38 Electabuzz

(Base Set, 1999)

The most Energy-efficient attacker from the early years of the game, the only thing that stopped Electabuzz from being hands-down the best attacker was the fact that it was weak to the popular Fighting-type Hitmonchan. Needing only one Lightning Energy to use either of its attacks allowed Electabuzz to easily splash into multi-type decks through 2000.

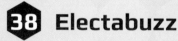

37 Garchomp C LV.X

(Platinum—Supreme Victors, 2009)

The ultimate attacker of SP decks, Garchomp C LV.X went from being a very strong card to every deck's nightmare when Double Colorless Energy was reprinted in the HeartGold SoulSilver expansion in 2010. With Double Colorless Energy and the Energy Gain Pokémon Tool, all it took for Garchomp to deal 80 to any Pokémon was a single Double Colorless Energy. When you are reminded that all non-SP decks relied on an 80 HP Claydol to set up, you realize just how strong Dragon Rush (and Garchomp in general) are. The healing Ability was just overkill.

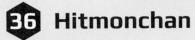

36 Hitmonchan

(Base Set, 1999)

The pressure created by 20 damage for a single Fighting Energy was enough to allow Hitmonchan to dominate the first year of the game. With 70 HP, Hitmonchan easily ran through the much weaker Basic Pokémon of the format. To deal with the Lightning-weak Pokémon that resisted Fighting, Hitmonchan could be paired with Electabuzz, creating one of the most dominant Pokémon decks of all time: The Haymaker deck.

35 Ultra Ball

(Black & White—Dark Explorers, 2012)

Ultra Ball quickly became a favorite of players as a way to fetch out any Pokémon without wasting your one Supporter card of the turn. Clever players are able to attenuate the drawback of discarding two cards, both by building decks that can recover these discarded cards, and also by pitching cards that would be useless in a particular match-up.

34 Pokémon Catcher

(Black & White—Emerging Powers, 2011)

Pokémon Catcher allowed fast, aggressive strategies to thrive into 2012, as players could use it to pick off weak Basic Pokémon from the opponent's Bench before they could evolve. The card was so powerful that it eventually would receive an errata requiring a coin flip to work.

33 Gardevoir

(Diamond & Pearl—Secret Wonders, 2007)

Once Gardevoir was in play, players could repeatedly use its Telepass Ability to create impressive boards with multiple Stage 2 Pokémon. Making Gardevoir even stronger was the fact that Gallade (Diamond & Pearl—Secret Wonders) could easily be splashed into the deck, offering the deck a strong attacker that could one-hit KO anything it encountered. Gardevoir/Gallade was one of the most dominant decks of all time, and won both U.S. Nationals and the World Championships in 2008.

32 Feraligatr

(Neo Genesis, 2000)

Feraligatr didn't see much play in the Standard format, where Energy Removal and Super Energy Removal kept it at bay. In the game's first Modified format, however, Feraligatr absolutely dominated, using its Riptide attack to one-hit KO anything it faced.

The strength of Feraligatr stemmed from the fact that it could use Trainer cards like Misty's Wrath and Trash Exchange to replenish the discard pile with Water Energy, allowing it to repeat heavy-hitting Riptide attacks.

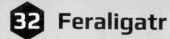

31 Broken Time-Space

(Platinum, 2009)

Being able to evolve on the first turn of the game allowed players to achieve impressive—almost ridiculous—setups. Since you could immediately evolve into the card-drawing Claydol, you could then continue drawing cards until you were able to evolve into an attacking Stage 2. If you won the opening coin flip, all of this happened before your opponent even got a turn.

30 Cyrus's Conspiracy

(Platinum, 2009)

Cyrus's Conspiracy was the card that held SP decks together, providing players everything they needed: an Energy, a Supporter, and an Item. It wasn't uncommon to play Cyrus's Conspiracy to search for another Cyrus's Conspiracy, and then repeat the process again next turn.

29 Scyther

(Jungle, 1999)

All it takes to recognize Scyther's strength is a quick glance: it's a Basic Pokémon with an impressive 70 HP, it retreats for free, resists Fighting, and attacks for any kind of Energy. This versatile card could be splashed into just about any deck, and it offered a solid defense against the Hitmonchan that had dominated the earliest format of the game.

28 Darkrai-EX

(Black & White—Dark Explorers, 2012)

Since its release, Darkrai-EX has managed to show up in Championship-winning decks year after year. It's not used only for its impressive Night Spear attack, but also because of its Dark Cloak Ability. Decks that play Darkness-providing Energy cards (like Prism Energy) can utilize Dark Cloak, giving free retreat to whichever Pokémon need it.

27 VS Seeker

(EX—FireRed LeafGreen, 2004)

VS Seeker was a competitively viable card when it was first released in 2004. It wasn't until more recently in 2015, after a plethora of other strong Trainer cards were released, that it became common to play 4 in decks. Being able to re-use Supporter cards allows players to get away with a single copy of situational Supporter cards, like Teammates, AZ, and Hex Maniac.

26 Lass

(Base Set, 1999)

Lass could be used multiple ways. You could use it on the first turn, hoping to deprive your opponent of key draw cards, and go for a quick win. Alternatively, if you had perfect timing, you could play it on a turn when you had the advantage, protecting your Pokémon from Energy Removal and Super Energy Removal, ensuring you maintained that advantage. Yet another way to use Lass was to avoid decking, shuffling Trainers back into your deck. Lass was always good, but when Cleffa debuted in 2000, Lass became even stronger, as you could play a Turn 1 Lass to cripple both players' hands, then immediately draw a new hand with Cleffa's Eeeeeek attack.

25 N

(Black & White—Noble Victories, 2011)

N is often the first step in an attempt at a comeback win, but it also doubles as a great draw card during the first turns of the game. It adds an exciting blend of skill and luck, forcing players to pitch useless cards from their hand to lower the odds of drawing a weak hand from an eventual N. Countless Pokémon games continue to be decided by what one player will draw from a suspenseful N to 1.

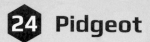

24 Pidgeot

(EX—FireRed LeafGreen, 2004)

When one player got out a Pidgeot, and the other didn't, you could almost always be sure the player with Pidgeot would win, even if the player with Pidgeot was a weaker player. Pidgeot allowed Evolution decks to thrive in 2005, when Rare Candy permitted evolving to a Stage 2 on the first turn of the game. The expansions that followed shortly after FireRed LeafGreen brought a lot of glaringly anti-Pidgeot cards, but it still continued to see play in successful decks.

23 Seismitoad-EX

(XY—Furious Fists, 2014)

180 HP, and it can stop players from playing Items for a Double Colorless Energy, while also hitting for 30 damage? When Pokémon players first saw Seismitoad-EX, there was little doubt that the card would be a top contender. Quaking Punch was often boosted by Trainer cards like Muscle Band and Hypnotoxic Laser, with the quick damage and No-Item limitation being too much for decks to handle.

22 Sneasel

(Neo Genesis, 2000)

Sneasel's Beat Up attack was incredibly strong, able to use a full Bench and the damage-boosting Darkness Energy (Neo Genesis) to average one-hit KOs on 70 HP Pokémon. In fact, the attack was so strong that in the first Modified format, where Energy Removal and Super Energy Removal were not around to keep Sneasel in check, it had to be banned. Another underrated attribute to Sneasel was its free retreat cost, which allowed players to easily retreat to the card-drawing Cleffa (Neo Genesis) whenever needed.

21 Rocket's Sneak Attack

(Team Rocket, 2000)

Rocket's Sneak Attack definitely changed the game, creating a significant advantage for the player opening first. Those fortunate enough to win the opening flip could use Rocket's Sneak Attack to strip away the key Trainer cards in their opponent's hand, preventing them from drawing additional Pokémon. This often resulted in quick wins. Though many players didn't like it, the bottom line was the card won games.

20 Battle Compressor

(XY—Phantom Forces, 2014)

Battle Compressor allows ridiculous first turns that would otherwise be virtually impossible to achieve. Among these are fueling the discard pile with the Joltik/Pumpkaboo/Lampent trio (XY—Phantom Forces), and hitting for as much as 220 damage on the first turn. It also sends powerful Evolved Pokémon to the discard pile, where they can then be put into play with Archie's Ace in the Hole or Maxie's Hidden Ball Trick. In addition to allowing powerful first turns, Battle Compressor also removes cards from the deck that have become useless in a match-up, giving players a better chance at drawing the cards they need.

19 Holon Transceiver

(EX—Delta Species, 2005)

The Holon Supporters were great cards, and even if Holon Transceiver didn't exist, they would have likely seen play. Holon Transceiver allowed decks to be much more consistent, increasing the odds of a key Turn 1 Holon Mentor. Even better, the card allowed players to re-use whatever Holon Supporters they needed. This allowed situational one-offs (like Holon Scientist) to be used as many as five times in a game!

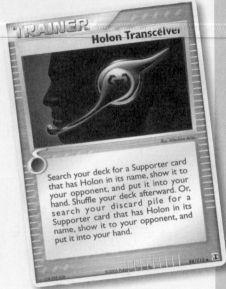

18 Dark Vileplume

(Team Rocket, 2000)

Plenty of Trainer-limiting cards have existed throughout the game's history, but never were disabling Trainer cards stronger than in the first years of the game, when decks played 30 or more of them. While future versions of Vileplume were typically aimed at disabling only Item cards, remember that in 2000, Trainer cards meant all Trainers, Stadiums included. The card also gained strength from evolving from a strong Stage 1, with Dark Gloom able to use its Ability to confuse the opponent's Active Pokémon.

17 Item Finder

(Base Set, 1999)

The Base Set era was filled with powerful Trainer cards, so it's no surprise a card that could recover these Trainer cards would be one of the best cards of its time. Pay attention to the Top 10 cards on this list, as you'll be seeing the powerful Trainer cards Item Finder was used to retrieve from the discard pile.

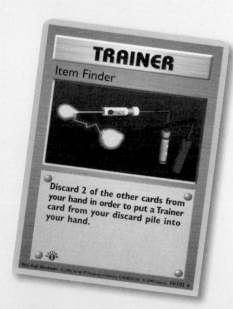

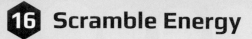

16 Scramble Energy

(EX—Deoxys, 2005)

The ultimate comeback card, Scramble Energy was so strong that players were sometimes placed in stalemate situations where neither wanted to take the first KO. A great strategy players used with Scramble Energy was to attack with Pokémon that spread damage (without taking KOs), so that after their Pokémon was knocked out, they could activate Scramble Energy and easily KO the damaged Pokémon that remained on board.

15 PlusPower

(Base Set, 1999)

PlusPower would see reprints in more recent formats, but the card's competitive zenith was during Base Set, when 10 damage was more likely to put an attack in KO range. (Obviously, today, with 180 HP Basic Pokémon, an extra 10 damage isn't as big of a deal.) PlusPower not only helped achieve game-changing KOs that would otherwise be just out of reach, but also could be stacked for a game-winning attack on the first turn of the game.

14 Double Colorless Energy

(Base Set, 1999)

In early years, it helped power Scyther's Slash and Wigglytuff's Do the Wave. A decade later, it was used with Garchomp C LV.X to unleash devastating Dragon Rush attacks. In today's Standard format, it fuels the massive Night March attacks that one-hit KO EX Pokémon for a single Energy card. Double Colorless Energy has seen several reprints, but unlike other reprinted cards, it has remained powerful in every single format it has seen.

13 Claydol

(Diamond & Pearl—Great Encounters, 2008)

Claydol was the draw engine of just about every deck in 2008. As if drawing cards until you had six wasn't good enough by itself, Claydol's Cosmic Power had the added bonus of allowing you to place 1 or 2 cards from your hand to the bottom of your deck, allowing you to replace cards that weren't useful at the moment with new cards.

12 Mewtwo

(Promo, 1999)

Issued alongside three other promo cards at Pokémon: The First Movie, this Mewtwo quickly became the strongest attacker in the game. Not only was it fast, able to hit for 40 damage on the second turn, but its Energy Absorption attack made it virtually immune to the barrage of Energy Removal and Super Energy Removal cards that dominated early Pokémon. Another bonus? It one-hit KO'd the Psychic-weak Hitmonchan that had dominated the first year of the game.

11 Uxie

(Diamond & Pearl—Legends Awakened, 2008)

Uxie allowed decks explosive first turns, and as a built-in bonus, it could use its attack to restore itself into the deck, where it could be retrieved to again use its Set Up Poké-Power. The card was used in every deck during the 2009–2010 season, allowing Pokémon-searching Supporter cards like Pokémon Collector to double as draw cards. As if all of that wasn't good enough, it could also Level Up into Uxie LV.X and fetch even more cards from the deck.

10 Shaymin-EX

(XY—Roaring Skies, 2015)

When you compare Shaymin-EX to Uxie, it seems like Uxie was simply better. After all, it drew one more card than Shaymin, had a Level Up card, and it didn't give up two prizes when KO'd. However, you have to remember a card is only as strong as the format it's released in. Since Shaymin-EX exists in the same format as Ultra Ball, and doesn't require burning your one Supporter card per turn to retrieve it, Shaymin allows for even more explosive turns than Uxie.

09 Rare Candy

(EX—Sandstorm, 2003)

Without Rare Candy, few Stage 2 Pokémon would have seen competitive play from 2003 onward, but because of it, we saw a variety of dominant Stage 2 decks throughout the years, some of which managed to win World Championships. Rare Candy not only allowed Stage 2 decks to keep up with faster decks, but also to get away with playing multiple Stage 2 Pokémon, since Rare Candy could be used to evolve into either of them.

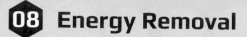

08 Energy Removal

(Base Set, 1999)

How strong is Energy Removal? When it was reprinted as a coin flip, it continued to see play. When you're limited to one Energy a turn, discarding an opposing Energy card with no drawback is a no-brainer for decks, and it defined the early years of the game.

07 Computer Search

(Base Set, 1999)

Computer Search was the key search card of the early years of the game, and though Basic Pokémon dominated this era, the few Evolution-based decks that saw success relied on this card to help evolve their Pokémon. However, all decks benefitted from the consistency boost it offered.

06 Murkrow

(Neo Genesis, 2000)

Mean Look—arguably the best attack in the history of the game—could strand a weak or Psychic-type Pokémon active, while Trainer-blocking Pokémon like Slowking (Neo Genesis) or Dark Vileplume (Team Rocket) could prevent Trainers like Switch from allowing the trapped Pokémon to escape. This allowed Murkrow to then repeatedly Feint Attack until the opponent's board was wiped out. With Murkrow, no game was out of reach until your opponent had drawn their sixth prize.

05 Gust of Wind

(Base Set, 1999)

No card in the history of the game ended more games than Gust of Wind. It's one of those cards that had it never been printed, the game would have been entirely different. Gust helped ensure that decks that relied on slower strategies of evolving Pokémon could not thrive during the early years of the game. It could also be used to stall your opponent for a few turns by trapping active Pokémon with a high retreat cost.

04 Slowking

(Neo Genesis, 2000)

A mistranslation from Japanese to English allowed Slowking's Pokémon Power to function on the Bench, instead of just the active position, as originally intended. This otherwise unplayable card then became incredibly overpowered, as players could stack their bench with multiple Slowking to significantly reduce their opponent's chances of successfully playing a Trainer card. The card would eventually be banned in 2003, but not before dominating events.

03 Super Energy Removal

(Base Set, 1999)

No card in Pokémon had more impact on the game than Super Energy Removal. For years, countless Pokémon were rendered useless because of this card. Being able to strip two Energy cards off of a Pokémon kept most Pokémon that needed 3+ Energy to attack unplayable in any format where this card was legal. Had Super Energy Removal never been printed, the game would have seen many more strategies based around Evolved Pokémon.

02 Professor Oak

(Base Set, 1999)

The ability to simply pitch your hand and draw 7 new cards for no cost is fairly unique to Pokémon, and it was part of the reason the early years of the game were so fun to play. Professor Oak allowed players to refill their hands after exhausting them of their useful Trainers and Energy cards. The card allowed players to be aggressive, and to draw through their deck in search of that crucial, often game-winning card. It was a staple in every deck.

01 Cleffa

(Neo Genesis, 2000)

No card changed the game more than Cleffa. Since it was released, the card was used in quite literally every deck, in every format that it was legal (and most of the time, decks were maxing out at four). Able to draw a fresh hand of 7 cards for a single Energy, Cleffa negated the power of cards like Rocket's Sneak Attack, which were aimed at crippling a player's hand early in the game. The best strategy with Cleffa was to drop a Turn 1 Lass to cripple your opponent's hand, while you use Eeeeeeek to draw a new one!

TOP 25 MOST VALUABLE ENGLISH POKÉMON CARDS

by Bill Gill

In celebrating the 20th Anniversary of Pokémon, we decided to share our take on the Top 25 Most Valuable English Pokémon Cards. These are all cards you can reasonably collect. These are cards that appeared in booster boxes, booster packs, and/or starter sets. Typical Pokémon fans could have plausibly obtained these cards through auctions, trades and/or blind luck pulls.

There are many "extremely rare" English cards that would be difficult to collect that we omitted from our list, like: Pokémon Art Academy Winner Cards; Pre-release Raichu, World Champion Trainer Cards; Tropical Mega Battle Cards; Trophy Cards; etc. These rarely come up

at auction and you certainly won't find one sitting in an old Pokémon Binder at a Garage Sale. Prices on our List are taken directly from actual eBay sales during the 2nd quarter of 2016. We may be missing a few cards here and there, but we feel this list is pretty accurate. Our prices are based on professionally-graded, gem mint cards, which are independently certified. We had an article on "Card Grading" in our *Pojo's Ultimate Pokémon* book which was released earlier in 2016.

So … without further ado, here are our Top 25 Most Valuable English Pokémon Cards:

---

25 Dark Tyranitar

2002 – 1st Edition, Holo – Neo Destiny – $250

I like this card as a collectible for several reasons - it's awesome looking; the attacks don't totally suck; and it's almost 15 years old now.

24 Charizard EX

2014 – Full Art Charizard, Flashfire Holo – $275

All PSA 10 Charizard cards are extremely collectible. Full art Charizard cards are relatively new, they look fantastic, and command high prices.

23 Lugia

2000 – 1st Edition, Holo – Neo Genesis – $300

This card is totally unplayable for competitive decks. But it's been a great collectible for over 15 years. Lugia is a Legendary Bird, has starred in a movie, and was featured on a video game cover. All add up to collectible status.

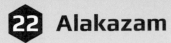

22 Alakazam

1999 – 1st Edition Holo, Base Set – $325

A rare holofoil from the Base Set. *Pssst* … come here … a little secret from Pojo … All 1st Edition cards from the Base Set are valuable in Mint form. Even Commons and Energy cards will fetch $30 these days!

21 Articuno

2002 – Holo, Legendary Collection – $350

Articuno fits very nicely into Blastoise Rain Dance decks. A beautiful and strong card from the early days of Pokémon.

20 Mew δ Gold Star

2006 Holo – EX Dragon Frontiers – $400

The first Gold Star Pokémon to appear on our Top 25 list. The card features beautiful artwork, but was not strong enough for competitive play. For collector's only.

19 Shining Tyranitar

2002 – 1st Edition, Neo Destiny – $400

There are about 10 Shining Pokémon Cards, and all are collectible. Shining Pokémon have alternate colors, and were incredibly difficult to pull from packs.

18 Machamp

1st Edition Holo, Base Set – $400

A beautiful fighting card from the original Base Set. There are more 1st Edition Machamps than any other 1st Edition rare card in the Base Set. A 1st Edition Machamp was found in every Two Player Starter set.

17 Pikachu Gold Star

Holo, EX Holon Phantoms – $400

There are about 30 Gold Star Pokémon cards, and all are good collectibles.

16 Dragonair

1999 – 1st Edition, Base Set – $410

This is the highest valued card from the original Base Set that is not a holo. I personally would collect all the foils from Base Set before this one, but the market is what the market is. Maybe it's the cuteness factor?

15 Mudkip Gold Star

Holo – EX Team Rocket Returns – $425

An extremely rare card from the Team Rocket Returns set. Star cards are unique, as their body is usually protruding out of the character window.

14 Espeon Gold Star

2007 – Pop Series 5 – $580

This card was very difficult card to pull from Pop Series 5 boosters. Pop Series 5 was the last EX Series released for Pokémon Organized play.

13 Charizard

2003 – Holo, Skyridge – $600

This Crystal Charizard was a secret rare from the Skyridge set. Another Charizard card for collector's only.

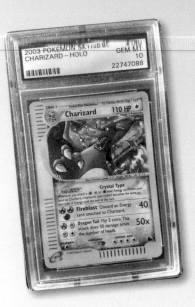

12 Umbreon

2001 – 1st Edition Holo, Neo Discovery – $610

An extremely cool looking Umbreon perched in the night sky. This is a card from many moons ago. Get it … many moons? Eh … let's move on …

11 Umbreon Gold Star

2007 – Pop Series 5 – $620

This card was very difficult card to pull from Pop Series 5 boosters. Pop Series 5 was the last EX Series released for Pokémon Organized play. This has the same rarity as the Espeon Gold Star.

10 Charizard EX

2004 – Holo, Fire Red Leaf Green – $660

This is a beautiful Holo Charizard card with a silver foil border. The attacks on this Charizard resemble the attacks on the Base Set 1 Charizard.

9 Nidoking

1999 – 1st Edition Holo, Base Set – $690

This card is a beautiful Stage 2 Pokémon from the original Base Set. He's beefy and his Toxic attack causes 20 poison damage instead of 10.

8 Mewtwo

1999 – 1st Edition Holo, Base Set – $700

This card was the basis of a hilarious deck idea when it first came out: the "Mulligan Mewtwo" deck. The deck consisted of 59 Psychic Energy and 1 Mewtwo. It uses Mewtwo and its attack "Barrier" to prevent damage, and hopefully your opponent runs out of cards before you do.

7 Charizard δ Gold Star

2006 – Holo – EX Dragon Frontiers – $710

This Charizard looks cool and that's about it. It wasn't playable whatsoever in 2006. It's for collectors only. It was going for $80 in 2006, and the value has gone up about 10 times since then.

6 Gyarados

1999 – 1st Edition Holo, Base Set – $715

This was once one of the most fearsome cards in the late 90's. It fit perfectly into a Blastoise Rain Dance deck. Dragon Rage is an awesome attack. Your only problem, you have to evolve it from Magikarp.

5 Shining Charizard

2002 – 1st Edition Holo, Base Set – $725

This card is not strong whatsoever for TCG Play. This is a collectors' card only. It's shiny, it's pretty old, it's rare, and it's really valuable in Mint form.

4 Zapdos

1999 – $750 – 1st Edition Holo, Base Set

What makes Zapdos so valuable?

Base Set 1? Check!
Holofoil? Check!
Legendary Bird?! Check!
An attack that does 100 damage? Check!
Looks awesome? Check!

3 Venusaur

1999 – $1,500 – 1st Edition Holo, Base Set

A rare holofoil for the original Base Set. Stage 2 Pokémon from the original Base Set are all pretty valuable.
This wasn't all that great for TCG play in the late 90's. Blastoise Rain Dance decks and Hitmonchan Haymaker decks were simply better.

2 Blastoise

1999 – 1st Edition Holo, Base Set – $2,000

Another rare holofoil from the original Base Set. Blastoise's Rain Dance Pokémon Power was the basis for one of the strongest Pokémon Decks in the late 90's.

1 Charizard

1999 – 1st Edition Holo, Base Set – $5,000

The Granddaddy of all Pokémon Collectibles – A 1st Edition
Base Set Charizard card. The funny part is that this card isn't
all that strong for using while playing the TCG. But it was the
coolest looking card in the set, and that's why everybody wants
one. If you saved yours, you were a very wise person!

TRADING CARD GAME HISTORY

The Top 5 Cards From Every Pokémon TCG Set

By Joseph Lee and Andrew Cornell

In February 1996, the Pocket Monsters Red and Green video games were released in Japan. They introduced the concept of collecting, trading and battling with Pocket Monsters.

Eight months later, thanks to the success of the Game Boy games, the Pocket Monsters Trading Card Game (TCG) was released. The Pocket Monsters TCG turned into a craze in Japan. TCGs were still a relatively new phenomenon in the world. Magic the Gathering debuted in 1993 and was easily the most popular TCG at the time. Magic the Gathering had a pretty strong teenage/young adult following. But common folk didn't even know that TCGs existed. Pocket Monsters / Pokémon really changed that.

The Japanese "Pocket Monsters" franchise name was changed to "Pokémon" in the United States due to copyright/ trademark laws. There was already a media franchise in the U.S. named "Monsters in My Pocket".

The Pokémon Trading Card Game hit North America in December 1998 and it took the U.S. by storm! Many kids simply collected the cards like baseball cards because they liked the video games or loved the anime. But soon, people realized that a beautifully designed beast of a game lived inside. The TCG was initially played by grade school children and their parents. So many children started bringing Pokémon Cards to school, that many schools decided to ban Pokémon.

Wizards of the Coast Mall Tours became a huge deal around the country. Pokémon Leagues started popping up at places like libraries, Toys R Us, Zany Brainy', etc. Wizards of the Coast opened Official Stores in large Malls. The game turned into so much more than a crazy children's fad. Teenagers and Young Adults quickly flocked to the game and flooded local tournaments. Local tournaments grew into State Tournaments. State Tournaments grew into Regional Championships. Regional Champions led to National Championships. And National Championships grew into World Championships. And twenty years later, the trading card game is still going strong.

There have been 69 set releases in the United States since the original Base Set hit the streets in 1998. We have a look back at The Top 5 Cards from every Pokémon TCG set that has ever been released in the U.S. These are the cards that made the biggest impact in the competitive Pokémon scene.

Jason Klaczynski
vs Amy Gill

STS Qualifier Finals

Pojo.com's "Pokémon Card of the Day" Reviewers have reviews of all the sets for you. Joseph "Otaku" Lee looks at Sets 1-47, while Andrew "Aroramage" Cornell reviews Sets 48-68. If you have never visited Pojo's Pokémon Card of the Day, we highly recommend it. Monday through Friday we review a new Pokémon Card for you. We've been doing it for 16 years now, and have reviewed over 3200 Pokémon cards in detail for you. It was an idea that 3-time World Champion Jason Klaczynski and I came up with in October of 2000, and we still keep it going today. You can find our Pokémon COTD page at www.pojo.com. We also actively review cards for Magic: the Gathering, Yu-Gi-Oh! And Cardfight!! vanguard.

Base Set

Release Date:
January 9, 1999

1) Professor Oak

Discarding your hand to draw seven cards sounds scary but it really isn't. Many decks manage it now before using a Supporter like Professor Sycamore. In the early days of the game when all Trainers worked like Items, it was even easier to burn through your hand.

2) Computer Search

Three-for-one might sound like a bad deal at first, but it is great! Get the exact card you need when you need it even if it you only run a single copy.

3) Gust of Wind

Nicknamed "Gust of Win" by early players for good reason. Bench-sitters with Pokémon Powers, Evolving Basics, or a Pokémon being prepped to attack could be forced Active. With Evolving Basics, this often lead to an easy OHKO (One Hit Knock Out).

4) Energy Removal/Super Energy Removal

As you could only attach one Energy card per turn in most decks, Trainer cards that could discard said Energy were potent. These two Trainers made opponent's attacks that needed more than one Energy card hard to pull off.

5) Item Finder

Another three-for-one deal that could often set up for Professor Oak. This time you can get a Trainer from the discard pile instead of a card from your deck.

JUNGLE

Release Date:
June 16, 1999

1) Scyther

Being a Grass Type Basic with 70 HP, Fighting Resistance, free Retreat Cost, and a 30-for-three attack, made Scyther a near deck staple. It was a pivot Pokémon, opener, and cleaner all in one.

2) Wigglytuff

Do The Wave could do 60 damage for any three Energy with a full Bench. Filling the Bench was easy with the Trainers of the time. One PlusPower made it 70 damage, enough to OHKO Haymaker Pokémon.

3) Mr. Mime

Though small Mr. Mime was very hard to OHKO due to its Pokémon Power. Decks would use it to stall or include healing so that it was hard to KO at all.

4) Clefable

Metronome allows Clefable to copy the attacks of the Defending Pokémon for any one Energy instead of the usual attack cost. Its Fighting Weakness and status as a Stage 1 kept it from the top, but it still saw play.

5) Jigglypuff

Used by some decks to deal with Mr. Mime before later sets. 60 HP, Psychic Resistance, and an attack that does 20 for any two Energy wouldn't be useful for long, but was needed at the time.

FOSSIL

Release Date:
October 10, 1999

1) Ditto

The Pokémon Power on Ditto copies what is printed on the other player's Active Pokémon and causes all Energy attached to itself to count as all Types. Toss in Double Colorless Energy and Gust of Wind for some potent plays.

2) Muk

Muk has a Pokémon Power that stops all other Pokémon Powers just by Muk being in play. Some decks were built around Pokémon Powers and only a few had none at all. This lead Muk to become a common partner for those without.

3) Articuno

Decks built around Blastoise at first used Stage 1 Pokémon for their offense. This left little room for Trainers. Articuno and Lapras were big Basic Pokémon from Fossil allowing Rain Dance decks even more trainers.

4) Magmar

Magmar was a 70 HP Basic Fire Type great for opening because the first attack could stall. Both of the cards attack Fire Energy, but only one or two. This meant Magmar showed up in off Type as even crowded Haymaker decks found room for it and a few Fire Energy.

5) Aerodactyl

Its Pokémon Power kept both players from playing Evolution cards. This left many decks without their best attacks or Pokémon Powers. Not all decks used Evolutions though.

Base Set 2

Release Date:
February 24, 2000

1) Hitmonchan

One of the two main Pokémon in Haymaker decks. Hitmonchan had good HP and a single Energy attack that did 20 damage. Its bigger attack was not bad either. The amount of early Fighting Weak Pokémon made both attacks even better.

2) Electabuzz

Another Basic Pokémon of Haymaker decks with the same HP as Hitmonchan, but it made use of Lightning Weakness. It too had low cost attacks that hit hard.

3) Blastoise

This was one of the few Stage 2 Pokémon that could compete with Haymaker decks. It let you attach as many Water Energy as you wanted from your hand to your Water Pokémon. This meant more power and speed, but only after it hit the field.

4) Double Colorless Energy

Not every deck could use Double Colorless Energy well, but those that could did and were better off because of it. Entire decks like those built around Wigglytuff would not have worked without it.

5) PlusPower

Many attacks were just 10 or 20 points shy of a OHKO or 2HKO. PlusPower solved that problem. It was very important to Haymaker decks and their explosive opens.

Team Rocket

Release Date:
April 24, 2000

1) Rainbow Energy

Even though it did 10 damage (later placed a damage counter) on the Pokémon to which it was attached to, this card was great and is still very good to this day. It provides one unit of Energy that counts as any type of Basic Energy, allowing more decks to run extra Types of Pokémon.

2) Nightly Garbage Run

This was the first Trainer to put multiple cards from your discard pile back into your deck. It made discarding Pokémon and basic Energy a much safer option. It was risky to leave out.

3) Imposter Oak's Revenge

This was a key card in the Trapper decks that arose after the Gym Heroes set. Making the other player shuffle his or her hand away and draw four didn't mean much on its own. You were supposed to use it after you played Erika and follow up with more cards to destroy the other player's hand.

4) Rocket's Sneak Attack

See the other player's hand and shuffle one of his or her Trainer cards away. Not bad but what made it so good was using it after Imposter Oak's Revenge and then follow it up with the Rocket's Trap. A little luck to destroy the other player's entire hand.

5) Dark Vileplume

A 60 HP Stage 2 was an awful thing even back when this card was new, but Dark Vileplume had a Pokémon Power that kept both players from playing Trainers. It was strong even in decks that did not include a trick to shut the Pokémon Power off during your own turn.

GYM HEROES

Release Date:
August 14, 2000

1) Erika

Erika allows you to draw three cards but the other player may also draw three. Seems like a risky play but you get first crack at using the cards you draw. Follow up with an Imposter Professor Oak and kiss the drawback goodbye.

2) The Rocket's Trap

This is a "tails fails" card, but remember it works like an Item. You use it after an Imposter Professor Oak and Rocket's Sneak Attack to do away with the other player's entire opening hand. It was okay to use more than one copy if the first failed.

3) No Removal Gym

Energy Removal and Super Energy Removal gain a two card discard cost while this Stadium is in play. Energy Removal and Super Energy Removal were still great when this card was released so it became a common play.

4) Trash Exchange

Though you don't come out ahead in terms of card count, Trash Exchange gives you a chance at getting cards back from your discard pile at the cost of some from your deck. Some decks could use this quite well.

5) Misty's Wrath

Getting two from the top seven cards of your deck while discarding the rest was only worth it in certain decks. Feraligatr (Neo Genesis 5/111) was one such deck, and ended up being one of the best for a good while.

GYM CHALLENGE

Release Date:
October 16, 2000

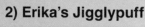

1) Rocket's Zapdos

A big Basic with two good attacks. For one Energy it could do 20 damage while building up for its second attack that did 70 damage for four Energy. That second attack also damaged itself, but Defender and later the first version of Metal Energy took care of that.

2) Erika's Jigglypuff

Decks often had low Pokémon counts to make room for more Trainers. Few Basic Pokémon had more than 70 HP. Double Colorless Energy, PlusPower, and the draw/search cards of the time allowed Erika's Jigglypuff to star in a version of Haymaker that rarely failed to take a KO first turn.

3) Chaos Gym

One of the most potent Stadium cards ever released. With decks still made of half to two-thirds Trainers, having to flip a coin to make them work right was bad enough, but it did create chaos when the other player got a chance to use your own Trainers against you.

4) Warp Point

Warp Point acts like a Switch for both players. Sometimes this would backfire or make no difference but it could also be a strong play. The current card Escape Rope is just Warp Point with a new name.

5) Koga's Beedrill

There are other Pokémon as strong as Koga's Beedrill, but Feraligatr (Neo Genesis 5/111) would release and begin to dominate next set. Feraligatr is Grass Weak and Koga's Beedrill and other Grass Type cards gained a big edge because of it.

Neo Genesis

Release Date:
December 16, 2000

1) Slowking

This is the second non-promo card ever banned from Standard Play. The Japanese version let you flip a coin to block the other player's Trainers while it was Active. All other versions were worded wrong and let the Pokémon Power work from the Bench and thus stack.

2) Sneasel

Sneasel was the first non-promo card banned from Standard Play. It could hit hard if you filled your Bench and didn't get poor results from your coin flips. This appears to be due to "when" and "with what" it was released, as an almost identical Sneasel was released in HS - Undaunted and caused no problems.

3) Cleffa

Cleffa was one of the best openers during its time and more or less a deck staple. Its attack was as strong as the best draw Trainer of the time. With its free Retreat Cost and protection from the Baby Rule, it was great at stalling while setting up.

4) Focus Band

"Tails fails" cards tend to be really good or really bad. Focus Band arrived at a time when it was hard to discard Pokémon Tools and few decks would Poison with their main attacker. A 50% chance to not only deny your opponent a Prize, but keep what you ought to have lost was a game changer.

5) Professor Elm

Professor Elm was the main draw card of its time since it shuffled your hand away to draw seven cards. Sounds great but the cost was you could not use any Trainer cards for the rest of your turn. Until we gained a better option in Expedition, this meant a much slower format.

Neo Discovery

Release Date:
June 1, 2001

1) Tyrogue

This tiny scrapper was not used quite as much as Cleffa from the last list but it came close. Able to hide behind the Baby Rule and retreat for free, the single Energy attack that did 30 on a coin flip was well worth it.

2) Unown D/Unown M/Unown N

These Unown each have a Pokémon Power that reduces the damage from attacks done to your Pokémon by one Pokémon Type. Unown D did it for Darkness, Unown M for Metal, and Unown N for Colorless.

3) Kabutops

Kabutops has an attack that does damage based on coin flips and gives more flips for extra attached Energy. Aquapolis would give us Boost Energy for three extra flips.

4) Eevee

Searching your deck for an Evolution is handy. Evolving you Pokémon the turn you play a card, even the first turn of the game, is potent. It required a coin flip and attaching the right Energy, but this Eevee had a Pokémon Power that did both.

5) Igglybuff

Its Pokémon Power shut off the Pokémon Power of one of the other player's Benched Pokémon. Mostly this meant Slowking from Neo Genesis.

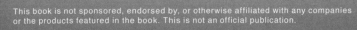

Neo Revelation

Release Date:
September 21, 2001

1) Magcargo

Magcargo has an attack that allows you to do extra damage by discarding Energy from itself. As you could discard a lot to OHKO Evolutions, or none to OHKO Baby Pokémon this proved very good.

2) Entei (6/64)

Though it ended your turn and cost you five cards from the top of your deck, the Howl Pokémon Power on Entei let it fuel Magcargo decks by attaching up to five extra Fire Energy.

3) Crobat

Feraligatr (Neo Genesis 5/111) was still one of, if not the, top deck. Its Grass Weakness made Crobat stronger than it ought to have been, just as it did for Koga's Beedrill.

4) Kingdra

Thanks to its own attack called Genetic Memory, Kingdra could use the attacks from a Horsea or Seadra under it. A promo version of the Trainer card Pokémon Center allowed for a deck that could hit and heal with ease.

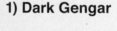

5) Suicune (27/64)

Its Pokémon Power kept Suicune, and Energy attached to it, safe from the Trainer cards, other than Stadiums. It also has a free Retreat Cost. Together this let you make Double Gust act like Gust of Wind.

Neo Destiny

Release Date:
February 28, 2002

1) Dark Gengar

Hiding behind the Baby Rule made Baby Pokémon tough. Dark Gengar had an attack that could get around the Baby Rule, which made people want to play it.

2) Dark Tyranitar

The first attack on Dark Tyranitar could do damage while milling cards from the other player's deck. The attack made you flip coins but you flipped more for each Energy attached to it. The second attack had an option to help deal with Baby Pokémon.

3) Light Dragonite

Light Dragonite has a solid attack with a potent Pokémon Power. Only a certain Standard Format decks used Special Energy at the time, but Light Dragonite itself would use its Pokémon Power to keep things like Boost Energy from discarding itself!

4) Broken Ground Gym

Many decks would count on the free Retreat Cost found on Baby Pokémon and some other Basics. Broken Ground Gym would thwart that plan without adding to the Retreat Cost of Evolutions.

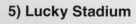

5) Lucky Stadium

A good, general purpose Stadium card that happens to have Japanese Pokémon mascot Imakuni in the artwork.

LEGENDARY COLLECTION

Release Date:
May 24, 2002

1) Bill

Most decks ran Bill when it first came out in Base Set but its use faded with time. Its rivals were not brought back so Bill again became a staple.

2) Pokémon Breeder

The Standard Format of this time was heavy on Stage 2 Pokémon. Pokémon Breeder got them into play a turn sooner and some of them had low enough Energy costs to attack right away.

3) Pokémon Trader

One of the best search options for the Pokémon heavy decks of the time. Get any Pokémon from your deck for the low cost of a Pokémon from your hand.

4) Dark Blastoise

Though small for a Stage 2, Dark Blastoise had good attacks. It first came out in Team Rocket and saw some use. Now it was back without its main rivals and counters but with new support!

5) Venusaur

Venusaur saw some play when first released in Base Set. Now just like Dark Blastoise, it and its old support were back, but not the worst of its rivals and counters.

EXPEDITION

Release Date:
September 15, 2002

1) Professor Oak's Research

Though some players were slow to come around, Professor Oak's Research was Professor Elm done right. You drew two less cards but you could still use any non-Supporter Trainer cards after using it.

2) Copycat

A Supporter that had you shuffle away your hand to draw a new one the same size as the other player's. The amount you drew was not set and a savvy opponent could turn it against you, which is why I rated Professor Oak's Research above it. Still a great card.

3) Ampharos

Moving Energy cards around your side of the board may not be as good as attaching an extra Energy, but that does not mean it is bad. Ampharos became a key player in decks that could attach extra Energy to the Bench and was the "A" in BAR decks.

4) Venusaur (30/165, 68/165)

Speaking of getting to attach an extra Energy card, this Venusaur did just that. It had to be when you attached an Energy to your Active, but more Energy meant more options and often more power.

5) Strength Charm

Strength Charm provides +10 damage but was not very good at first as Focus Band was still legal. Over time, not only was Focus Band gone, but more cards were released where that 10 damage was a huge deal.

AQUAPOLIS

Release Date:
January 15, 2003

1) Boost Energy

Boost Energy is a triple Colorless Energy. Though it had many restrictions, this much Energy all at once was potent with the right cards.

2) Scizor

Soon there would be decks that focused on Poison, so the Poké-Body on Scizor became important. The first attack could use Strength Charm to OHKO Baby Pokémon that had been on the Bench, while the second attack took advantage of the Poké-Power on this set's Furret for easy set up.

3) Town Volunteers

Though your Supporter was precious, it could be used for more than draw or search. Town Volunteers gets back five cards from your discard pile (either Pokémon, Basic Energy, or a mix of both). It also get back an entire Stage 2 and some of its Energy in one shot!

4) Pokémon Fan Club

Neo-era Baby Pokémon were great and are still here. Other Basics were getting better or needed so they could Evolve, and so it was worth your Supporter to get the exact two you wanted.

5) Juggler

While still allowed, Bill was better for quick draw. After it was gone or in decks that needed to get Energy into the discard pile, Juggler became a potent play.

SKYRIDGE

Release Date:
May 12, 2003

1) Oracle

It was not worth your Supporter to search your deck for two cards only to leave them on top of said deck. We did have Bill and later certain Poké-Powers so we could draw them right away. This made Oracle one of the best Supporters of this time.

2) Fast Ball

You had to risk showing the other player a lot of your deck but Fast Ball meant you would get an Evolution. As long as you did not run too many Evolved Pokémon, you could make sure you got something you wanted.

3) Desert Shaman

Desert Shaman let you draw just one less than Professor Oak's Research but made the other player do the same. At this time in the game, it was common to prep your hand for many turns in advance, so this could be hard on the other player.

4) Starmie (44/144)

Starmie punished heavy Special Energy usage. Though it was a Stage 1, it could use any Energy Type for its Core Blast attack. Thus it was worked into many decks.

5) Beedrill

Poison plus Paralysis is a deadly combo as a Poké-Power. Super Scoop Up and Hyper Devolution Spray let you spam Beedrill, so this version saw play in both the Unlimited and Standard Formats of the time.

EX RUBY & SAPPHIRE

Release Date:
June 18, 2003

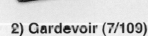

1) Blaziken (3/109)

Blaziken became famous for its Firestarter Poké-Power which attached a Fire Energy from your discard pile to one of your Benched Pokémon. It was the "B" in BAR decks.

2) Gardevoir (7/109)

Gardevoir also became famous for its Poké-Power which could attach a Psychic Energy from the deck to any of your Pokémon. This came with an added cost as it placed two damage counters on the Pokémon that received the Energy.

3) Delcatty (5/109)

Delcatty was a common sight on Benches at this time. For the low cost of discarding an Energy card from your hand, its Poké-Power let you draw three cards.

4) Swampert (13/109)

The Poké-Power on Swampert allowed you to attach a Water Energy to your Active Pokémon from hand. It would get some help in later sets but was never as good as BAR or Gardevoir decks.

5) Sceptile (20/109)

Sceptile brought back Energy Trans though as a Poké-Power this time. While it still had many of its tricks, the Energy Trans decks of this time were only somewhat strong.

EX SANDSTORM

Release Date:
September 17, 2003

1) Rare Candy

Before errata in recent years, Rare Candy let you Evolve your Basic Pokémon right away into either its Stage 1 or Stage 2 form. This let many decks run more than one Stage 2 and be stronger for it.

2) Dunsparce

A strong Pokémon with which to open due to its Strike and Run attack. This made it easy for decks to fill their Bench and set up quickly.

3) Gardevoir-ex

Gardevoir-ex could hit hard based on either the other player's cards in hand or the total Energy in play. The Gardevoir from the last set made both easy to afford.

4) Wobbuffet

The first of the Safeguard Pokémon when it was a Poké-Power. Safeguard kept the attacks of Pokémon-ex (instead of Pokémon-EX) from working on Wobbuffet. It was used in many decks.

5) Wynaut

Wynaut could use its Poké-Power to Evolve into Wobbuffet while healing all damage from itself. Gardevoir from Ruby & Sapphire could attach extra Energy but it did damage to that Pokémon. Using one with the other, you could end up with a Wobbuffet ready to attack sooner but with no damage on it.

EX Dragons

Release Date:
November 24, 2003

1) TV Reporter

TV Reporter became a staple for decks thanks to its draw-three-discard-one effect. Sometimes you just needed to draw without shuffling, while some decks just needed certain cards in the discard pile.

2) Rayquaza-ex

At last we have come to the "R" in BAR decks. Rayquaza-ex has an attack that hits harder the more Fire or Lightning Energy you discard from it. Blaziken would attach the Fire Energy from the discard, while Ampharos would move it back to Rayquaza-ex to keep attacking.

3) Kingdra-ex

Kingdra-ex is like the Kingdra from Neo Revelation but with more HP and a better second attack. It was even the better choice in Unlimited where both were an option.

4) Mr. Briney's Compassion

Bounce a Pokémon and all cards attached to your hand as long as it wasn't a Pokémon-ex. Mr. Briney's Compassion was like a Super Scoop Up without the flip, but at the cost of your Supporter for the turn.

5) Magneton

Though its attack was decent, the reason to run Magneton was for its Poké-Power. Magnetic Field let you discard a card to add two basic Energy cards from your discard pile to your hand. A key piece of support in certain decks.

EX Team Magma vs Team Aqua

Release Date:
March 15, 2004

1) Blaziken-ex

BAR decks did not need help but they got it from this set. Blaziken-ex gave the deck a super sniper that could take out something with 100 HP or less on the other player's Bench in one shot.

2) Suicune-ex

Swampert from Ruby & Sapphire at last got the heavy hitter it needed. Suicune-ex could do more damage with its main attack by bouncing all its attached basic Energy to your hand. Swampert made it possible to attack with Suicune-ex turn after turn.

3) Double Rainbow Energy

Double Rainbow Energy was worth two units of Energy that each counted as all Types at once, though it also made that Pokémon do 10 less damage. It could not be attached to Basic Pokémon or Pokémon-ex.

4) Team Aqua's Manectric (4/95)

Team Aqua's Manectric could move as many basic Energy cards attached to it as you wanted to another of your Pokémon. This led it to replace Ampharos in BAR decks (which got a new name).

5) Team Magma's Groudon

You needed to back Team Magma's Groudon with several Team Magma Pokémon, just so its Poké-Body would not prevent it from attacking. Good thing there were Team Magma Pokémon and Trainers to fill your field and even help with Energy.

EX Hidden Legends

Release Date:
June 14, 2004

1) Ancient Technical Machine [Rock]

This card was a way to bounce the top Stage of all of the other player's Evolved Pokémon to his or her hand. It might mean a KO or two if lucky but the big draw was if those Pokémon had been put into play via Rare Candy.

2) Steven's Advice

Steven's Advice let you draw up to six cards, one for each of the Pokémon the other player has on the field. You could not use it if you had more than seven cards in your hand, so while almost every deck ran it they only used about two copies.

3) Desert Ruins

Desert Ruins punished both players for using big Pokémon-ex as it placed a damage counter on Pokémon-ex with a max HP score of 100 or higher between turns. This often KO'd cards a turn faster.

4) Jirachi

Though you had to attack and even place a damage counter on Jirachi to do it, "Make a Wish" let you search your deck for an Evolution to put onto its lower Stage right away. It even worked first turn.

5) Milotic

Milotic healed all damage on all Pokémon in play when you Evolved into it, except for Pokémon-ex. Smart players turned that drawback into a bonus, running no Pokémon-ex while facing decks with many.

EX FireRed LeafGreen

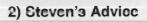

Release Date:
August 30, 2004

1) Pidgeot

A free card search each turn boggles the mind, and the Poké-Power on Pidgeot did just that. Most decks ran Pidgeot, though only one or two because the Poké-Power was truly once per turn (it would not stack).

2) VS Seeker

VS Seeker is a top card right now because it lets you reuse a Supporter from your discard pile. Back then it did not have Battle Compressor but it was still a great card!

3) Nidoqueen

Though it took some time, Nidoqueen would become the main offense of a deck built around it and its Power Lariat attack. There were many helpful Evolutions to have sitting on your Bench to feed it.

4) Blastoise-ex

A card that also saw heavy play but not right away. Blastoise-ex had a Poké-Power that let you attach as many Water Energy as you wanted to your Pokémon but each placed a damage counter on that Pokémon. It was the "B" in BLS decks.

5) Electrode-ex

Its Poké-Power KO'd itself, but then attached five Energy cards from your discard pile to the Pokémon you had left in play. Players soon learned how to use this to exploit the many cards meant to help a player come from behind.

EX Team Rocket Returns

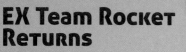

Release Date:
November 8, 2004

1) (Almost) All Trainers

Copycat, Pokémon Retriever, Pow! Hand Extension, Rocket's Admin., and Swoop! Teleporter saw use in many if not most decks. The ones that saw little play were Venture Bomb and Here Comes Team Rocket! with the rest falling in between.

2) Dark Dragonite

Dark Dragonite had a Poké-Power that could move [D] Energy around the field: while Dark Electrode had one that let you attach a [D] or Dark Metal Energy card from your deck to itself if it had no Energy already. By their Poké-Powers combined many events were won.

3) Dark Tyranitar (both)

The two Dark Tyranitar in this set were strong enough to use separately, but thanks to Surprise! Time Machine they also saw play together in the same deck.

4) Dark Hypno

Dark Hypno teamed up with three other Stage 1 Pokémon in a deck known as Four Corners. The goal was to cover four often seen Weaknesses. Some versions used other Dark Pokémon but many did not.

5) Dark Metal Energy/R Energy

There were no basic Darkness or Metal Energy cards at the time of this set. Dark Metal Energy thus had a simple purpose. R Energy provided a speed and damage boost to Pokémon with Dark or Rocket's in their name, but not for long as it would discard itself at the end of the turn.

EX Deoxys

Release Date:
February 14, 2005

1) Jirachi

If Active, Jirachi could use its Poké-Power to add a card to your hand from the top five cards of your deck. This left it Asleep but that would not matter as the decks using it would play Swoop! Teleporter. As long as Jirachi had been in play long enough, you would then Evolve the Pokémon you just swapped in for Jirachi.

2) Scramble Energy

One more card to reward players who knew how to get ahead in terms of setup but look behind in terms of Prize count. Scramble Energy would act like a triple Rainbow Energy if you had more Prize cards in play than the other player, though Pokémon-ex and Basics could not use it.

3) Magcargo (20/107)

One more Pokémon with a Poké-Power to search your deck. Magcargo did not add the card to hand but put it on top of your deck. You needed draw power to get it but this was only a Stage 1.

4) Ludicolo (10/107)

Ludicolo had a Poké-Power to draw a card and its big attack did damage based on how many Pokémon each player had in play. This made it work well with the above Magcargo.

5) Manectric-ex

The first attack on Manectric-ex kept your opponent from playing any Trainer that was not a Supporter during his or her next turn while doing 40 damage. This led to some lock decks.

POJO'S UNOFFICIAL BIG BOOK OF POKÉMON

EX Emerald

Release Date:
May 9, 2005

1) Battle Frontier

Battle Frontier shut down Poké-Bodies and Poké-Powers on Evolved Colorless, Darkness, and Metal Type Pokémon. Soon we would be getting some strong Metal Type Pokémon for this to counter and we already had Pidgeot from EX FireRed/LeafGreen and multiple Darkness Type Pokémon from EX Team Rocket Returns.

2) Scott

Great Scott! This Supporter might be too slow now, but at the time getting up to three Stadiums, Supporters, or a mix of both was quite handy. It let you plan ahead and controlling what Stadium was in play had again become key.

3) Medicham-ex

A fast Stage 1 card, Medicham-ex was about control. While Active, its Poké-Power shut down other Poké-Bodies and Poké-Powers (except on Pokémon-ex). Its first attack could target the Bench while the second did not just ignore Resistance but increased the damage done to more than compensate.

4) Mr. Stone's Project

Most decks could use a way to reliably add a particular basic Energy card to hand. Getting two at once from either deck or discard proved worth a Supporter.

5) Deoxys-ex

The all Colorless Energy cost for Fastwave allowed decks to splash in Deoxys-ex in order to deal with protective effects.

EX Unseen Forces

Release Date:
August 22, 2005

1) Lugia-ex

The highest printed HP score was 200, so little could survive the attack of Lugia-ex. The Poké-Body was nice as well but unreliable. This would be combined with Blastoise-ex to become the "L" in BLS decks.

2) Steelix-ex

Though the massive Energy cost was a huge turnoff, next set we would see something to help Blastoise-ex keep Steelix-ex up and running. The "S" in BLS decks was scary because not even your Bench was safe from its Mudslide attack.

3) Eevee

Remember the Eevee from Neo Discovery? Consider this the updated version. A few drawbacks like less HP, but Energy Evolution was back as a Poké-Power, and it no longer needed a coin flip.

4) Solid Rage

Solid Rage could only be used by Evolutions that were not Pokémon-ex, and the effect only triggered when you had more Prize cards left than the other player. Even needing all of this, the +20 damage was potent.

5) Energy Root

+20 HP was very good at this time, even if you could not use it with Pokémon-ex and those with "Dark" or an owner in their names. Shutting off any Poké-Body or Poké-Power, the Pokémon in question might be good, bad, or not matter at all.

EX Delta Species

Release Date:
October 31, 2005

1) Holon's Electrode/Holon's Magneton

You could attach either of these Pokémon from hand as if they were an Energy card, but you had to return another already attached Energy if you did. When used like this they provided two units of Energy that counted as all Types. They were the final piece of BLS decks.

2) Dragonite δ

Dragonite δ had a Poké-Power to attach [L] Energy from the discard pile to one of your Benched Pokémon while being a solid attacker. As a Pokémon δ, it was both Metal and Lightning Type at the same time instead of being Colorless.

3) Metagross δ

Metagross δ was used with Dragonite δ to form the deck known as "Metanite". Its Poké-Power could help with set up and field maintenance; but the main draw was its attack, as it could discard Energy from any of your Pokémon in play to up its damage.

4) Holon Transceiver

Holon Transceiver could get a Supporter from your deck or discard pile so long as it had "Holon" in its name. The Holon Supporters covered draw, search, and recycling effects. The "Holon Trainer Engine" became a typical part of Standard decks of this era.

5) Jolteon-ex

When you Evolved an Eevee into Jolteon-ex, its Poké-Power would place a damage counter on each of your opponent's Pokémon. Jolteon-ex was also a solid attacker.

EX Legend Maker

Release Date:
February 13, 2006

1) Mew-ex

Mew-ex had a Poké-Power that let it copy the attacks of any Pokémon in play. As you might expect this proved strong, and a deck built around it and Manectric-ex even won the 2006 World Championship.

2) Cursed Stone

A way to counter the heavy use of Poké-Powers, Cursed Stone placed a damage counter on each Pokémon with one. Unlike Desert Ruins, this move did not care about max HP.

3) Banette-ex

A strong attack and solid Poké-Power got people looking at Banette-ex. In two sets, the Shuppet with the Ascension attack and a regular Banette with the Safeguard Poké-Body would give it a strong deck.

4) Solrock

This Solrock could stop Colorless Pokémon other than Pokémon-ex from using their Poké-Powers with its Poké-Body. It and Lunatone (below) were run as singles, while the older versions from EX Deoxys would attack and provide even more support with their own Poké-Bodies.

5) Lunatone

This Lunatone could stop Fire Pokémon other than Pokémon-ex from using their Poké-Powers with its Poké-Body. It was part of a top deck with Solrock (above), plus the Lunatone and Solrock from EX Deoxys, but was also a budget deck!

HOLON PHANTOMS

Release Date:
May 3, 2006

1) Raichu δ

Decks were heavy on Poké-Bodies and Poké-Powers, so 20 to each Pokémon with one, the other, or both at the low price of just one Energy proved too good to resist. The second attack and rest of the card were solid as well, and soon it was partnered with Exeggutor δ in a deck known as RaiEggs.

2) Exeggutor δ

Exeggutor δ was a solid Stage 1 with two great attacks. The first did damage based on how many Pokémon δ you had in place and the second could hit two targets on the Bench. Both worked well with Raichu δ and additional Pokémon δ support.

3) δ Rainbow Energy

When attached to a Pokémon δ, this card provides one unit of Energy that counts as all Types. Yet if needed to slap it onto something that was not a Pokémon δ, you actually could. It would only provide [C] instead of all Types.

4) Flygon δ

Its Poké-Power allows you to attach a basic Energy card or δ Rainbow Energy card to your Pokémon δ. It also stacks so two Flygon δ and your manual Energy attachment got a lot ready in a single turn.

5) Holon's Castform

Remember Holon's Electrode and Holon's Magneton? As they were Stage 1 cards, there was no danger of getting stuck with them as your opening Basic. Holon's Castform is at risk of being your opener, but has a solid enough setup attack that some preferred it to the others.

EX CRYSTAL GUARDIANS

Release Date:
August 30, 2006

1) Windstorm

At the cost of just a "normal Trainer" (or as we call them now, an "Item") you could take out up to two Pokémon Tools or a Stadium and a Tool. Two-for-one trades are good in general and this was at a time when both Tool and Stadium cards were important.

2) Cessation Crystal

Cessation Crystal could not be used by Pokémon-ex and only did something while the Pokémon it was attached to was Active. Its effect was amazingly strong; Cessation Crystal shut off both Poké-Bodies and Poké-Powers while it was working.

3) Castaway

Get a replacement Supporter for next turn plus a Pokémon Tool and basic Energy card you could use this turn. Some decks didn't need much more than this to keep going and would play Castaway after Castaway.

4) Crystal Beach

Cards that could provide more than one Energy at the time were potent plays. While Crystal Beach was on the field, things like Boost Energy, Double Rainbow Energy, and Scramble Energy would only yield [C] instead of their usual Type and amount of Energy.

5) Fearow δ

There were quite a few decks that ran heavy on Pokémon δ. A Stage 1 which could add a Pokémon δ to your hand ended up being worth the space.

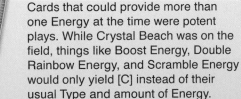

EX DRAGON FRONTIERS

Release Date:
November 8, 2006

1) Rayquaza-ex δ

Due to its Poké-Body, the somewhat pricey attacks by Rayquaza-ex δ became steals when you had more Prizes left than your opponent. Another example of how being behind in Prizes does not guarantee you are actually losing.

2) Flygon-ex δ

A master of damage spread as both its Poké-Power and attack placed damage counters across your opponent's Bench. The attack also did a solid bit of damage to the Defending Pokémon; and players found the right back up to make Flygon-ex δ part of a top flight deck.

3) Gardevoir-ex δ

Gardevoir-ex δ was the only Pokémon capable of placing Imprison Counters on another. A Pokémon with an Imprison Counter couldn't use its Poké-Bodies or Poké-Powers. They were hard to get rid of as well; other than bounce your only option was Tropius δ.

4) Tyranitar-ex δ

Tyranitar-ex δ could place a Shockwave Counter on one of your opponent's Pokémon with its first attack. Its third attack let you select a Pokémon with a Shockwave counter and KO it. It was the only source of Shockwave Counters and (again) only Tropius δ could get rid of them.

5) Holon Energy FF

If a basic Fire Energy was attached, Holon FF removed the Weakness of that Pokémon while a basic Fighting Energy let it ignore Resistance. It was part of a series of similar Special Energy cards reprinted in this set.

EX POWER KEEPERS

Release Date:
February 14, 2007

1) Absol-ex

A Poké-Power that moved three damage counters from one of your opponent's Pokémon to another, enables some nice tricks. You could avoid wasting damage by moving it off of something that will be KO'd even without it and/or put it on something to KO it.

2) Jolteon*

Read as "Jolteon Star" this special version of Jolteon used its alternate or "Shiny" color scheme and was a Basic Pokémon. There were other Pokémon* but Jolteon* earned a place in decks because its Poké-Power placed a damage counter on both Active Pokémon.

3) Delcatty

This set contained several reprints of cards from sets that had already rotated from Standard play. Delcatty brought back its reliable draw power and could now be used alongside Delcatty-ex.

4) Gardevoir

Gardevoir returned alongside some of its old deck mates like the Wobbuffet with Safeguard that was first released in EX Sandstorm.

5) Blaziken

Yet another familiar card; Blaziken did not have the presence it once did, but attaching Energy from the discard pile is an enticing thing.

DIAMOND & PEARL

Release Date:
May 23, 2007

1) Lucario

What did Lucario have going for it? Two low cost attacks, with the second hitting both the Active and a Benched Pokémon; being a Fighting Type to better exploit Weakness; PlusPower to increase damage; and Rare Candy still worked for Stage 1 cards at this time.

2) Machamp

The first attack on this card made it. For just one Energy, Machamp could score big damage if your opponent had KO'd one of your Pokémon the previous turn (via attack damage). Lucario was its usual dance partner and together they formed "Mario" decks.

3) Empoleon

Its first attack can hit anything in play while its second attack hits both the Active and something on the Bench. Even the Prinplup in this set could spread damage, and this led to a very focused deck that backed this Evolution line with many Trainers.

4) Dusknoir

Dusknoir was used in some decks for its Poké-Power; unless your opponent played with a Bench of three or less Pokémon, there was a constant threat of shuffling something needed away. Warp Point meant even Actives were not safe.

5) Infernape/Infernape LV.X

Infernape and Infernape LV.X could hit fast and hard with low Energy attacks. The biggest attack needed 8 Fire Energy in your discard and returned that Energy to your deck; Delcatty with Energy Draw helped with that.

DP MYSTERIOUS TREASURES

Release Date:
August 22, 2007

1) Blissey

The main draw for Blissey was its attack as it started with one Energy but attached more to itself, and then hit harder based on the amount of Energy attached. It was easy to fit into other decks. On its own it relied on control elements.

2) Time-Space Distortion

There was a chance it would fail entirely, but the odds were in your favor you would get at least one Pokémon back from the discard pile and upwards of three, making it a strong play. It was a Secret Rare though and hard to get.

3) Team Galactic's Wager

Each player shuffles away their hand and draws a new one of either three or six cards, determined by who wins a quick game of Rock-Paper-Scissors. Some just trusted their luck while others trusted in their Ability to read opponents, but it was a fearsome card when it worked.

4) Alakazam

Its Poké-Power let you discard two cards to cancel the effects of a Poké-Power being used by an opponent's Pokémon. An Alakazam meant uncertainty and your opponent did have to pay for Poké-Powers before knowing if they would work.

5) Kricketune

Swarm Kricketune and Kricketot and then keep recycling them to keep up the damage with their second attack. It could be built as a budget deck and had a straightforward strategy, making it good for beginners.

DP Secret Wonders

Release Date:
November 7, 2007

1) Gallade

Its first attack set up anything to be KO'd by its second attack, but that second attack isn't always needed because it could reveal face down Prize cards for a damage boost. Used with the next entry.

2) Gardevoir

A second Supporter per turn is powerful and this card's Poké-Power basically does just that, as it copied the effect of a Supporter from your opponent's discard pile. The attack could lock down an opponent's Poké-Powers as well.

3) Roseanne's Research

Roseanne's Research fetches two Basic Pokémon or two basic Energy cards or one of each from your deck. A good draw card would likely provide the same but this was guaranteed.

4) Magmortar

Magmortar has a Poké-Power that heals it when you attach Fire Energy from your hand, and an attack that hits harder if you attach extra Energy to it. It also had access to Magmortar LV.X from DP Mysterious Treasures.

5) Absol

Abso had a great hand disruption attack: decks were Trainer heavy so odds were in your favor of a double discard. Its second attack was decent for damage as well.

DP Great Encounters

Release Date:
February 13, 2008

1) Claydol

The Poké-Power on Claydol let you draw until you had six cards in hand. It also let you put two cards from hand on the bottom of your deck first, increasing your draw. A staple while legal.

2) Unown G

From your Bench Unown G could attach itself to one of your Pokémon like a Tool. The equipped Pokémon were protected from attack effects (but not damage), which was a problem for more technical decks.

3) Togekiss

The "Serene Grass" Poké-Power lets you attach as many basic Energy cards as you found in the top 10 cards of your deck to your Pokémon when you played it from your hand. This was used in a deck with attackers like Garchomp from DP Mysterious Treasures and Ho-Oh from Secret Wonders.

4) Beedrill

Get up to 120 damage for just [G] using this card's "Band Attack", 30 per Beedrill you have in play. It was the main focus of the 2009 Masters Division World Championship winning deck "Luxdrill".

5) Porygon2

Its Poké-Power let you discard a Supporter to copy its effect. This made it a useful support card and it is one of the few used in Unlimited even today, enabling certain first turn win strategies.

DP Majestic Dawn

Release Date:
May 21, 2008

1) Unown Q

Another Unown that (while on the Bench) could be attached to one of your Pokémon as a Tool, Unown Q reduced the Retreat Cost of that Pokémon by [C]. Why is that so good? It lets several key Pokémon retreat for free!

2) Call Energy

While it only provides [C] for Energy costs, if the Pokémon to which Call Energy is attached is your Active, you can search your deck for two basic Pokémon to add to your Bench. It made any Basic an opener.

3) Empoleon

Another Empoleon that went on to do well, this time winning the 2008 World Championship in the Senior Division. Its first attack can hit two Pokémon in play while the second does more damage the larger your Bench.

4) Scizor

Scizor tag-teamed with Toxicroak from this same set in a deck that won the Junior Division for the 2008 World Championship. Both Stage 1 attackers had strong, single Energy attacks and were backed by cards like Cessation Crystal and Crystal Beach to further disrupt the opponent.

5) Leafeon LV.X

Leafeon LV.X allowed you to attach an extra Energy card from your hand with its Poké-Power. This saw use with various partners, among them Magmortar from DP Secret Wonders and Magmortar LV.X from DP Mysterious Treasures.

DP Legends Awakened

Release Date:
August 20, 2008

1) Uxie/Uxie LV.X

Uxie and Uxie LV.X allowed decks to be less reliant upon Supporters to draw thanks to their Poké-Powers. Their attacks were also good, with the one on Uxie giving you a chance of reusing the Poké-Power (eventually).

2) Kingdra

Its first attack required no Energy attached to use, though the damage does depend on how many Water Energy cards are in your discard pile. The second attack requires a single Water Energy, but could deal solid damage while letting you discard up to two cards from hand.

3) Mewtwo LV.X

The important thing about Mewtwo LV.X is its Poké-Body that protected it from the attacks of Basic Pokémon. A Level X Pokémon had the same Stage as the Evolution under it, so this could wall against a good chunk of the metagame.

4) Azelf

Get a look at all your face down Prize cards, you'll have the option of swapping a card from your hand for a Pokémon among them. It only worked once though, when you played Azelf from your hand to your Bench.

5) Cynthia's Feelings

Shuffle your hand into your deck and draw four cards, or eight if one of your Pokémon had been KO'd the turn before. The four cards were better than nothing, while the eight were great.

DP STORMFRONT

Release Date:
November 8, 2008

1) Sableye

Sableye has a killer Poké-Body to make you go first. Impersonate allows a second Supporter for the turn. Finally, it has an attack that could hit harder if the Defending Pokémon had less HP than Sableye, at a time when you could attack first turn.

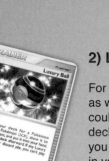

2) Luxury Ball

For the cost of a "normal Trainer" (or as we call them now, an Item) you could get any Pokémon from your deck sans a Pokémon LV.X, unless you had a copy of Luxury Ball already in your discard pile. People learned to just run and enjoy one.

3) Dusknoir LV.X

This complicated Poké-Power took an awful lot to make it work, not only was it the Level-Up form of a Stage 2, but it had to be damaged from an opponent's attack that finished off Dusknoir LV.X. A one-sided Stadium was worth it, though.

4) Gyarados

This card wouldn't truly shine until we got Broken Time-Space, letting you Evolve instantly while doing big damage for no Energy. A deck built around it took second in the Senior Division of the 2010 World Championship.

5) Poké Drawer+

Poké Drawer+ had one effect if played normally on its own, but a second if you used two at once (which its wording enabled). Drawing one card was okay but a double deck search was amazing!

PLATINUM

Release Date:
February 11, 2009

1) Broken-Time Space

Broken-Time Space let players ignore the "once per turn" Evolution rule. Evolutions of this time were typically stronger but slower than Basics, and this removed the "slower" part. It still took more cards, though.

2) Team Galactic's Invention Cards

This was a series of Trainers (Items), most of which had strong effects. Even the ones that didn't might get played because of theme support for Team Galactic's Invention cards.

3) Cyrus's Conspiracy

Speaking of which, Cyrus's Conspiracy would search your deck for a Supporter, a basic Energy card, and a Trainer (Item) with "Team Galactic's Invention" in the name. It was common to use one Cyrus's Conspiracy to get another for next turn.

4) Crobat G

As a Pokémon SP this was a Basic instead of a Stage 2. The Poké-Power placed a damage counter on the target of your choice and with Team Galactic's Invention G-105, Poké Turn could easily bounce to hand to reuse.

5) Dialga G/Dialga G LV.X

Dialga G could attack to block an opponent from playing Trainers (Items) and Stadium cards while doing 10 damage. Dialga G LV.X added a Poké-Body that shut off other Poké-Bodies on cards that weren't Pokémon SP. It made for a vicious lock.

PL RISING RIVALS

Release Date:
May 20, 2009

1) Luxray GL LV.X

Luxray GL LV.X has a "Gust of Wind" like Poké-Power that activated when you Level-Up while it is Active. It had a good attack and a free Retreat, so not a big problem.

2) SP Energy

While attached to a Pokémon SP, SP Energy provided one unit of Energy that counted as all Types. Less impressive, though still handy, it could still provide [C].

3) Nidoqueen

Nidoqueen has a Poké-Body that removes a damage counter from each of your Pokémon between turns, but worded so it can't stack. It also had some solid attacks, but the healing was its main thing.

4) Beedrill

Used to back up the Beedrill from DP Great Encounters, because its Poké-Power allows you to search your deck for a Grass Pokémon to add to hand. Thanks to Broken Time-Space this could lead to a blisteringly fast set up.

5) Flygon/Flygon LV.X

Flygon has a handy Poké-Body to aid in retreating, an attack to discard Stadium cards and wall, and an attack for big damage. Flygon LV.X has a Poké-Body to mill the opponent's deck and an attack that snipes opposing Pokémon LV.X for 150 damage!

PL SUPREME VICTORS

Release Date:
August 19, 2009

1) Garchomp C LV.X

Mass healing for your Pokémon SP when you Leveled-Up and strong sniping attack made Garchomp C LV.X potent. With Luxray GL LV.X, it won the Masters Division at the 2010 World Championships.

2) Dragonite FB

Dragonite FB was designed to counter other Pokémon SP. With Team Galactic's Invention G-101 Energy Gain and Double Colorless Energy, you could swing for 80 in one turn against them with its first attack.

3) VS Seeker

Reprinted this set, VS Seeker provided extra flexibility with how your deck was run.

4) Chatot [G]

Chatot [G] let you rearrange the top four cards of your opponent's deck when you Benched it, through its Poké-Power. Specialized for hand control decks but well worth it there.

5) Staraptor FB LV.X

Its Poké-Power let you add the Supporter of your choice from deck to hand. VS Seeker compliments this as well, but Luxray GL LV.X made the whole thing risky.

PL ARCEUS

Release Date:
November 4, 2009

1) Expert Belt

Getting +20 HP is good. Doing +20 damage is great! Giving up an extra Prize when KO'd is a serious risk, but the pros often outweighed the cons. It helped the underlying Pokémon score or avoid key KO amounts.

2) Spiritomb

Its Poké-Body kept both players from using Items while Spiritomb was Active. Its first attack Evolved one of your in play Pokémon, including searching your deck for said Evolution. Useful for buying time to set up.

3) Charizard

Charizard is a popular Pokémon and this one had a great Poké-Body that let it hit harder for each Fire Pokémon on your Bench. Thanks to Broken Time-Space, its good single Energy attack and good three Energy attack did not go to waste.

4) Department Store Girl

Great but only for certain decks, hence why Department Store Girl is number four. There were some great Pokémon Tools then, a lot like now. In the modern game we have an Item (Eco Arm) which does the same thing.

5) Gengar LV.X

Its Poké-Power let you remove the Level-Up card from one of your opponent's Pokémon and stick it on the bottom of his or her deck. You might score a KO as the target's HP drops, and either it isn't as good or they burn resources setting it back up.

HEARTGOLD/ SOULSILVER

Release Date:
February 10, 2010

1) Professor Oak's New Theory

Shuffle your hand into your deck and draw six cards. So simple, but so effective. This gave a stability to decks where you could get good, reliable draw without a massive discard cost or other conditions.

2) Pokémon Collector

When this card was released, Uxie from DP Legends Awakened was still legal so you got to search then play Uxie to draw. Later we got Smeargle to kind of do that, plus decks built around Basic Pokémon combos.

3) Jumpluff

With Broken Time-Space, a Stage 2 could be fast with the right attack. Jumpluff had that attack, as for [G] it did 10 damage times the number of Pokémon in play. Your opponent had to choose between a skimpy Bench or Jumpluff hitting harder.

4) Donphan (107/123)

A.k.a "Donphan Prime", its Type, Stage, HP, Resistance, Poké-Body, and first attack made it potent alone or with partners. It was used in the Masters Division 2011 World Championship winning deck "The Truth".

5) Double Colorless Energy

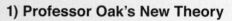

There are so many cards with more than one Colorless Energy requirement, and/or attacks that do more damage based on how many Energy are attached. It once again makes Double Colorless Energy a fantastic card.

HS Unleashed

Release Date:
May 12, 2010

1) Shaymin

When Benched from hand, the Poké-Power of this Shaymin let you move around your in-play Energy. Useful in general, it was vital to a deck built around Zekrom from the Black & White expansion, Pachirisu from Call of Legends, and itself.

2) Kingdra (85/95)

Kingdra "Prime" had a Poké-Power that allowed you to place a damage counter on one of your opponent's Pokémon once per turn that stacked. It had a solid attack that did 60 for one Water Energy (except against Fire Types).

3) Engineer's Adjustments

Great for decks that were heavy on basic Energy and/or wanted said Energy in the discard pile. Engineer's Adjustments let you discard an Energy card to draw four, letting you enlarge your hand without discarding or shuffling it away first.

4) Judge

Desert Shaman by a new name, Judge was useful for providing decent draw power while shrinking or at least disrupting your opponent's hand. It made for great decks with Poké-Power draw effects and for Yanmega "Prime", which we will discuss in another Top 5.

5) Dual Ball

A reprint, Dual Ball is worth mentioning now for the same reason Pokémon Collector made the previous list: this was a format for combos with Basic Pokémon. Get up to two Basic Pokémon without burning a Supporter.

HS Undaunted

Release Date:
August 18, 2010

1) Vilepiume

Not quite as powerful as it looks because this was when "Trainers" only referred to what we now call Items. It was still the backbone of the 2011 World Championships winning Masters Division deck "The Truth".

2) Smeargle

See your opponent's hand and copy the effect of a Supporter there via its Poké-Power. Smeargle was a common sight in decks, but you had to be careful as you had to copy a Supporter, even if its effect was bad for you.

3) Rotom

Players would use the Alph Lithograph from HS Triumphant to see an opponent face down Prizes. They would then Poké-Power on Rotom to swap the top card of their decks for one of any Prize cards needed for key combos, though not in all decks.

4) Scizor (84/90)

Not only could the attack on Scizor "Prime" increase its damage with extra [M] Energy, but its Poké-Body protected it from attack damage if the attacker had any Special Energy attached.

5) Rayquaza & Deoxys LEGEND

Its Poké-Body let you take an extra Prize when it KO'd an opponent's Pokémon and its attack hit quite hard. The attack was also expensive, so it was reserved for decks like those using the Emboar with Inferno Fandango.

HS Triumphant

Release Date:
November 2, 2010

1) Seeker

This Supporter forces both players to bounce a Benched Pokémon to hand. Reuse coming-into-play Poké-Powers, as well as potentially stealing a win by leaving an opponent with no Bench before you KO their Active.

2) Junk Arm

Discard two cards to reuse an Item from your discard pile. Even though there were Item blocking cards like Vileplume from HS Undaunted, there were also enough great Items from this period to make it a staple.

3) Magnezone (96/102)

Magnezone "Prime" combines a killer Poké-Power that let you draw with an attack that sent Energy from your in-play Pokémon to the Lost Zone to do big damage. It was seen in multiple decks, though they worked in a similar fashion.

4) Yanmega (98/102)

Yanmega "Prime" has two solid attacks, one which can even hit the Bench. What made it so strong was that its Poké-Body zeroed out the Energy costs for those attacks, so long as both players had the same hand size.

5) Twins

As long as you are behind on Prizes, Twins fetches two cards of your choice from your deck. Incredible if your deck was slow to start and pretty good in general as insurance.

Call of Legends

Release Date:
February 9, 2011

1) Lost Remover

Don't just discard a Special Energy for the cost of playing an Item, but send it to the Lost Zone where your opponent can't get it back. Some decks used no Special Energy, but most had at least a few.

2) Pachirisu

When you Benched Pachirisu, you can attach two Lightning Energy to it from your hand. Players would follow up with Shaymin from HS Unleashed to move that Energy to an already in play Zekrom from Black & White. Use your manual Energy attachment and Zekrom can swing for 120 damage.

3) Lost World

This Stadium provided a new win condition; if six of your opponent's Pokémon were in the Lost Zone, you won! Potent but it needed a deck built around it to work, and unless you used the correct effects, you'd be better off winning by KO.

4) Sage's Training

We look at a reprint because it was in a set with several other good cards. Sage's Training let you get two of the top five cards from your deck. The rest are discarded, which limited its general appeal but certain decks made good use of both parts of the effect.

5) Ninetales

This was another reprint from this set that had so many. Ninetales saw some use as an additional source of draw power, especially in decks that made use of Fire Energy from your discard pile.

BLACK & WHITE

Release Date:
April 25, 2011

1) Professor Juniper

Juniper was an instant classic in every deck once she came out, getting run at the full four copies in every deck. Discarding unwanted cards and drawing out 7 more from you deck is always a good thing, and Juniper is the essence of a good draw card!

2) Zekrom/Reshiram

The two dragon mascots of the Black and White era were also the big mascots of the great decks from the format. Each had the Outrage attack, which could deal more damage the more they took without getting Knocked Out. If they weren't beaten, they could defeat anything easily, and that led them to dominate the game!

3) Emboar

An interesting take on the classic "Rain Dance" Ability. Inferno Fandango could power up Reshiram instantly, and thus it was a key part of Reshiboar decks! Without Emboar, Reshiram would've been on even footing with his brother Zekrom, but with Emboar he was the better of the two.

4) Klinklang

Klinklang wasn't a big deal right out the gate, but his Shift Gear Ability was not to be underestimated. As time went on, it became popular to use it alongside cards like Prism Energy and Rainbow Energy in order to shift them around before using a Max Potion.

5) Reuniclus

Reuniclus embodied the "Damage Swap" Ability that made Alakazam from Base Set an interesting beast. By moving damage counters around, Reuniclus was another means of healing Pokémon with the future Max Potion.

EMERGING POWERS

Release Date:
August 31, 2011

1) Pokemon Catcher

At the time of its printing, Pokemon Catcher was an updated Gust of Wind. It allowed the player to choose his or her target that they'd then attack, rather than simply getting stuck with the opponent's Active.

2) Max Potion

Max Potion remains as one of the best healing cards out there. Even with the cost of discarding all of the Pokémon's Energy, using it to completely recover their HP is an amazing effect. Never mind that there are several different ways to avoid the downside! Max Potion is an amazingly powerful card.

3) Crushing Hammer

Crushing Hammer was one of a few cards that could discard Energy. Even though a coin flip was involved, the potential to get rid of any kind of Energy is always appealing. As a result, it saw lots of play in decks aiming to cripple the opponent's Pokémon by constantly denying them Energy.

4) Gothitelle (#47)

Her Magic Room Ability could ensnare the opponent's Item cards as long as she was Active, keeping them from using some of the more powerful effects in the game. And with Madkinesis as a Psychic-typed "Hydro Pump", she could prove to be formidable in her own right.

5) Tornadus

Tornadus would play a major part in one of the decks at the time of its release, ZPST. He was a crucial part of the deck, being a back-up attacker to Zekrom against its main Weakness of Fighting types.

NOBLE VICTORIES

Release Date:
November 16, 2011

1) N

As one of the many draw Supporters, N immediately found a home in many decks. As a Supporter that could reshuffle your opponent's hand back into their deck and give them less cards, N was an instant classic. As a card featuring the suave character of the same name, N is amazing.

2) Eelektrik

Eelektrik has become one of the more iconic Pokemon in the card game simply for its Ability. With it, he can charge up other Pokemon with Electric Energy from the discard pile! While Eelektrik wasn't gifted with a powerful offensive move, his supporting role has been noted as one of the best in the game that's seen wide play in many decks.

3) Archeops

In a time when Evolution Pokemon were relevant, Arcehops could become a devastating lockdown for such cards. Ancient Power prevents any more Evolutions from occurring, so once Archeops is down, there's no way any more Pokemon can evolve.

4) Virizion

Early Grass decks in the Black & White era got a big boost with Virizion. Double Draw could nab more cards for the player while Leaf Wallop could deal more damage on consecutive turns.

5) Victini (14)

Victini wasn't always the one to bring victory, but he could make things easier. With Victory Star, it became easier for different attacks such as Vanilluxe's Double Freeze to hit the heads they needed. For decks reliant on coin flips, there's no better card than Victini.

NEXT DESTINIES

Release Date:
February 8, 2012

1) Mewtwo-EX

While Psydrive was a pretty decent attack, it was X Ball that caught people's attention, which could deal damage based on the number of Energy on both Active Pokemon. With that kind of firepower and a hefty 170 HP, Mewtwo-EX became the central focus of the game, leading to the infamous "Mewtwo Wars".

2) Skyarrow Bridge

Powerful Pokemon-EX - which counted as Basic Pokemon - made Skyarrow Bridge amazing, and it became a must-run in any EX-based deck.

3) Level Ball

Retrieving Pokemon with 90 HP or less gave the card a wide usage and made it worthwhile, especially with cards like Eelektrik. It could search out instantly and make things run even more smoothly for players.

4) Prism Energy

Prism Energy works a lot like Rainbow Energy, and Rainbow has a lot of utility. Similarly, Prism provides every color of Energy at once, but it only really applies to Basic Pokemon. It could give your Pokemon-EX anything they need without taking damage.

5) Shiftry

While not too powerful on its initial release, Shiftry is an example of one of those cards that got better with time. In fact, it got SO much better it's now banned in Expanded play because of a combination between a Stadium that came out years later and its Ability, Giant Fan.

DARK EXPLORERS

Release Date:
May 9, 2012

1) Darkrai-EX

The big leader of Dark decks in the BW era, Darkrai-EX gave them something that most other cards haven't given to Pokemon: free Retreat Cost. As long as they had a Dark Energy, Darkrai-EX could make any Pokemon disappear beneath his Dark Cloak.

2) Dark Patch

One of the biggest things about Dark Explorers was the support for Dark Pokemon, and Dark Patch was no exception. It could immediately attach a Dark Energy from the discard pile right onto a Dark Pokemon at no extra cost.

3) Entei-EX

An oddity among other decks, Entei-EX was powerful enough that some people ran only 4 Entei-EX and nothing else in their entire decks. With Grand Flame to cycle back Fire Energy and even a basic Fire Fang to inflict the rare Burn, Entei-EX embodied the idea of, "if you want something done right, do it yourself."

4) Enhanced Hammer

This hefty hammer is a bit of an upgrade to something like Crushing Hammer. It gets rid of the need to flip a coin in exchange for limiting itself to Special Energy. Of course the widespread use of Special Energy made it playable for a long time.

5) Ultra Ball

Pitching two cards from your hand to grab any Pokemon you need made Ultra Ball an absolute must-run in many decks. It's not every day you can just nab whatever you want.

DRAGONS EXALTED

Release Date:
August 15, 2012

1) Rayquaza-EX

Rayquaza-EX sported a tremendous attack in the form of Dragon Burst, which could deal 60 damage per Energy discarded of either Fire or Electric. Combined with Eelektrik, he became his own major deck archetype, soaring to the top alongside Mewtwo-EX and Darkrai-EX!

2) Terrakion-EX

Terrakion-EX was one of the better Fighting-EX to come out. With Rock Tumble to avoid the occasional Resistance and Pump-Up Smash to accelerate Energy onto others, he became a very necessary part of early Fighting decks.

3) Blend Energy GFPD/WLFM

The two Blend Energies were made in the wake of Dragon-types that needed more than one kind of Energy. They would become integral to early Dragon decks and anything that wanted to run something outside of a mono-Type build.

4) Mew-EX

Mew-EX came out as probably the weakest Pokemon-EX in terms of HP, but don't let that fool you! He can move Energy around to give him just what he needs to use his Versatile Ability and unleash any attack on the field.

5) Emolga

With his initial Call to Family, he could easily bring out 2 Basic Pokemon from the deck, and with no Retreat Cost, he could easily switch out before getting hurt! Up until the rule change where the first player couldn't attack, Emolga was a key part in the strategy of early EX decks.

BOUNDARIES CROSSED

Release Date:
November 7, 2012

1) Computer Search

If Ultra Ball's ability to get any Pokemon was good, Computer Search's ability to grab any card for the same cost was even better! Discarding two cards to get whatever you need is a must-have!

2) Skyla

The Flying-type Gym Leader from Unova soars into the TCG with the Ability to grab out any Trainer card from the deck. Again, these kind of searching effects are always good, and Skyla quickly found a home in many decks.

3) Keldeo-EX

Keldeo made his TCG debut not only as a normal card but as an EX too! Rush In could bring him out in a flash, and Hydro Pump could stack on Water Energies for massive damage. He became a quick mainstay in many decks simply for his Rush In Ability, a much needed power in the sets to come.

4) Landorus-EX

At the time of his release, Rayquaza-EX was arguably the most powerful deck out there. So what happens when you can take out two Tynamo trying to evolve into Eelektrik in one turn? Landorus-EX's Hammerhead provided a quick answer - attack!

5) Blastoise

Blastoise pushed for the rise of Water decks by bringing back his old power with a new name, Deluge. Letting Water rain from one's hand and fuel one's Pokemon, Blastoise became a major part of Keldeo-EX's own deck archetype in much the same way as Eelektrik did for Rayquaza-EX.

PLASMA STORM

Release Date:
February 6, 2013

1) Hypnotoxic Laser

Hypnotoxic Laser, alongside Virbank City Gym, made an immediate impact upon its release. With the ability to instantly Poison a Pokemon and maybe even put it to Sleep, HTL would become the most game-changing card of its time.

2) Colress

Draw power has always been a powerful resource to have, and Colress is among the best. While he does shuffle your hand into your deck, you can draw cards based on the number of Benched Pokemon in play. Consider how many Bench-sitters were around in that format.

3) Black Kyurem-EX

Black Kyurem-EX saw a good amount of play alongside Blastoise. With Black Ballista capable of dealing 200 damage and wiping out anything in the format, Blastoise was the perfect partner to fuel Black Kyurem-EX's heavy 3-Energy discard.

4) Lugia-EX

Lugia-EX was one of the first to use Plasma Energy. Plasma Gale could deal a powerful 120 damage by discarding one such Energy, and combined with Overflow, he took a lot of Prizes away in a single stroke. Upon his release, he became the flagship ace of the Plasma decks.

5) Bicycle

While most draw power was given over to Supporter cards, Bicycle showed that Items could also have draw power. With the ability to draw up to four cards, Bicycle could speed up decks even faster than before!

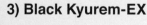

Plasma Freeze

Release Date:
May 8, 2013

1) Thundurus-EX

Thundurus-EX became the new headliner with Raiden Knuckle allowing him to retrieve Plasma Energy from the discard pile along with any other Energy he wanted. Thunderous Noise provided a quick one-two punch to most any Pokemon.

2) Deoxys-EX

Power Connect increased the damage subtly by 10 for each Deoxys-EX in play on every Plasma Pokemon's attacks... save for another Deoxys-EX. In a pinch, he could even use Helix Force to knock out an opposing Pokemon, but he was usually relegated to the Bench.

3) Float Stone

Float Stone is one of the most useful Tools in the game, taking care of the Retreat Cost of any Pokemon by making it free. While it doesn't come up that often, it can be crucial at times. This made Float Stone a key part in a lot of decks.

4) Flareon

Flareon doesn't seem to be that big of a deal at first, but his Vengeance attack could do more damage based on the number of Pokemon in the discard pile. While it wasn't always at the top of the list, Flareon Vengeance decks did become a prominent part of the format.

5) Garbodor

Though Garbodor technically came out in Dragons Exalted, it did get a reprint in Plasma Freeze, and with Float Stone's arrival, it became a force to be reckoned with. Its main appeal is the Garbotoxin Ability, which kept all other Abilities on lockdown while Garbodor had a Tool attached.

Plasma Blast

Release Date:
August 14, 2013

1) Virizion-EX

Virizion-EX is half of what made the VirGen deck great. Verdant Wind made the then-popular HTL completely useless against any Pokemon with Grass Energy. With Emerald Slash capable of powering up something quick, Virizion-EX played an amazing supportive role in Grass decks.

2) Genesect-EX/G Booster

Genesect-EX made up the other half of the VirGen deck, as well as its main attacker. Megalo Cannon worked out pretty nicely on its own, but with G Booster, Genesect-EX could wipe out any other Pokemon in the game completely unopposed.

3) Jirachi-EX

Jirachi-EX is currently the Pokemon-EX with the lowest HP score, at only a mere 90. It's also one of the most versatile Pokemon-EX and was easily put in every deck for one reason: Stellar Guidance. With the Ability to pull out any Supporter needed, Jirachi-EX became an integral part in every deck.

4) Suicune

With Safeguard, Suicune was one of the only Pokemon that could successfully stand up to Pokemon-EX without being threatened with a KO. And while Aurora Beam isn't exactly something to write home about, it was a solid move for Suicune to use in combination with HTLBank to get the KOs it needed.

5) Silver Mirror

With Plasma Pokemon on the rise, Silver Mirror was one of the only cards that could stand up to threats like Lugia-EX and Thundurus-EX. It effectively gave a Safeguard effect to any Pokemon against anything Team Plasma, making it a relevant if not niche tech card to use.

Legendary Treasures

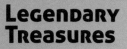

Release Date:
November 6, 2013

1) Meloetta-EX

Meloetta-EX provided a very niche support to a very niche deck archetype: The Round deck. While most of the other Pokemon with Round needed Evolutions, Meloetta-EX could just come right into play thanks to her status as a Basic.

2) Spiritomb

While its Ability limits some of the least playable cards in the game, it does prevent players from making huge plays with an instant search. Taking Spiritomb in some form could easily become priority #1 for VirGen players.

3) Mewtwo-EX

This reprint allowed Mewtwo to stick around for a few more years until Legendary Treasures rotated out, letting him reign over the early XY era as another one of the powerful EXs. With X Ball still an ever-present threat, Mewtwo-EX continues to live on to this day through Expanded play and remains one of the best Pokemon-EX ever printed.

4) Darkrai-EX

Darkrai-EX's reprinting meant that Dark decks would continue seeing major support, which was necessary once Dark Explorers rotated out. Without cards like Dark Patch around, Darkrai-EX was essential to keep Dark Energy bearers with free Retreat.

5) Keldeo-EX

With the reprint of Keldeo-EX, the ongoing fight to fend off HTLBank was guaranteed to continue for years to come. By keeping him in the format, Rush In could still be used as a counter to HTLBank's sinister Poison damage combo.

XY

Release Date:
February 5, 2014

1) Muscle Band

This handy little Tool came out with the XY Base Set and became a standard in any deck. Attaching it added an extra 20 damage to every attack the Pokemon made. This could push some moves into 2HKO and even OHKO range when they wouldn't have normally!

2) Yveltal-EX

With Evil Ball, it could dish out even more damage while the Energy to use it limited its usage to mostly Dark decks. Not that that stopped anyone from playing him - especially in combination with his Basic non-EX version!

3) Trevenant

With Forest's Curse, he could lock out an opponent from using any Item cards...so long as he was Active. He'd eventually see major play once the right support came out, but until then he was merely a niche Pokemon.

4) Roller Skates

Much like Bicycle was in its day, Roller Skates was Item-based support that could accelerate decks to a new level. Unlike Bicycle it relied on a coin flip, and ultimately it didn't pan out terribly well in the long run.

5) Yveltal

Yveltal became the new Dark Patch for Dark decks, with Oblivion Wing taking them straight to the top. Accelerating Energy out of the discard pile and dealing damage at the same time was a fantastic way to set-up.

FLASHFIRE

Release Date:
May 7, 2014

1) Lysandre

While some of the more useful Supporters have been based on draw power, Lysandre focuses more on switching things up by switching Pokemon around for your opponent. With Pokemon Catcher's errata, Lysandre became the balanced version that could be guaranteed to work.

2) Fiery Torch

Fiery Torch was part of the Fire-type support in the set, and it became a staple in many new Fire decks at the time. All that was needed was a discard of Fire Energy, and Fiery Torch snagged the player two new cards.

3) Pyroar

Pyroar had the unique Ability to keep any Basic Pokemon at bay with his Intimidating Mane. Not only did this include smaller Basics, but it also included the mighty Pokemon-EX!

4) Blacksmith

Blacksmith could cycle back the Fire Energy discarded by Fiery Torch or a Fire Pokemon's attack. Not only could it grab two Fire Energies, but it could also put them onto any Pokemon you have.

5) Druddigon

With Revenge, Druddigon could do more damage when you lost a Pokemon, meaning he could counter for 90 damage - or 180 against Dragons like Rayquaza-EX.

FURIOUS FISTS

Release Date:
August 13, 2014

1) Strong Energy

Strong Energy not only set a trend for future sets but became yet another game-changer. Providing a Muscle Band-like effect while at the same time powering up every Fighting move on any Fighting type, it did for Fighting decks what cards like Blacksmith did for Fire decks.

2) Seismitoad-EX

From the day he was previewed, Seismitoad-EX was the hype. And he lived up to that hype. Quaking Punch was an aggressive form of Trevenant's Forest's Curse Ability, and it made Seismitoad-EX into his own archetype. Combined with the Hammers, he was almost unstoppable.

3) Lucario-EX

With three attacks of various degrees of usefulness for every stage of the game, Lucario-EX has a nice bag of tricks. All the Fighting support makes him just as viable in some cases as Landorus-EX!

4) Landorus

With his hefty Shout of Power, he can call out a Fighting Energy card from the discard pile to attach onto one of your Benched Pokemon, powering up their attacks quickly! He's a must-run for any Fighting deck working to muster up a quick one-two punch!

5) Fighting Stadium

Fighting Stadium had the unique Ability to do even more damage against opposing Pokemon-EX! Not only did this make even the smallest Fighting-types able to do massive damage alongside Strong Energy and Muscle Band, but it brought a huge power boost to the non-EX Fighting decks working their way up!

Phantom Forces

Release Date:
November 5, 2014

1) Lysandre's Trump Card

A card that was so powerful it ended up being banned, Lysandre's Trump Card was the ultimate reset button. Once a player used it, any cards in the discard pile aside from Lysandre's Trump Card were put back into the deck, letting players recycle everything they used.

2) Battle Compressor

Battle Compressor is the physical embodiment of deck-thinning in Pokemon. Using it meant you could toss out any three cards into your discard pile easily, getting access to Energy and Supporters in ways unseen before its appearance.

3) Bronzong

Bronzong could do for Metal decks what Eelektrik did for Lightning decks, bringing out Energy from the discard pile with ease. Metal Links made Bronzong extremely playable, and soon he would become a force to be reckoned with.

4) M Manectric-EX

One of the first playable Megas, M Manectric-EX had a lot of advantages that earlier Megas - and even current Megas - don't really have. The first was the access to Spirit Link cards, which allowed a player Mega Evolving to forego the rule that would immediately end their turn upon playing it.

5) Gengar-EX

Gengar-EX was used frequently with Trevenant as a sneaky striker. Using Dark Corridor, the player could Poison the Active Pokemon while dealing damage, switch Gengar-EX with Trevenant to keep the opponent from playing Item cards doing their next turn, and then switch the two back with a Float Stone attached to Trevenant to repeat the cycle again.

Primal Clash

Release Date:
February 4, 2015

1) Primal Kyogre-EX

Primal Clash brought with it the advent of Ancient Traits, alongside two of the best users of it. Primal Kyogre-EX was armed with Alpha Growth, allowing the player to attach two Basic Energies to him each turn. Combined with Tidal Storm's overwhelming damage and the ability to not only move two Energy to a Benched Pokemon but deal another 30 damage to an opposing Bench-sitter, Primal Kyogre-EX made an immense splash on impact.

2) Archie's Ace-in-the-Hole/ Maxie's Hidden Ball Trick

Both of them can only be played when they're the last card in your hand, both bring back a Pokemon from your discard pile for free, and both let you draw 5 cards.

3) Silent Lab

Having the power to shut down all Abilities on Basic Pokemon? Pretty good. Having the attributes of a Stadium to compete in the ongoing Stadium Wars? Nice to have. Getting played at the right time to knock out your opponent's Safeguarding Suicune or turn off their Wobbuffet's Bide Barricade to get the KO for the win? Priceless.

4) Primal Groudon-EX

With Omega Barrier protecting it from the power of Trainer cards, he could walk out unopposed once the sun shined bright on his time. And with the powerful Gaia Volcano, he could deal lots of damage in a moment's notice!

5) Acro Bike

Like the Acro Bike in the games, it was less about speed and more about technicality. And while limiting itself to only two cards could be seen as detrimental, Acro Bike still has a glorious place in aggressive fast-drawing decks.

ROARING SKIES

Release Date:
May 6, 2015

1) Shaymin-EX

With Set Up grabbing up to 6 cards and Sky Return letting you put him back in your hand to re-use Set Up again and again, he became an easy "one-of" in every deck.

2) Double Dragon Energy

At the time of the release of the Dragon-type in the TCG, the best Energies to use with them were cards like Prism Energy and the Blend Energies. Now they have access to their own personal Double Rainbow Energy, without the restrictions or limitations aside from the Pokemon being a Dragon-type.

3) Trainers' Mail

You know what's better than drawing cards? Grabbing exactly the card you need, and Trainers' Mail does just that. So long as whatever Trainer you need is in the top 4 cards of your deck, you're set to do whatever you need to do!

4) M Rayquaza-EX (76)

M Rayquaza-EX got two iterations in this set, and one of them came out as a Colorless form. It also carries the Delta Evolution trait, which allows the player to evolve even if Rayquaza-EX just got put into play.

5) Sky Field

Sky Field possesses the unique ability to change how many Benched Pokemon each player could have. While normally it was limited to 5, as long as Sky Field remained in play, it could be up to 8 Benched Pokemon.

ANCIENT ORIGINS

Release Date:
August 12, 2015

1) Giratina-EX

Giratina-EX became a Swiss-Army-Lock Pokemon of sorts, having a variety of counters to a variety of cards. His Renegade Pulse powered on against the Mega Evolutions, safeguarding him from their attacks. His Chaos Wheel locked out Tools, Special Energy, and Stadium cards to keep the opponent slower and from gaining the upper hand.

2) Hex Maniac

Hex Maniac curses all Pokemon with Abilities to have them cancelled out for the next turn. This can be useful for getting past annoying Abilities and keeping your opponent from benefiting off of theirs, making Hex Maniac a crazy gal to have around!

3) Hoopa-EX

The moment he was revealed; Hoopa-EX became a blip on everyone's radar. With Scoundrel Ring able to grab any Pokemon-EX that one needs, he was essential for any strategy that needed to retrieve those Pokemon-EX from the deck.

4) Vileplume

Vileplume brought back the Ability to completely lock down Item cards. While Seismitoad-EX is arguably better with Quaking Punch, Vileplume did find an immediate use in Giratina-EX decks as a way of covering one of the few types of cards that he didn't cover.

5) Lugia-EX

Lugia-EX is effectively a Colorless version of Mewtwo-EX. Aero Ball is another version of X Ball, meaning Lugia-EX is a lot like Mewtwo-EX. Of course he's also got the advantage of Deep Hurricane, which is stronger when a Stadium is in play to be discarded, making him far more relevant!

BREAKThrough

Release Date:
November 4, 2015

2) Parallel City

With two different effects depending on which side was facing you, Parallel City was a curious way to renew the Stadium concept. With the effect of either reducing your Bench to only 3 Pokemon or making 3 Types' attacks do less damage, Parallel City is easy to use, but difficult to master.

4) Mr. Mime

Mr. Mime provides an incredibly useful Ability with Bench Barrier. By protecting the Bench from damage, Mr. Mime keeps all of one's Pokemon from taking damage from sniping attacks. This prevents future KOs from getting set-up, and ultimately this makes Mr. Mime a neat tech card against those decks.

1) Zoroark

Not only does he have "Stand In", which embodies Keldeo-EX's own Ability, but he also has the advantage of a great BREAK Evolution, a mechanic introduced in this set. He's certainly one of the best in the set to use, even as a Stage 1 Evolution.

3) M Mewtwo-EX (64)

At long last, M Mewtwo-EX came to finish what Mewtwo-EX started. What's better than an X Ball doing damage based on the Energy attached to both Pokemon? Having Psychic Infinity deal 10 damage plus 30 more for every Energy attached to both Pokemon. Nuff said.

5) Brigette

Brigette is a search Supporter with options, making her flexible in a variety of decks. One can either put a Basic Pokemon-EX or 3 Basic Pokemon non-EX onto the Bench. This makes for some interesting plays that Brigette can make happen very, very fast.

BREAKpoint

Release Date:
February 3, 2016

1) Psychic's Third Eye

First it reveals your opponent's hand, giving you insight into his or her strategy. Then it lets you discard anything you don't need to draw into the same amount that you discarded. This makes Psychic's Third Eye an astonishing preparatory card.

2) Fighting Fury Belt

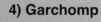

As an alternative to Muscle Band, Fighting Fury Belt gives up a little damage for another big boost. It gives out 10 extra damage instead of 20, but it also gives 40 extra HP to the Pokemon it's attached to. This makes Fighting Fury Belt a fine substitute for Muscle Band if need be, though depending on the format, one will probably be better than the other.

3) Garbodor

What starts to look like a reprint of the infamous Garbodor, turns out to be something slightly different. Not only does he have Garbotoxin, but he's also got Offensive Bomb, a decent attack that can Confuse and Poison. It may not be much to keep Garbodor off the Bench, but it's good to have if he's forced to take an active role.

4) Garchomp

Turbo Assault can bring out Energy onto a Benched Pokemon while Bite Off can utterly destroy Pokemon-EX, making Garchomp a competent and powerful threat.

5) Puzzle of Time

When played with just one copy, it can let the player look through the top 3 cards of their deck. When two copies are played at the same time, they can add 2 cards from the discard pile back to their hand. This gives Puzzle of Time a lot of flexibility, and it has found its way into some decks as a result.

Generations

Release Date:
February 22, 2016

1) Jolteon-EX

Jolteon-EX quickly proved popular thanks to its Flash Ray attack. Like Regice (AOR)'s Resistance Blizzard, the attack prevents Jolteon-EX from being hit by a certain type of Pokemon's attacks, namely Basic ones.

2) Revitalizer

Revitalizer is a great card for Grass decks, having the ability to put 2 Grass Pokémon back from the discard pile to one's hand. This can recycle some Pokemon or quickly gather the Evolutions for a line-up to use with Forest of Giant Plants.

3) Olympia

Olympia doesn't do a whole lot, but she does provide a quick switch and heal to one Pokemon. This makes her fairly impressive in some regards, though it may not be worth one's Supporter for the turn.

4) Flareon-EX

Flareon-EX is notable for one of its Hydro Pump-esque Blaze Ball and supportive Flash Fire Ability. Using Flash Fire to move Fire Energy over to Flareon-EX, he can power up his Blaze Ball attack to impressive levels before incinerating the competition.

5) Imakuni?

Clearly not the best card in the set, or even in the game, but Imakuni? has a large cultural importance in the world of Pokemon. While the card itself only confuses your Active Pokemon, it represents a popular real world entertainer for Pokemon in Japan.

Fates Collide

Release Date:
May 4, 2016

1) Regirock-EX

Regirock-EX provides a damage boost of 10 to all Fighting Pokemon's attacks, making their already impressive amount of damage-boosting even greater. Throw in Bedrock Press which dealt heavy damage while preventing some from hurting him, and Regirock-EX is a solid Pokemon to work with.

2) Carbink BREAK

Arguably the best BREAK Evolution printed yet. Combined with either of the two Carbinks printed in this set - one of which has Safeguard - makes Carbink BREAK an effective addition to Fighting decks that need the acceleration.

3) Zygarde-EX

Zygarde-EX itself isn't that impressive at first glance. He possesses 3 attacks, similar to Lucario-EX but none of which compare to them. On the other hand, he also has Power Memory, a Tool similar to Genesect-EX's G Booster with similar damage output and a much higher cost.

4) Mew

Appearances can be deceiving, and Mew hardly looks intimidating. A low HP score and a meek copy of its EX version's Ability makes Mew questionable at first. However, it combines extremely well with the Night March deck archetype, giving Mew a great spot in the deck to use.

5) Glaceon-EX

Glaceon-EX worked to copy her brother Jolteon-EX's success by pulling out a similar move to his Flash Ray, Crystal Ray. The main difference is Crystal Ray only affects Evolved Pokemon, giving Glaceon-EX a unique mix-up on Jolteon-EX's attack but with less availability in some cases.

POKÉMON TCG JARGON

BY JOSEPH "OTAKU" LEE

Like most hobbies, the Pokémon TCG has developed its own jargon. Some of these are official terms, but obscure. Others were coined by players, which means they can vary from place to place, like Pokémon leagues and message boards. They can make discussion easier by expressing complex concepts in just a few words or make things confusing because no one is using them the same way. This is true whether you're a new player or a long time veteran. For the fan derived terms there is no authority to prove which use is correct, but we can look at not only what is the most common or useful; the two are not always the same. Unless it had an additional slang meaning, terms found in the Glossary of the Rule Book were not included.

2-On-2 Battle: Rules variant where each player has two Active Pokémon. Unsanctioned but official rules exist for league, side events, etc.

4-Copy Rule: Rule that restricts you to running no more than four copies of a non-basic Energy card in your deck for Constructed play.

30-Card: Rules variant that uses 30 card decks. Unsanctioned but official rules exist for league, side events, etc.

+39: In a Limited Format event, sometimes you can pull a Basic Pokémon so potent your best bet is to simply run it with 39 other non-Basic Pokémon cards to ensure you open with it.

#-#-#: Notation for a related set of cards, usually an Evolution line. In the case of the latter, start with either the lowest Stage or the highest Stage. Replace # with actual quantity of that card.

#HKO: Replace # with the actual number of turns it takes to score a knockout. So two turns are a 2HKO – A "2 Hit Knock Out".

(X): Text representation of an Energy symbol; replace "X" with the appropriate letter for that Type. Can also be used to represent a generic non-Colorless Energy requirement. See also "[X]". Letters used in these designations can be found later in this article. Example: "G".

[X]: Text representation of an Energy symbol; replace "X" with the appropriate letter for that Type. Can also be used to represent a generic non-Colorless Energy requirement. See also "(X)".

Acceleration: Anything that speeds up an aspect of gameplay, most commonly Energy or Evolution.

Aggro: Short for "aggressive". Usually an aggro deck tries to take Prizes quickly and doesn't worry about long term strategy or performance. Typically wins fast or not at all.

Archetype: A foundational deck concept from which others are derived or a deck list/skeleton in widespread use.

Auto Win: A matchup so favorable it is quite probable you will win. Usually references the relative strengths of the decks being used against each other, not the players.

Auto Loss: A matchup so unfavorable it is quite probable you will lose. Usually references the relative strengths of the decks being used against each other, not the players.

Bait: Card you want your opponent to focus attention or resources on instead of something more important.

Basic: A Basic Pokémon or Energy card; differentiated in card text by always using a capital "B" for Pokémon but not for Energy.

BCIF: Best Card In Format. Difficult to prove; often used hyperbolically.

BDIF: Best Deck In Format. Difficult to prove; often used hyperbolically.

Beatstick: An uncomplicated attacker. Easy to run with good damage and affordable attack costs, at least in a given deck.

Bench: Besides being the location of your non-Active but in play Pokémon, this term is also used to describe putting a Pokémon into play apart from Evolving.

Bench-Hitter: A Pokémon that does damage or places damage counters on one or more Benched Pokémon. Includes spread or snipe but also covers those that fall in between.

Bench Out: When you lose because you have no more Pokémon in play.

Bench-sitter: A Pokémon a player prefers to keep on the Bench, usually because it has an effective Ability it can use from there.

Board: Cards currently in play. Sometimes includes all things known such as all cards currently in play, hand size, deck size, cards in discard, etc.

Booster Draft: Similar to a Sealed Deck event but players separate into groups of eight, taking turns opening a pack, selecting a card from it, then passing the pack around for the others to also select a card. Pack contents are not public knowledge.

Bounce: An effect that returns an in play card to hand.

Broken: An incredibly potent card, usually one seen as threatening or destroying game balance.

Burn: The name of a Special Condition; also used to describe using up a resource for little or no gain, as in "Burn a card." Done intentionally for certain combos.

C: Colorless, especially as a replacement for an actual Colorless Energy symbol when typing. Often put in parenthesis or brackets. See also "Pokémon SP".

Casual Play: Playing just for fun. Cards that are great for Casual Play may be terrible in Competitive Play.

CC: City Championship, part of the Championship Series.

CCG: Collectible Card Game

Championship Series: The string of organized play events that end with the World Championships.

Cleaner: Pokémon used to finish off an opponent while you are in a favorable position, especially if it is independent of your main strategy.

Clock: Also sometimes "the clock", references the time allotted for a match in competitive play. "Winning by the clock" is the same as "winning by time".

Closer: Pokémon used to finish off an opponent regardless of position, especially if it relies heavily on your main strategy.

CP: Championship Points, earned through playing in Championship Series events. Lets you qualify to play in the World Championships.

Combo: Small group of cards that work better together.

Competitive Play: When players are focused on winning with optimal deck builds and plays, especially if that is how they enjoy the game.

CotD: The Card of the Day is a card evaluation popularized by Pojo.com where one or more reviewers discuss and rate a single card every day. Check it out!

Consistency: How reliably your deck provides you the cards you need to set up and maintain your strategy.

Constructed: When you play using a deck built from your own cards and not those provided at the event. Includes Unlimited, Standard, Expanded, and Legacy Formats.

Control: Effects that influence or restrict the actions your opponent can take, usually as part of a larger strategy. Often has a focus such as Energy Control, Hand Control, etc.

Counter: The use of an effect, mechanic, or tactic to reduce or completely eliminate the effectiveness of an opponent's card, effect, use of mechanic, or tactic. Also applied to what was actually used to counter.

CREATURES: Creatures, Inc. is a Japanese videogame company affiliated with TPC.

D: Darkness, especially as a replacement for an actual Darkness Energy symbol when typing. Often put in parenthesis or brackets.

DARK: An old mechanic, some Pokémon showed affiliation by having "Dark" as part of their card name, in front of the actual Pokémon name. Not to be confused with the Darkness.

DEAD CARD: A card that you cannot currently use at the moment (possibly the rest of the game) except as discard fodder.

DEAD DRAW: When you draw into something not particularly useful to your current situation, especially dead cards.

DECK LIST: A write up of the contents of your deck.

DECK MATCHUP: The likelihood of a deck winning assuming all other factors (build, luck, player skill, etc.) are equal.

DECK OUT: When you lose because you cannot draw a card at the start of your turn.

DENIAL: Preventing an opponent from significantly utilizing a particular resource by blocking it or quickly eliminating it; a form of control.

DISRUPTION: Effects that alter the opponent's game state to reduce their effectiveness and/or sabotage any plans, usually as part of a larger strategy. A form of control.

DONK: FTKO that results in a win; effective but disliked by many players.

DCE: Double Colorless Energy

EARLY GAME: The first few turns of the game relative to the overall length, especially while players are still setting up their fields.

ENERGY ACCELERATION: Increasing your effective supply of Energy in play. This can be accomplished in several ways, including some that do not actually change the quantity of Energy in play.

EXPANDED: A rotating format similar to Standard Format, but allowing sets from further back and rotating less frequently.

EVOLUTION ACCELERATION: Getting Evolutions into play without the normal wait and/or investment of cards required.

F: Fighting, especially as a replacement for an actual Fighting Energy symbol when typing. Often put in parenthesis or brackets. Does not apply to the mechanic name "Pokémon Tool F".

FIZZLE: When an effect does nothing due to another in game effect preventing it from working.

FLIPPY: Descriptor for something relying on coin flips; often derogatory.

FORMAT: The specific rules for play, usually determining which cards are legal for use in your deck.

FTKO: First Turn Knock Out.

FTK: First Turn Kill. More violent sounding version of First Turn Win.

FTW: First Turn Win. As it sounds, winning on the first turn but in particular having that as the actual focus of your deck.

G: Grass, especially as a replacement for an actual Grass Energy symbol when typing. Often put in parenthesis or brackets. Example: "(GG) – might represent the energy cost of at an attack that requires 2 Grass Energy".

Game Freak: Game Freak, Inc. is a Japanese game developer and the primary developer of the Pokémon series of games.

GG: Good game. Common expression to show respect to opponent after finishing a game, however careless use or intentional misuse can be seen as an insult.

GLASS CANNON: An attacker with good damage output and/or attack effects but which is very easily KO'd.

GOING ROGUE: Using a rogue deck at an event.

HARD LOCK: A lock that is very difficult to break.

INVITE: Invitation to participate in the World Championships. Earned through CP.

JANKEN: Another name for Rock-Paper-Scissors.

JUNIOR DIVISION: Age bracket for players 10 and under.

KO: Knock Out.

L: Lightning, especially as a replacement for an actual Lightning Energy symbol when typing. Often put in parenthesis or brackets.

LATE GAME: Last few turns of the game, especially when it is apparent someone will soon win.

LC: League Challenge, part of the Championship Series.

LEAGUE: Pokémon League, a place where players regularly meet to play, trade, etc. Can be sanctioned by TPCi.

Legacy: A PTCGO exclusive format using cards from the HS series of sets and promos, Call of Legends, and BW series of sets and promos.

Limited: When players build decks to use at an event from cards supplied there. It includes Sealed Deck, Booster Draft, Rochester Draft, and Solomon Draft Formats. Deck size is 40 cards and players only set aside 4 Prize cards.

Line: Short for Evolution Line, the series of cards from which the final one Evolves.

Lock: A strategy where you prevent an opponent from using at least one of a certain card, effect, or game mechanic. Part of control and disruption tactics.

Loose Staple: A card run in many decks; or a card regularly considered but not always run in nearly all decks.

Lucksack: Gaining significant advantage or the win primarily through chance. Also a derogatory term for a person who just seemingly won through luck.

M: Metal, especially as a replacement for an actual Metal Energy symbol when typing. Often put in parenthesis or brackets.

Masters Division: Age bracket for the 15+ in organized play.

Meta: Short for metagame.

Metagame: The current competitive play environment, including both cards and tactics commonly used by players.

Metagaming: Countering the metagame.

Mid Game: The middle of the game, generally after the field has set up but before someone appears close to winning.

Mill: To discard a card or cards from your opponent's deck, usually from the top.

Misplay: Making a less than optional move in the game, especially bad plays.

Mulligan: When a player's opening hand contains no Basic Pokémon and s/he must shuffle it back into the deck and try again.

Multi-Lock: Multiple lock effects stacked together.

N: Well-known supporter, but also "Dragon", especially as a replacement for an actual Dragon Energy symbol when typing. Often put in parenthesis or brackets.

Nats: National Championships for a particular country. Part of the Championship Series.

Ness: Jason Klaczynski, a player with several high profile wins including winning the Masters Division of the World Championships three times! Most people regard him as the Best Pokémon TCG Player of all time due to his resume. He also wrote the "Top 100 cards of All Time" article in this book. *Pojo Note: He's also a very likeable person. ;-)*

Net-Decking: Copying a deck from an online source, especially card for card. Formerly derogatory, now seen as a common sense practice.

Nintendo: Well known game company. One of three to jointly own the copyright to Pokémon.

OHKO: One-Hit Knock Out. When you score a KO with a single attack or use of an effect. Often used loosely, permitted if multiple things score a KO in one turn.

OP: Organized Play. This refers to non-casual play, especially when a league, tournament, or other event is sanctioned by Play! Pokémon. Alternatively, it can be short for "overpowered" and refer to a broken card.

Opener: Active Pokémon when you begin the game. Alternatively, Pokémon run specifically to be your opening Active.

Opening: A chance to gain an advantage. Also used to describe the first few turns of the game.

Opening Hand: The initial seven cards drawn from your deck. Sometimes your mandatory first turn draw is also included.

Otaku: An obsessive fan, especially of things pertaining to Japan. Often derogatory.

P: Psychic, especially as a replacement for an actual Psychic Energy symbol when typing. Often put in parenthesis or brackets.

P!P: Play! Pokemon, the division of TPC that handles organized play for both the TCG and the video games.

P#: P1 for the player going first, P2 for the player going second, up to P4 for the player going fourth if using Team Battle rules.

Perfect Lock: A lock that cannot be broken; very rare.

Pivot Pokémon: Pokémon promoted to Active because it is easy to retreat. Usually has a free Retreat Cost and aids in combos.

Play Style: A player's natural tendencies when building or using a deck; can be a strength or weakness. Often incorrectly used as an excuse for poor decisions.

Play Test: Using a deck specifically to learn how to best run or counter it.

Pojo: Pokémon Dojo. Also used to refer to the owner and administrator of pojo.com.

Pokémon Professor: A special class of judge/support staff for Pokémon organized play, named after the iconic "Professor" characters in the video games and the anime.

Pokémon SP: An older game mechanic. Pokémon SP have different symbols after their name a stylized, "C" for "Champion", "FB" for "Frontier Brain", "G" for "Team Galactic", "GL" for "Gym Leader", or "四" (a Japanese character for the number four) for the "Elite Four". Shorthand might put the letters in brackets or parenthesis. Do not confuse for Energy symbol shorthand.

POP: Pokémon Organized Play, a former name for P!P.

Porter: Attack that Benches your Active Pokémon, usually while doing damage or some other useful effect.

Pre-Release: Sealed Deck Limited Format event using booster packs from the newest set before its official release.

Promote: Moving a Pokémon into the Active spot from your Bench.

Prop 15/3: Predecessor to the original Modified Format; players could use cards from any set but only 15 Trainers and no more than three copies of a card.

Proxy: Using one card to represent another. This is usually done because you can't find a certain card, or that card is too expensive to buy, but you still want to test it out. Illegal in sanctioned play except to replace a card damaged during play in order to finish out an event.

PTCGO: Pokémon Trading Card Game Online, the official online Pokémon TCG service run by Nintendo/TPCi.

Pull: When you get a card in a booster pack.

R: Fire, especially as a replacement for an actual Fire Energy symbol when typing. Often put in parenthesis or brackets.

Regionals: Regional Championships, part of the Championship Series.

Reprint: When a card is released more than one time, even if the art is significantly different.

Revenge: Effect that requires your opponent KO'd one of your Pokémon on the prior turn, either to work at all or to work better.

Rochester Draft: Similar to a Booster Draft but the chosen player opens two packs at a time, with contents being public knowledge for the group. Players then take turns selecting cards until all booster packs are opened.

Rogue Deck: An unanticipated deck being used in a particular metagame. Some definitions prefer the deck to perform well at the event and/or be largely unknown beforehand.

Rotating Format: When the legal card pool adds new releases while removing older ones; not necessarily at the same time.

Rotation: When the legal card pool has sets removed (but not added).

Rules Lawyer: Player who attempts to use the rules to his or her gain in violation of their intent. Often but not always knowledgeable about said rules.

Rush: An aggro swarm strategy.

Rushing: Fast play on your part and/or trying to get your opponent to play faster in a timed event to avoid running out of time. Alternatively, see "Rush".

Scoop: When a player forfeits by picking up his cards from the field. Usually done because a player knows he cannot win, based on the current board position, and doesn't see the point in wasting anyone's time.

Sealed Deck: A Limited Format event where each Player receives the same amount of booster packs to open and uses the contents, plus basic Energy, to build a 40 card deck to use.

Senior Division: Age bracket for players 11 to 14 years old.

Shred: Attacks that ignore protective effects. Named after one such attack.

Shrink: As in "Shrink your hand"; when you are trying to use as many cards as you can from your hand to lower its size.

Skeleton: An incomplete deck list intended for others to flesh out. Sometimes called a Deck Skeleton.

Slow Play: Playing slower than the rules permit, usually in an attempt to win by time. Often used interchangeably with "stall".

Sniping: Attacking a single target on the Bench, preferably for a OHKO.

Soak: When a Pokémon can safely absorb damage either by reducing, preventing, or quickly healing it; sometimes used for taking damage in general without being KO'd.

Soft Lock: An easily broken lock.

Solomon Draft: A Limited event where players are given their packs and paired up in groups, using a specific procedure to select cards from a pile made from the contents of both their packs.

Spam: Using a card, or effect, over and over again, particularly in an attempt to overwhelm the opponent through sheer volume.

Spread: Damaging or placing damage counters on more than one of your opponent's Pokémon at a time.

Stall: Tactic where a player tries to win by outlasting his opponent's resources or the clock. Often used interchangeably with "Slow Play", causing arguments.

Standard: A rotating format where approximately the last two years' worth of sets are allowed. New sets join as they become legal, while older sets rotate out once per year. Originally a term for the default format used in formal play under WotC.

Staple: A card run in nearly all competitive decks.

Starter: Cards based on the Pokémon you start with in the video games, or their Evolutions. Alternatively, can be another name for an opener.

States: State/Province Championships, part of the Championship Series.

Structure: How your deck is built, sometimes specifically with regards to its consistency.

Swarm: Quickly filling your field with Pokémon, especially the same Pokémon.

T#: "T" is short for "Turn"; replace # with the current turn count.

Tank: A wall Pokémon capable of a slow but strong offense.

Tails Fails: Effects that require a coin flip but do nothing if you get "tails".

TCG: Trading Card Game

Team Battle: Rules variant where players compete with each other in teams of two. All four players play simultaneously in a single game. Unsanctioned but official rules exist for league, side events, etc.

Tech: Technical Advantage. When you lower a deck's consistency to run a card (or combo) as a single (or singles) for a useful strategy, especially to counter a problem matchup.

Theme Deck: An official pre-made deck sold in stores, usually meant for beginners. Also a Format in the PTCGO, where players face each other only with Theme Decks.

Theorymon: Speculating about card or deck performance. Initially derogatory, but it is actually a vital skill to avoid wasting time when play testing.

Tier: Method of ranking decks. Sometimes refers to a deck's potency but can also reflect usage trends instead.

Time: Tournaments almost always have a time limit so it is possible to win by meeting certain conditions once time has expired. Also referred to as "winning by time" or "winning by the clock".

Top Cut: The best performing players in a tournament. In many forms of tournament play, the top cut will play it out against each other to determine final placement.

Top Deck: The top card of your deck. Sometimes used as a verb when placing a card on top of your deck or drawing something useful when you had no hand.

TPC: The Pokémon Company, created jointly by Nintendo, Game Freak, and Creatures, Inc. to market and license the Pokémon franchise.

TPCi: The Pokémon Company International, the division of TPC that handles Pokémon in most regions outside of Japan.

Turbo: An older term for aggressive play or card effects.

VG: Video game, usually referring to the Pokémon video games.

Variants: An alternate version of a card; or an alternate version of a deck that does not differ enough in build or strategy to be seen as something separate.

W: Water, especially as a replacement for an actual Water Energy symbol when typing. Often put in parenthesis or brackets.

Wall: Pokémon using soak (either meaning) damage.

Whiff: When an effect or desired does nothing or when a desired result does not occur, due to nothing more than chance.

Worlds: World Championships, the invitation only final event of the Championship Series.

World Championship Decks: Pre-made decks which are not legal for sanctioned play. Based on decks which did well during the previous World Championships. Nice as a learning tool or souvenir.

WotC: Wizards of the Coast, former license holder for the international handling of the Pokémon TCG, before Nintendo/TPCi took over.

Y: Fairy, especially as a replacement for an actual Fairy Energy symbol when typing. Often put in parenthesis or brackets.

WHO'S WHO IN THE POKÉWORLD

By Anna Gill & Bill Gill

The Pokémon anime saga is populated by a mind-numbing number of Trainers, Villains, Scientists, Gym Leaders and Bosses. There are nearly 400 recurring characters in the Pokémon World. It can be tough to keep everyone straight after more than 900 episodes.

For this reason, and because we're gluttons for punishment, we've compiled brief biographies of every recurring character in the Pokémon Anime Universe. For simplicity and reference, we made this an Alphabetical Index of everyone who has appeared in at least two different episodes, from Johto to Kalos. Enjoy!

Aaron
A Pokémon trainer who has a passion for bug Pokémon. Ash and his friends meet him as he is training for his championship battle against Cynthia.

Agatha
Temporary Gym Leader for the Viridian Gym. Ash Challenges her to a Gym battle. Ash loses to her, and it is later revealed that she is a member of the Elite Four.

Alder
A Pokémon Champion who Ash and his friend Trip encounter in Unova and have the opportunity to battle. He is shown as being very forgetful and often flirtatious with beautiful women.

Alder

Aldith
A high ranking member of Team Plasma. She is often in charge of monitoring Team Plasma's mind-controlling experiments.

Alexa
A journalist from the Kalos region. She can often be clumsy and forgetful, but her Pokémon Gogoat is very helpful to her. When Ash travels to the Kalos region, she accompanies him there.

Alexa

Aliana
A scientist for Team Flare. She is very confident in her skills and makes fun of her other fellow scientists when they fail.

Alouette
A Pokémon Performer who participates against Jessie and Shauna in the Coumarine City Showcase.

Anabel
The Frontier Brain of Battle Tower in the Hoenn region.

Angie
A girl who lives in the Sinnoh region. She is more of a tomboy, and becomes a rival and friend for Ash.

Aliana

Angus
A trainer from the Unova region who participates in the Clubsplosion Tourney along with his siblings, Betty and Getty. He gets the opportunity to fight Ash in the event.

Anthea
Along with Concordia, sisters of N and children of Ghetsis. They are very protective of their brother as well as the Pokémon around them, as they believe all humans are vile and hurt them.

Archie

Anthony
A trainer in the Hoenn Region who claims to have the strongest Pokémon, his Pelipper. Ash decided to battle him, but finds out Anthony is trying to scam them.

Antonio
A trainer who participates in the Club Battle.Tournament and the Vertress Conference.

Archie
The boss of Team Aqua, the enemies of Team Magma. He gains control of the legendary Pokémon Kyogre by using a Red Orb

Aria
A famous Pokémon Performer and the current Kalos Queen. She became famous in the Kalos region for her Pokévision videos. She has a joyful and energetic personality and strives to spread that joy to the people who watch her.

Aria

Ash Ketchum

Ash Ketchum
Ash is the 10-year-old main character of the Pokémon Anime. He has always dreamed of becoming a Pokémon master. The friends he travels with throughout the series frequently change, but his constant and loyal companion is his Pikachu. He has a very determined personality. He is very good at befriending Pokémon and has no sympathy for people who mistreat them.

Aya
A ninja at the Fushia City Gym. She is the younger sister of Koga, the City's Gym Leader, and has studied under him since they were younger.

Aya

Barret
Barret is a member of Team Plasma. Ash and his friends encounter him during their battle to stop the group's evil plans. He follows orders and reports to Colress.

Barry
A Pokémon trainer in the Sinnoh region who becomes a minor rival for Ash. Barry's idol is Paul, Ash's main rival in the region. Unlike Paul, Barry is very caring toward his Pokémon.

Bertha
A member of the Elite Four in the Sinnoh region. Ash and his friends help save her nephew from Team Rocket. She believes observation skills are very important when working with Pokémon.

Barry

Betty
A Pokémon trainer who participates in the Clubsplosion event. Her brothers, Getty and Angus, also compete. She battles Getty, as well as Ash later on in the tournament. Her main Pokémon in Simipour.

Bianca
A Pokémon trainer and one of Ash's rivals in the Unova region. She is very clumsy, and often runs and tackles people into pools of water. Bianca has a love for cute Pokémon.

Billy
One of Brock's younger brothers.

Bianca

Billy Jo
Part of the band "Roxie and the Toxics." She plays guitar during Roxie's Gym Battles to create ambience and increase the tension of the fight.

Blaine
Gym Leader of Cinnabar Island. He specializes in fire type Pokémon. He likes to disguise himself and give riddles to visitors of the island about his hidden Gym.

Blanche
A Pokémon Performer first seen at the Coumarine Showcase. She performs with her two Meowstic.

Blaine

Blossom
A Furisode Girl who is loyal to Valerie, the Laverre Gym Leader. Blossom and her friend Katherine are fans of Valerie's fashion collection.

Bonnie
Clemont's little sister. She travels with Ash in the Kalos region. She has big plans to become a Pokémon trainer when she is old enough. Bonnie has a strong relationship with her brother and often tries to find him a wife.

Brandon
The Frontier Brain of the Battle Pyramid in the Hoenn region. Trainers must battle all the other Frontier Brains in the Battle Frontier before they can encounter Brandon.

Bonnie

BRAWLY

Gym Leader of Dewford Town in the Hoenn region. He uses fighting-type Pokémon in his battles. Brawly surfs with his Pokémon, and he uses surfing techniques during battles to deflect damage. He has a laid back personality and prefers to go with the flow.

Brawly

BRIANNA

A Pokémon Performer who develops a relationship with May after she sends her a letter with a rose in it.

BROCK

Gym Leader at the Pewter City Gym. After meeting Ash, he decides to join him on his journey. Brock dreams of becoming a great Pokémon Breeder. He later wants to become a Pokémon Doctor. Brock is very flirtatious, and tries to win the heart of every pretty girl he meets.

Brock

BRODIE

A member of Team Magma. He is a master of disguise and gained the nicknames "Brodie the Phantom Thief" as well as "The Man of a Thousand Faces". He uses his disguises to steal various items.

BRUNO

A member of the Elite Four in the Indigo League. Ash and Brock idolize him and want him to take them on as students. Bruno believes that Pokémon and humans should care for each other.

Bruno

BRUTELLA

The owner of a restaurant in Johto. She's mean and tries to sabotage a neighboring restaurant.

BRYCEN

Gym Leader of the Icirrus City Gym. He specializes in Ice-type Pokémon. Brycen and his partner Beartic were once famous movie actors, but they are now retired.

BRYONY

One of the five scientists who works for Team Flare. She takes orders from Xerosic and often teams up with Celosia.

Burgh

BUGSY

Azalea Town Gym Leader who specializes in Bug-type Pokémon. Ash challenges him to a battle in order to earn the Hive Badge.

BURGH

Gym leader of Castelia City. He uses Bug-type Pokémon in his battles. He also designs clothes which are inspired by Bug-type Pokémon. Because he loves bug Pokémon so much, he is very protective of them.

BURGUNDY

A Pokémon and Pokémon Connoisseur (See Cilan). She can be a brat. She can be quite abrasive and does not take criticism well, especially from Cilan. She becomes Cilan's rival after she is defeated by him.

Burgundy

BUTCH

A member of Team Rocket along with his partner, Cassidy. He can be arrogant, and often makes fun of Jessie and James. Throughout the series, Butch frequently gets annoyed when other characters can't get his name right.

Butch

BYRON

Gym Leader of Oreburgh City. Byron is the father of Roark. Byron has an obsession for fossils, and left the gym for a short time to pursue that passion.

CAITLIN

A member of the Unova Elite Four. She specializes in Psychic-type Pokémon. She battles very gracefully.

Cameron

Carrie

Cassidy

Charlene

Charon

Cheren

Cameron
A young Pokémon trainer who Ash and friends encounter in the Unova region. He often doesn't have his facts straight about Pokémon training and makes a lot of errors.

Candice
Gym Leader of Snowpoint City. She has known Zoey since childhood and tries to help her become a better coordinator.

Captain Aidan
A firefighter who works with a group of Wartotle to put out fires.

Cara
She and her husband, Izzy, are Dawn's neighbors in Twinleaf Town.

Caroline
May and Max's mother and Norman's wife. She is a very cheerful person and loves her children deeply.

Carrie
One of Olympia's apprentices who has Psychic powers.

Casey
A new Pokémon trainer from New Bark Town. She and her family are fans of the Electabuzz baseball team, and because of that she has a love for Pokémon that have Black and Yellow stripes.

Cassidy
Part of Team Rocket. She is partners with Butch. She is very arrogant and vain. She is a rival of Jessie's, and whenever they meet, they argue.

Cassie
A trainer who competes in the Pokémon World Tournament Junior Cup.

Cedric Juniper
Professor Juniper's father. He used to be an expert Pokémon researcher of Unova.

Celosia
One of five scientists who works for Team Flare.

Charlene
A Psychic and one of Olympia's apprentices. She seems to be of higher rank than all of the other apprentices.

Charles
A motorcyclist in Driftveil City. When the town is in trouble, he changes into Accelguard, a hero who protects the city.

Charles Goodshow
The president of the Pokémon League Torch Committee.

Charon
One of Team Galactic's four commanders and lead scientists. He is the most laid back of all of the commanders, and this often causes Saturn to get in squabbles with him.

Chaz
A Pokémon coordinator who competes with his Venemoth. He is rivals with Janet.

Cheren
The Aspertia City Gym Leader as well as a teacher at the Trainer's school. Because he is a new Gym Leader, he fears not being good enough.

CHERYL
Born into a family of treasure hunters, she uses her Pokémon Mothim to search for honey in the trees of the Eterna Forest.

Cheryl

CHILI
One of the Gym Leaders in Striaton city along with his brothers Cress and Cilan. Chili specializes in fire Pokémon.

CHRISTOPHER
Was once a student of the Team Rocket Academy, but later was inspired to create a chain of Noodle Shops after Jessie and James invited him for ramen to cheer him up.

CHUCK
Gym Leader of the Cianwood Gym. He uses fighting type Pokémon. He battles and wrestles around with them to improve their concentration and skills.

Cilan

CILAN
One of three brothers who run the Striaton City Gym. After Ash defeats him in a Gym battle, Cilan decides to join him on his journey. Cilan is an A-class connoisseur meaning is highly capable in seeing compatibility between Pokémon and their trainers.

CINDY
One of Brock's younger sisters.

CISSY
Mikan Island Gym Leader. At her gym, Pokémon trainers must compete with her in accuracy and surfing contests in order to gain the Coral-Eye Badge.

Clay

CLAIR
Gym Leader at the Blackthorn City Gym. She specializes in Dragon-type Pokémon including Dragonair and Dragonite.

CLARICE
A Pokémon Performer. She enters contests in Pokémon XY.

Clembot

CLAY
Driftveil City Gym Leader. He specializes in Ground-type Pokémon. He dresses like a cowboy and was a miner before becoming a Gym Leader.

CLEAVON SCHPIELBUNK
A famous movie director. He creates movies with Pokémon in the starring roles.

CLEMBOT
A robot that was built by Clemont. Clembot fills in for Clemont as the Lumiose City Gym Leader while he is away traveling with Ash.

CLEMONT
Gym Leader of Lumiose City. He specializes in Electric type Pokémon. Clemont is very smart and also an inventor. He joins Ash during some of his travels.

Clemont

COLONEL HANSEN
An evil-doer who has plans to take control of the Mirage Kingdom by using Misty's Togepi. He enlists Team Rocket's help to steal Togepi.

COLRESS
A scientist for Team Plasma. He uses a machine to manipulate Pokémon and bring out their "true power".

CONCETTA
A Pokémon Performer. She enters contests in Pokémon XY.

Colress

Concordia

Concordia and Anthea are the sisters of N and children of Ghetsis. They are very protective of their brother as well as the Pokémon around them, as they believe all humans are vile and hurt them.

Connally

A Black Belt who trains at Maylene's Gym in Veilstone City. After Maylene lost in a Pokémon battle to Paul, Connally keeps her confidence high.

Conway

An intelligent Pokémon trainer who becomes a rival for both Ash and Dawn. His knack for strategy makes him very effective in Pokémon battles. Conway also has a tendency to appear out of nowhere.

Cosette

One of Professor Sycamore's assistants and helps her with research.

Crasher Wake

Gym Leader at Pastoria Gym. He specializes in Water-type Pokémon. He also is a judge in the town's Coagunk festival.

Cress

One of the three Gym Leaders of Striaton City Gym (along with Cilan and Chili). He specializes in Water-type Pokémon, and awards the Trio Badge. He's also a waiter, and sports an apron.

Cynthia

The Pokémon Champion of the Sinnoh region. She has a strong personality and won't hold anything back in a Pokémon battle. She believes that the bonds humans make with Pokémon are more important than training them to be strong.

Cyrus

The leader of Team Galactic. He is completely emotionless and one of the cruelest villains to appear in the anime. He wants to create a new world and wants to rid the world of anyone he thinks would blemish it.

Daisy

One of Misty's older sisters. Daisy and her sisters Violet and Lily act as the Gym leaders of the Cerulean gym when Misty is away. For a while, Daisy, Violet and Lily perform water ballet with their Pokémon and neglect the gym.

Danny

Navel Island's Gym Leader. Instead of a tradition Pokémon battle, he challenges trainers to work together with their Pokémon to build a bobsled and race down the side of a mountain to earn his badge.

Davy

A rescue worker. He is the older brother of Virgil and son of Jeff. He cares a lot for his brother Virgil and watches out for him.

Dawn

Dawn is one of Ash's main traveling companions (along with Brock) in Diamond and Pearl. She aspires to be a great Pokémon Coordinator like her mother. She tries to remain confident even when she does poorly in contests.

Delbert

A Pokémon trainer who participates in the Clubsplosion Tournament. He uses his Pokémon Mienshao in the tournament.

Delia Ketchum

Delia Ketchum is Ash's mother. She is a kind and caring mother, an always reminds Ash to change his underwear. She has a Mr. Mime named Mimey who helps her with housework.

Diantha
A famous actress as well as the Pokémon Champion of the Kalos region. Because of her fame, she often wears disguises in public to get around. Diantha is a calm and honorable woman. She cares about the people of Kalos and tries to protect them.

Diantha

Dino
A Pokémon trainer who participates in the Club Battle tournament

DJ Mary
A radio personality who works at Goldenrod Radio Tower. She interviews people involved in the Pokémon world.

Don George
Each Don George are family members and look identical. They all run Pokémon Battle Clubs across the Unova region.

Don George

Dr. Abby
A Pokémon doctor who was previously a top Pokémon coordinator. She specializes in natural medicine.

Dr. Kenzo
The director of the Oreburgh Mining Museum and its Fossil restoration program.

Dr. Namba
A scientist who works for Team Rocket.

Dr. Zager
A Team Rocket scientist who studies and analyzes the meteorite that crashed in the Unova region. He later becomes Team Rocket's leading official for most activities in the region.

Drake

Drake
Orange Crew Supreme Gym Leader of the Orange League. He is considered the strongest trainer in the Orange Islands. Any trainer who defeats him will enter the Orange League Hall of Fame.

Drayden
Opelucid City Gym Leader. He specializes in Dragon-type Pokémon. He believes education to be extremely important, and he cares deeply for the renowned Opelucid Academy.

Drayden

Drew
A friend and rival of May. He is a Pokémon coordinator like May. He is very confident in his skills and determined to become the best.

Duplica
A Performing Pokémon trainer and impressionist. She performs using her Ditto.

Drew

Elder
She is the elder of the Village of Dragons. She is the one who gave Iris her Axew.

Elesa
Gym Leader of the Nimbasa Gym. Along with being a Gym Leader, she is also a fashion model. She specializes in Electric-type Pokémon and takes a liking to Ash's Pikachu.

Elma
A Pokémon Performer who participates in several different showcases.

Elesa

Emmanuel
A Pokémon trainer who participates in the Club Battle tournament and the Vertress Conference.

Emmet

Emmet
A Subway Boss in the Unova region. He cares about the Nimbasa City's underground and its safety. He is very intelligent and is very capable of maintaining the railway system.

Enta
The mayor of Hearthome City, as well as the announcer during the City's Tag Battle Tournament. He also is the commentator at the Hearthome Collection Contest too.

Erica
A Pokémon coordinator who trains with her boyfriend, Joshua. They were training for the Pacifidlog Town Contest. She becomes jealous of May when she begins training with Joshua as well.

Erika
Gym Leader of Celadon City. She specializes in Grass-type Pokémon. She also runs a perfume shop in the city.

Erika

Eusine
A Mystery Man who has an obsession with Suicune and wishes to catch it.

Fantina
Heathome City Gym Leader. She specializes in Ghost-type Pokémon. She has a tendency to leave her Gym for long periods of time, making it difficult for Trainers to challenge her.

Fantina

Fennel
A scientist in the Dreamyard researching Mushama's Dream Mist. She is friends with Professor Juniper.

Ferris
Works at an excavation site, discovering fossils of Pokémon.

Flannery
Lavaridge Town Gym Leader. She took over the gym after her grandfather retired. Since she is new, she is inexperienced and is still learning how to be a great Gym Leader. She specializes in Fire-type Pokémon.

Flannery

Flint
Brock's father. He takes over Pewter City's Gym when Brock decides to travel with Ash. He specializes in Rock-type Pokémon.

Flint
A member of the Sinnoh Elite Four. He is rivals and good friends with Volkner, the Gym Leader of Sunyshore.

Flora
A Pokémon trainer who competes in the Clubsplosion tournament as well as the Vertress Conference.

Forrest

Forrest
One of Brock's younger brothers. He becomes the Gym Leader of the Pewter City Gym once Brock decides his parents are not fit to run the Gym anymore.

Forsythia
A girl that teaches cooking classes. She maintains her garden and home with the help of her Pokémon Roserade and Lotad.

Freddy O'Martian
One of the announcers for both the Don Battle Tournament and the Donamite Tournament.

Freesia Freesia
A maid that works for Princess Salvia.

Forsythia

Gail
A Pokémon trainer who competes in the Clubsplosion tournament. She dresses like a girl of high class, using a fan to cover up her face.

Gardenia
Gym Leader at the Eterna Gym. She has an obsession with Grass-type Pokémon, often becoming distracted by them and interacting with other trainer's Pokémon.

Gary Oak
Gary is Professor Oak's grandson and Ash's first rival. Gary can be very smug about his abilities as a Pokémon trainer. He often brags to Ash about his success which sends Ash into a rage.

Gary Oak

Gary's Cheerleaders
A group of girls that follow Gary around on his Pokémon journey. They cheer Gary on when he does well and burst into tears when he loses a match.

Gary's Cheerleaders

Gena
A famous Poké Puff maker and serves as a judge in the Poké Puff contest. She later is part of the judge's panel during the Denemille Town Pokémon Showcase.

Georgia
A rival of Iris. She is a "Dragon Buster" who seeks Dragon masters to defeat them. She is very confident, but when she is defeated she can be a sore loser.

Georgia

Geraldo
A Pokémon trainer who participated in the Pokémon World Tournament Junior Cup and later competed in the Vertress Conference.

Getty
A Pokémon trainer who enters the Clubsplosion tournament along with his siblings, Betty and Angus.

Ghetsis
The leader of team Plasma. He hungers for power and control of Unova. He lies to his adopted children, especially N, about his power to communicate with Pokémon. He counts on his lead scientist Colress because of his machine that allows them to control Reshiram.

Ghetsis

Giovanni
The head of Team Rocket and also the Gym Leader of Viridian City. He has plans to use strong Pokémon to obtain global domination.

Grace (Hoenn)
A Pokémon Coodinator. She competes in the Fallarbor Contest. Whenever May compliments her abilities as a Coordinator, she gets embarrassed and her face turns red.

Grace (Kalos)
Serena's mother. She is a Rhyhorn racer, and wants the same thing for her daughter. But when Serena decides to become a Pokémon Performer, Grace supports her wholeheartedly.

Giovanni

Grant
Gym Leader of Cyllage City. He specializes in Rock-type Pokémon and has a passion for climbing things.

Greta
Frontier Brain of the Battle Arena. She is energetic and passionate about Pokémon battles. She uses Fighting-type Pokémon in battles.

Gurkinn
Korrina's grandfather and a descendent of the first trainer who mega-evolved a Pokémon. He is a strict man who values honor.

Greta

Harley

Harrison

Holly

Ippei

Iris

James

Hanzo
Elder of the Ninja Village. He is very wise and has the power to choose the village chief. He is often seen next to Shinobu.

Harley
A Pokémon coordinator and rival of May. Harley finds May annoying and tries to humiliate her in order to beat her in Pokémon contests. He uses his Pokémon Cacturne in Contests.

Harrison
A Pokémon trainer and rival of Ash. He is good friends with Gary Oak. He competes in the Silver Conference and later convinces Ash to continue his journey to the Hoenn region.

Hawes
The vice-curator of the Nacrene Museum. He is a bit of a coward and claims to have seen a lot of supernatural activity. He is the husband of Lenora, the City's Gym Leader.

Heidayu
A man who lives in the Ninja village. He is a follower of Kagetomo. When Kagetomo leaves the village, Heidayu leaves with him as his loyal and dedicated follower.

Holly
A Pokémon trainer who participates in the Hearthome City Tag Battle Competition. She was paired up with Brock as battle partners. She develops a little crush on Brock as they battle together.

Horatio
A Pokémon trainer who participates is the Pokémon World Tournament Junior Cup.

Ian
The assistant to the Oreburgh City Gym Leader, Roark. He takes care of the Gym's Pokémon.

Ingo
A Subway Boss along with Emmet under the city of Nimbasa. Their job is to make sure the underground can run smoothly and safely.

Ippei
Ippei is the chieftain as well as the strongest ninja in Ninja village. He is the older brother of Sanpei and Nihei.

Iris
One of Ash's traveling companions. She was born in the Village of Dragons and aspires to be a Dragon Master. She has a wild and energetic personality.

Izzy
Dawn's neighbor in Twinleaf town along with his wife Cara.

J
A Pokémon hunter who steals and captures Pokémon and sells them on the black market.

Jack
Part of Rhonda's filming crew. He operates the microphone boom, which he often accidentally drops on Rhonda's head.

James
A member of Team Rocket and partner to Jessie and Meowth. They continuously try to capture Pikachu as well as other rare Pokémon. James is the most sensitive member of the trio. One of the main villains of the show.

Janina
Jasmine's apprentice at the Olivine Gym. When Ash comes to the Gym, she poses as Jasmine and battles him before Jasmine cancels the match.

Jasmine
The Olivine City Gym Leader. She has a tough but fair personality. She specializes in Steel-type Pokémon. She delays a match with Ash because her Ampharos was ill.

Jasmine

Jeeves
Madame Muchmoney's butler.

Jeffrey
A Pokémon trainer who challenges Jessie at Team Rocket's fake gym.

Jeremiah
Works for the Pokétch Company and is also a student at the Snowpoint Trainers' School.

Jeremy
A businessman who once was a Pokémon trainer and part of a traveling rock band. It had been his dream to enter a Pokémon Contest. He decides to enter the Silver Town Conference.

Jessebelle

Jervis
Cynthia's butler at her home in Undella Town.

Jessebelle
She was chosen by James' parents to be his fiancée. Jessebelle is extremely bossy and controlling. James is terrified of her.

Jessie
A member of Team Rocket with partners James and Meowth. She is the bossiest member of their group and has a hot temper. One of the main villains of the show.

Jessie

Jimmy Ray
A Pokémon trainer who participates in the Club Battle tournament. He wears a Watchog costume while he battles.

Johanna
Dawn's mother. She is an accomplished Coordinator and serves as inspiration for her daughter.

Juan

Joshua
Professor Birch's assistant in his lab.

Joshua
A Pokémon coordinator and boyfriend of Erica. When Erica becomes too intense, he begins to train with May instead. (Yes, there are two Joshuas in the anime. Maybe they should consult our Index here in the future?)

Juan
Sootopolis City's Gym Leader. He is quite the entertainer, putting on shows with his Pokémon. He uses Water Pokemon and awards the Rain Badge.

Jupiter
One of four commanders of Team Galactic.

Kagetomo

Kaburagi
A referee at the Blackthorn City Gym. He is also Clair's assistant.

Kagetomo
A member of the Ninja village. He was thought to be the most eligible to become the next chief after Hanzo, but he becomes power hungry.

Kai

Kai
Part of the Invincible Pokémon Brothers along with Kim and Kail. They use Fighting-type Pokémon. Kai is the heaviest of the 3 brothers.

Kail

Kail
Part of the Invincible Pokémon Brothers along with Kim and Kai. They use Fighting-type Pokémon. Kail is the tallest of the 3 brothers.

Kali
A Furisode girl who is a follower of Lavern City Gym Leader, Valerie. She along with other Furisode girls spot out potential models for Valerie's fashion show.

Katharine
A Pokémon Trainer, who shows up in Rival Destinies. She battles Ash a couple of times in the wild, and also enters some tourneys in Unova.

Katherine
A Furisode girl who is a follower of Lavern City Gym Leader, Valerie. She and Blossom spy on Serena and Bonnie and believe they would be great in Valerie's fashion show.

Kathi Lee
Diantha's manager who keeps track of her schedule.

Katie
A Pokémon trainer who battles in the Ever Grande Conference Victory Tournament. She likes to swap out her Pokémon often.

Kazalie
A Pokémon performer. She participates in the Fleurrh City Rookie Class Pokémon Showcase.

Keanan
The caretaker of the swamplands located between Lumiose City and Laverre City.

Kelly
A Pokémon Coordinator who becomes friends and rivals with May.

Kellyn
A top ranked Pokémon Ranger. He makes it his mission to protect Riolu while he travels home.

Ken
Part of the Pokémon Mystery Club duo along with Mary. Their goal is to prove that Pokémon are extraterrestrial lifeforms.

Kendall
A student at Professor Rowan's Pokémon Summer Academy. He also has a little crush on Dawn.

Kendrick
A Pokémon trainer who competes in the Vertress Conference.

Kenny
An assistant for Norman at the Petalburg Gym. He is close to May and Max's family.

Kenny
A Pokémon Coordinator in the Sinnoh Region. He is from Twinleaf Town and is a childhood friend and rival of Dawn. Yep, there are two Kennys in the anime.

Kenton
A Pokémon trainer who battles in Pokémon tournaments including the Pokémon World Tournament Junior Cup and the Vertress Conference.

Khoury
A Pokémon breeder who travels with Lyra. He asks Brock to mentor him and joins Ash and friends briefly on their travels.

Kali

Katherine

Katie

Kellyn

Khoury

Kim

Part of the Invincible Pokémon Brothers along with Kim and Kai. They use Fighting-type Pokémon. Kim is the shortest of the 3 brothers.

Kim

Koga

Gym Leader at the Fushcia Gym. He trains in ninjutsu, and his sister Aya is one of his students. He specializes in Poison-type Pokémon.

Korrina

Gym Leader of Shalour City Gym. She specializes in Fighting-type Pokémon, and awards the Rumble Badge. She joins up with Ash and gang for a while in hopes of finding a Mega Stone.

Koga

Koume

One of the Kimono sisters. All of the sisters have a different evolution of Eevee. Koume has a Flareon.

Kurt

A Poké ball smith (A person who makes custom Poké Balls). Professor Oak sends Ash with a GS Ball for him to study.

Kyle

A Pokémon Coordinator who competes in the Wallace Cup. He is very confident in his abilities and points out Ash's mistakes as they battle.

Korrina

Lance

A member of the Elite Four in the Kanto region. as well as the Champion in the Johto region. He is an expert with Dragon-type Pokémon.

Lenora

Gym Leader of Nacrene City. She specializes in Normal-type Pokémon. She and her husband, Hawes, also run the Nacrene City Museum.

Lewis

He helps tend to Milos Island and the Revival Herbs that grow there.

Lenora

Lila

A Pokémon Coordinator who was once Johanna's rival. She was the first person to defeat Johanna in a contest. She later became a Pokémon stylist.

Lilian Meridian

The announcer for Contests in the Kanto region. She is sisters with Vivian, the Hoenn Contest announcer.

Lily

One of Misty's sisters. She is the second youngest of the four of them. She participates in the water shows with her sisters at the Cerulean Gym. She looks down on Misty, teasing her for not being a stronger Pokémon trainer.

Lila

Lily

A Pokémon performer who competes in the Anistar City Pokémon Showcase and later the Gloire Pokémon Showcase. (Yes, there is more than one Lily. Actually there are three! One Lily appeared once as magician in the episode "Hocus Pocus" in the Hoenn region)

Linnea

A Furisode girl who works for Valerie, the Laverre City Gym Leader.

Liza

Along with her twin brother Tate, they are the Gym Leaders of Mossdeep City. Liza is the stronger trainer of the two. She makes a friend in May as they have much in common.

Lilian Meridian

Looker

Liza

The caretaker of the Charizard living in Charicific Valley in the Johto region. (Yep, there are two Lizas, too.)

Looker

A member of the International police. He travels around the world to investigate crimes and suspicious activity.

Luana

Gym Leader of the Kumquat Island Gym. The Gym also doubles as a luxury hotel that she runs.

Lucian

A member of the Sinnoh Elite four and a master with psychic-type Pokémon.

Lucy

The Frontier Brain in charge of the Battle Pike. She develops a little crush on Brock.

Lucy

Luka

A young girl who tries to search for the silver wing which her great-grandfather lost when his ship sank many years ago.

Luke

A film-maker who wants Ash, Iris and Cilan to play parts in his movie.

Lyra

A Pokémon trainer who joins Ash and his friends in their travels temporarily. During their travels she becomes good friends with Dawn.

Mable

Mable

A scientist working for Team Flare. She is very confident in herself and criticizes her fellow scientists when the fail to achieve their assigned tasks.

Macy

A Pokémon trainer who enters the Silver Conference. She is a fan of Fire-type Pokémon. She falls in love with Ash after he saves her from falling.

Madame Catherine

A custodian at Professor Sycamore's Summer Camp.

Macy

Madame Muchmoney

A very rich woman who owns a Snubbull. Her Snubbull is unhappy because Madame Muchmoney smothers her and doesn't give her enough freedom.

Maizie

Kurt's granddaughter. After Ash brings Kurt the GS ball, she helps them find Apricorns for custom Poké balls.

Malva

A member of the Kalos Elite Four and a master of Fire-type Pokémon. She is also a TV reporter.

Malva

Mandy

The wife of Jeremy. She does not understand her husband's dream of becoming a Pokémon Coordinator and begs him to come home.

Manning

A trainer who enters the Pokémon World Tournament Junior Cup and the Vertress Conference.

Maria

The Guardian of the Snowpoint Temple.

Marian

Marian

The Sinnoh Contest announcer. She is energetic and enthusiastic about her work.

Marlon
Gym Leader of Humilau City Gym. He specializes in Water-type Pokémon, and awards the Wave Badge. He battles Cameron in Black and White.

Marlon

Maron
The Ref at Battle Tower. He also is the announcer there.

Marris
A Pokémon Trainer, who is a regular on the Junior Cup Scene.

Mars
One of Team Galactic's four Commanders. Team Galactic are the villains in the Diamond and Pearl.

Mars

Mary
A DJ in Goldenrod Radio Tower. She hosts shows on Pokémon related topics.

Matori
Giovanni's Secretary. She is also a go-between delivering messages to and from Giovanni.

Max
Max is May's younger brother. He is a Pokémon Genius, who wants to a Pokémon Trainer. He tags along with Ash and May on their travels, and is an integral part of the team.

Max

Maxie
The Leader of Team Magma. Team Magma fights with Team Aqua for Pokémon World Domination.

May
May is training to become Pokémon Coordinator. A Pokémon Coordinator raises Pokémon to compete in Pokémon contests. She accompanies Ash, along with her brother Max, on many of Ash's journeys.

May

Maya
A Sea Priestess of the Whirl Islands. She watches over the Whirl Cup. She can communicate with Water Pokémon.

Maylene
Gym Leader of Veilstone City Gym. She awards Cobble Badge and specializes in Fighting-type Pokémon. She is a new Gym Leader and not cofident. Ash and gang build up her confidence in Diamond and Pearl.

Maylene

McGinty
A Photographer who runs a Photo Studio in Geosenge Town. He gives Korrina a Mega Stone.

Meyer
Father of Clemont and Bonnie. He is also the secrety indentity behind the Blaziken Mask. He acts like a Super-Hero when he sports Blaziken Mask.

Miette
A Pokémon Performer and a rival of Serena. She is kind of snobby at first, but eventually befriends Serena. She teases Serena about her crush on Ash.

Miette

Mikael
A Pokémon Trainer who appears in tournaments in the Unova League.

Miles
Grandfather of Skyla. He was once the Gym Leader of Mistralton Gym. He runs a cargo business and is an Assistant and Ref at Skyla's Gym.

Miranda
Caretaker of the Mirage Kingdom.

Misty

MISTY

Misty is the "Water Pokémon" Gym Leader from Cerulean City. Misty accompanies Ash and Brock on many of their journeys. She is great friends with Ash and Brock. Misty has a short temper, but deeply cares about her friends and Pokémon.

MITCHELL

A student at the Pokémon Summer Academy who befriends Brock.

MONSIEUR PIERRE

The Announcer of Pokémon Showcases. He's a Frenchman and speaks with a flamboyant accent.

Monsieur Pierre

MONTGOMERY

Champion of the Clubsplosion Tournament, he returns to defend his title in Rival Destinies. He eventually loses to Stephan.

MORRISON

A Pokémon Trainer from Verdanturf Town and a friendly rival of Ash. He likes to wear Japanese Samurai Kimonos. Friendship is more important than winning to Morrison.

MORTY

Gym Leader of Ecruteak City's Gym. He awards the Fog Badge and uses Ghost-type Pokémon. He also teaches classes on Ghost-type Pokémon.

Morrison

MR. BRINEY

A Retired Sailor. He's kind of an old sage with his advice and experience. He tells stories while boating Ash and Gang around Hoenn.

MR. HONCHO

Headmaster of Snowpoint Trainers' School.

MR. MOORE

Flannery's Granfather. Former Gym Leader of Lavaridge, and a retired member of the Elite Four. He's big into poetry in his old age.

Mr. Moore

MR. SUKIZO

President of the Pokémon Fan Club. And a Judge of most Pokémon Contests.

MRS. GRIMM

Mother of Timothy Grimm. She doesn't like Timmy playing Pokémon games, and wants him to study more in school.

NANDO

A Wandering Minstrel who plays a harp, and plays music to keep everyone calm, even in battle. He becomes a friend and rival of Dawn and Ash in Diamond and Pearl.

Nicholai

NICHOLAI

A Pokémon Trainer from Hoenn. He enjoys dressing up as a Pokémon while battling.

NICHOLAS

He dreams of becoming a Pokémon Master. He is the son of Jeremy and Mandy who try to convince him to give up that dream.

NICKY

The drummer of Roxie's band In Black 2 and White 2. The band is called "Koffing and the Toxics".

NIHEI

The younger brother of Ippei, and older brother of Sanpei. He is a strong Pokémon trainer and protects the Ninja Village from attacks.

Nihei

Nini

A Pokémon Performer and one of Serena's Rivals. She appears often in XY. She is polite and friendly with Ash's gang.

Nini

Noland

The Frontier Brain and runs the Frontier Battle Factory. Ash's Charizard has a terrific batter with Noland's Articuno in the Diamond and Pearl series.

Norman

Father of Max and May, and also the Gym Leader of Petalburg Gym. He uses Normal type Pokémon and awards the Balance Badge. He is good friends with Professor Birch.

Nurse Joy

There are actually many Nurse Joys in the World of Pokémon. Joy is their family name, not their first names. Each Nurse Joy has a different color "+" on their nursing caps. Nurse Joys are caring women and heal Pokémon.

Officer Jenny

Officer Jenny

A police officer who resides in every city. There are actually very many Jennys (Jenny is their last name). They are a massive family. It's hard to tell them apart, as there are very subtle differences in their uniforms.

Oliver

Oliver befriends Ash and Rich on Ogi Ilsand. He found a baby Lugia, and tried to protect it from Team Rocket. He works with Ash to free it.

Olympia

Gym Leader of Anistar City's Gym. She specializes in Psychic-type Pokémon, and awards the Psychic Badge. She is also a Psychic and predicts Ash's future a couple of times.

Olympia

Palermo

A former Kalos Queen, and now a famous Producer. She is rich and gets involved in many Pokémon Contests in XY.

Paul

A Pokémon Trainer from Veilstone City. He is Ash's main rival in Diamond & Pearl. He has a cold way of training his Pokémon. He only cares about their physical power and abilities, not the relationship he builds.

Paul

Pierce

A member of Team Rocket, showing up in the Unova Region.

Porter

Porter is a porter. He takes tickets and welcomes people aboard ships in several episodes in the anime.

Prima

A Pokémon Master, and member of the Elite Four in Kanto. She is "Lorelei" in the video games, but 4Kids thought her name was too hard to pronounce and changed it for TV. She uses Ice-Type Pokémon.

Prima

Princess Salvia

A Princess in the Sinnoh region. She looks exactly like Dawn, and switches identities with Dawn for a while.

Princess Sara

Princess of the Mirage Kingdom. She finds Misty's Togepi injured in her palace garden

Professor Birch

Pokémon Professor of Littleroot Town in the Hoenn Region. He specializes in Pokémon Habitats. He gives Sawyer his first Pokémon - Treecko.

Professor Birch

Professor Elm

Professor Carolina
A Pokémon Professor and also Cynthia's grandma. She heads the Celestic Town Historical Research Center.

Professor Elm
A Pokémon Professor from New Bark Town in Johto. He specializes in Pokémon Breeding. He was a top student of Professor Oak. He asks Ash to deliver a stolen Pokémon egg.

Professor Ivy

Professor Ivy
A beautiful Pokémon Professor from the Valencia Island. She gives Ash a GS Ball at the request of Professor Oak. Brock has a crush on her and eventually stays with her for a while to help her with her research.

Professor Juniper
Another beautiful Pokémon Professor in the Unova Region. She specializes in the origins of Pokémon. She gives Trip his first Pokémon. She is an old friend of Professor Oak, though she looks too young for that - wink.

Professor Juniper

Professor Oak
Professor Oak runs a Research Lab in Ash's hometown of Pallet Town and invented the Pokedex. Many consider him the utmost authority on Pokémon.

Professor Rowan
A Pokémon Professor in the Sinnoh Region. He gives Dawn her Piplup. He specializes in evolutions.

Professor Sebastion
A Professor for Team Rocket. He is smart and calm. He created the crystal system that traps electric type Pokémon.

Professor Oak

Professor Sycamore
A Pokémon Professor in the Kalos Region. He is a calm and helpful Pokémon tutor. He researches and teaches Ash about Mega Evolutions of Pokémon.

Proprietor
A former Pokémon Poacher. He was a rival of Volkner and Flint when they were kids, but now they're friends.

Pryce
Gym Leader of Mahogany Town's Gym. He specializes in Ice-type Pokémon. He awards the Glacier Badge. He was burned as a young Pokémon trainer. He became bitter and cold, like his Pokémon.

Professor Sebastion

Rachel
Jin's wife. She is also the sister of Tate and Liza, the Mossdeep City Gym Leaders.

Ramone
A recurring trainer who competes regularly in the Junior Division Cups.

Ramos
Gym Leader of the Coumarine City Gym. He uses Grass type Pokémon and awards the Plant badge. He is also a wise old gardener.

Raoul Contesta
One of the frequent judges of Pokémon Contests.

Reggie
Paul's older brother. After losing to Ash in a duel, and watching his brother lose a battle to Brandon, he decides to become a Pokémon Breeder.

Professor Sycamore

Rhonda
A TV Show host from the Sinnoh Region. She appears regularly in Diamond and Pearl to cover Pokémon News stories where Ash happens to be traveling.

RIDLEY

A descendant of ancient folks from the Abyssal Ruins. He is protecting the Meloetta that lived in harmony with the Ancient Civilization.

RILEY

A Pokémon Trainer from the Sinnoh Region. He uses Steel type Pokémon. He is also training to be an Aura Guardian.

RITCHIE

Richie is a young Pokémon Trainer. He is a friend and rival of Ash. Ritchie's main Pokémon and best friend is a Pikachu named Sparky. Ritchie is a very good trainer.

Ritchie

ROARK

Gym Leader of Oreburgh City's Gym. He uses Rock type Pokémon and hands out the Coal Badge to Trainers who defeat him. He battles Ash and Paul in the anime.

ROBERT

A Pokémon Coordinator from Silver Rock Isle. He defeats Drew to win the Ribbon Cup in Pokémon Advanced.

Roark

ROXANNE

Gym Leader of Rustboro City Gym. He gives out the Stone badge and specializes in Rock type Pokémon. She is friends with Brock and Professor Oak.

ROXIE

Gym Leader of Virbank City Gym. She uses Poison type Pokémon and gives out the Toxic Badge. She jams out on a Bass Guitar player while she duels Ash.

RUDY

Gym Leader of Trovita Island Gym. He specializes in teaching Pokémon moves they would not normally learn. He gives out the Spike Shell Badge. He duels Ash in a 3 vs. 3 battle.

Roxanne

RUSSET

A Pokémon Trainer from Inakano Town who battles in some of the Unova Region Tournaments.

SABRINA

Gym Leader of Saffron City. She uses Psychic Pokémon and hands out the Marsh Badge. Ash loses his first battle with her, but befriends a Haunter later to help win the rematch.

SAIZO

A Skilled Ninja and teacher from Ninja village in Pokémon XY.

SAKURA

A Pokémon Trainer who lives with her Kimono Sisters. She is friendly with Misty.

Roxie

SALVADOR

A Pokémon Trainer from Cherrygrove City. He battles Ash at Silver Conference.

SAMUEL

An assistant to Pyramid King Brandon. He also refs Brandon's matches.

Sabrina

SANDRA

Sandra wants to be a Pokémon Trainer, even though her mother is a very good Pokémon Coordinator and wants Sandra to also be a Coordinator.

SANPEI

A Ninja from Ninja Village in Pokémon XY. He becomes friends with Ash and trains Ash's Froakie for him.

SARA LEE

A Pokémon Performer. She enters contests in Pokémon XY.

Sanpei

Saturn

Satsuki

One of the five Kimono Sisters. They are skilled Pokémon Trainers using Eevee-lutions.

Saturn

One of Team Galactic's four Commanders. Team Galactic are the main villains in Diamond and Pearl.

Savannah

A Pokémon Coordinator from Rubello Town. She becomes friends and a rival for May in Pokémon Advanced.

Savannah

Sawyer

A Pokémon Trainer who becomes a friend and rival of Ash in XY. He is very studious and documents the results of all his battles in his notebooks.

Sayer

The coordinator of the Twinleaf Festival. He is friends with Team Rocket.

Schwarz

A member of Team Plasma. He works with Weiss to steal Pokémon and cause trouble for Ash.

Scooter

A competitive Trainer who battles Luke and Black and White.

Sawyer

Scott

Scott is the owner of the Battle Frontier. He recommended Ash take part in the Frontier Challenge, and offered Ash a job of a Frontier Brain.

Sebastian

Gym Assistant to Juan at the Sootopolis Gym. He is also a butler at Juan's mansion.

Serena

Serena is a Pokémon Trainer from the Kalos Region. Her goal is to become a top-class "Pokémon Performer". A Pokémon Performer is a female trainer who competes in dance routines with her Pokémon. She is kind and polite. Serena has a crush on Ash.

Sergio

Noland's assistant at the Battle Frontier Battle Factory. He takes care of Pokémon and refs the match between Noland and Ash.

Serena

Shauna

A Pokémon Performer from Vaniville Town, and a rival to Serena. She enters contests in Pokémon XY.

Sheila

An assistant to Pryce at the Majogany City Gym. She also refs the gym matches there.

Shelly

One of the Admins of Team Aqua. She leads squads on missions against Team Magma.

Shepherd

A young Pokémon Trainer. He battles in some of the Junior Cups in the series.

Shinobu

A member of Ninja Village. He assists the Village Elder - Hanzo.

Shulin

A Pokémon Performer. She enters contests in Pokémon XY.

Shelly

Sierra

A Pokémon Archeologist. She is a childhood friend of Ferris.

Simeon
A young Pokémon Trainer. He battles in some of the Junior Cups in the series.

Skyla
Gym Leader of Mistralton City. She uses Flying Type Pokémon and awards the Jet Badge. She battles Cilan and then Ash.

Skyla

Solana
A Pokémon Ranger. She bumps into Ash in several seasons and they work together to defeat Pokémon villains.

Solidad
A Pokémon Coordinator from Pewter City. She becomes a rival of May, and they battle at the Kanto Grand Festival.

Solana

Sophie
One of Professor Sycamore's Assistants.

Spenser
An elderly man who specializes in herbs. He also battles Ash to provide experience.

Stephan
A Pokémon Trainer from the Unova Region. He is one of Ash's main rivals and appears often in Black and White.

Steven Stone
A very skilled Pokémon Trainer who is also a collector of rare stones. He originally meets Ash in the Hoenn Region, but shows up in XY also. He is calm and assists trainers. He also battles them to help with their experience.

Stephan

Sumomo
One of the five Kimono Sisters. They are skilled Pokémon Trainers using Eevee-lutions.

Suzie
A famous Pokémon Breeder in the Kanto Region. She gives Brock a Vulpix to train.

Tabitha
One of the Officers of Team Magma. He confronts Ash several times during Pokémon Advanced.

Steven Stone

Tamao
One of the five Kimono Sisters. They are skilled Pokémon Trainers using Eevee-lutions.

Tate
Twin Sister of Liza, and one of the Gym Leaders of Mossdeep City. They specialize in Psychic Type Pokémon and award the Mind Badge. They eventually battle Ash in a double battle.

Thatcher
He runs a lighthouse in the Hoenn Region with his sister Alyssa. Ash helps him train his Plusle and Minun to help charge the lighthouse.

Suzie

Tierno
A Pokémon Trainer from Santalune City and one of Ash's Main Rivals in Pokémon X and Y. He is a dancer and likes to train Pokémon with dance skills.

Tilly
One of Brock's younger siblings.

Timmy
A little kid who befriends a Meowth that causes confusion with Team Rocket's Meowth is Season 1 for a couple of episodes.

Tierno

Timmy Grimm

A Pokémon Coordinator who battles disguised as the Phantom. He battles in disguise so his mother doesn't find out. But his Father encourages him.

Tobias

A Pokémon Trainer who competes in the Lily of the Valley Conference. He battles and defeats Ash in the Semi-Finals, and eventually wins the tournament.

Todd Snap

A professional photographer. He became famous for taking a picture of the supposedly extinct Aerodactyl. He travels with Ash intermittently.

Tommy

One of Brock's younger brothers.

Tommy Grimm

Timmy Grimm's Father. He helps his son pursue his dream of being a Pokémon Coordinator.

Tracey Sketchit

Tracey is a Pokémon Watcher (a person who studies Pokémon and observes them in their natural habitat). He is a gentle person. He travels with Ash at times, and studies with Professor Oak.

Trevor

A friendly rival for Ash during the course of the XY Series. He is also a Pokémon photographer. He gets forgetful of his immediate purpose when he sees a new Pokémon to photograph.

Trip

A Pokémon Trainer from the Unova Region. He is one of Ash's main rivals and appears often in Season's 14 and 15.

Tucker

The Frontier Brain and Commissioner of Frontier's Battle Dome. He has a double battle against Ash in the Battle Dome.

Tyson - Hoenn Region

A Pokémon Trainer from Mauville City and a rival of Ash in the Hoenn Region. He eventually wins the Hoenn League Conference.

Tyson - Team Rocket

An Officer of Team Rocket. He is confident and actually somewhat polite, but does what he needs to get the job done.

Ultimo

A Pokémon trainer who battles at the Vertress Conference.

Ursula

A Pokémon Coordinator and another rival of Dawn in the Sinnoh Region in Seasons 12 and 13. She is a very confident trainer, and somewhat dislikes Dawn.

Valerie

She is the Gym Leader of the Laverre City Gym. She specializes in Fairy Type Pokémon and gives out the Fairy Badge. She is also into the fashion scene, and gives advice to Serena and Bonnie.

Viola

A professional photographer and Gym Leader for the Santalune City Gym. She passes out the Bug Badge. Ash loses to her the first time around. Ash returns later after learning how to handle her immobilizing attacks.

Violet
She is one of Misty's Sisters. She was the Gym Leader of the Cerulean City Gym at one time. She writes the ballet performances for the Sensational Sisters, who do water ballets with Pokémon.

Virgil
A friendly rival for Ash. He specializes in Eevee-lutions, and shows up quite often in Season 16.

Vivian Meridian
The stadium announcer for the Hoenn Pokémon Coordinator Contest.

Vladimir
A Pokémon Trainer from Lilycove City. He is also known as Ralph and teaches Ash's Pokémon some moves.

Volkner
The Gym Leader for Sunyshore City Gym. He gives out the Beacon Badge and uses Electric Type Pokémon. He teams with Ash to defeat Team Rocket.

Volkner

Wallace
Wallace is a flamboyant Pokémon Master. He was the Sootopolis Gym Leader. He is now a judge for the Wallace Cup.

Wallace

Watt
An assistant to Wattson. He also officiates Gym Battles.

Wattson
Gym Leader from Mauville City. He uses Electric type Pokémon and passes out the Dynamo Badge. His gym is filled with puzzles and pranks. Ash defeats him easily. Team Rocket then steals all of his Pokémon, and Ash gets them back.

Wattson

Weiss
A member of Team Plasma. She works with Schwarz to steal Pokémon.

Whitney
Gym Leader of Goldenrod City Gym. She uses Normal Type Pokémon and gives out the Plain Badge. Ash loses to her the first time around, but strategizes better in a rematch to earn his badge.

Winona
Gym Leader for Foretree City Gym. She uses Flying Type Pokémon and gives out the Feather Badge.

Whitney

Wulfric
Gym Leader for Snowbelle City in the Kalos Region. Wulfric defeats Ash the first time around, but gives him some Pokémon Tips. Ash wins the rematch later in the season.

Xerosic
An evil scientist for Team Flare. He appears often in Season 19.

Wulfric

Yolanda
One of Brock's younger siblings

Yuzo
One of Professor Rowan's assistants, and a teacher at the Pokémon Summer Academy.

Zachary
He officiates the battles at the Foretree Gym. He runs the gym while Winona is away.

Zoey
A Pokémon Coordinator from Snowpoint City in the Sinnoh Region. She is Dawn's main rival. She is friendly and offers Dawn advice at times.

Zoey

20 POKÉMON GO TIPS AND TRICKS!

BY SCOTT GERHARDT

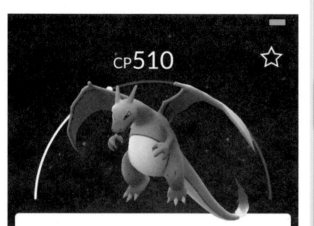

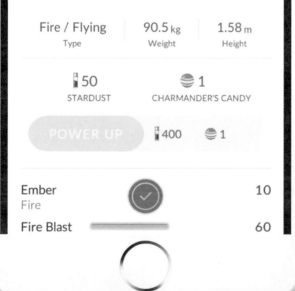

cp510

Charizard

HP 60 / 60

| Fire / Flying | 90.5 kg | 1.58 m |
| Type | Weight | Height |

50
STARDUST

1
CHARMANDER'S CANDY

POWER UP 400 1

Ember	10
Fire	
Fire Blast	60

Pokémon GO is the amazing new game that lets you do for real what you've been doing on the Game Boy and 3DS for 20 years now: be a Pokémon Hunter! Using Augmented Reality, you are able to find and catch Pokémon from your iPhone or Android.

Since its release, it's been bringing gamers out of their houses and out of the woodwork. Gamers who often might not leave home unless they have to, are now seen outside at local public gathering areas. People who were never gamers to begin with love this simple, yet thrilling game.

Of course, if you were a child of the 90s, you can't help but be nostalgic to want to catch them all! However, like any game, the more you know, the better you'll do. So, I want to share some tips that have really helped me.

1. LEARN HOW TO TIME YOUR THROWS RIGHT.

The farther away the Pokémon is, the harder you need to flick it. Green circles are Easy; Orange circles are Harder; and Red are the Hardest. You want to try to throw the ball right when the circle is the smallest – it gives you the best chance to catch them. The more you practice, the easier it gets. Also, if it's a rarer Pokémon, give yourself the best chance by feeding it a Razz Berry and use the best Pokéball you can. It's not perfect, though. Sometimes Pokémon will escape their ball and sometimes even run away. I've lost a Chansey and a Magmar this way. Don't get too frustrated by this.

2. POKÉSTOPS ARE YOUR FRIEND.

Besides giving you needed supplies, there is little way to farm Pokémon better than a Lured Pokéstop. Pokémon Lure Modules attract Pokémon for everyone. If a Pokéstop is raining pink petals, it means someone has used a Lure Module, so hang out there for awhile. The best is when you have two stops that overlap. If they are both lured, watch the Pokémon flock to you. Lured stops not only bring out Pokémon, but also bring out people, which brings me to my third point.

3. BE SOCIAL!

This is a game designed for everyone to help out. See that Hitmonchan in the area and not sure where it is? Ask to see if someone has seen it, or use a group to go out and try to find it. Remember to say thank you to someone if you know they used a lure – it might make them want to use another one again later. It can be very difficult finding some of the rare Pokémon just by yourself. People working together make things so much easier.

4. USE YOUR POKÉMON TRACKER!

That box in the bottom right of your screen is an amazing resource for you. Clicking on it will show you up to the 9 nearest Pokémon, with footprints below each one. Each footprint is about 100 meters (approximately 100 yards for those bad at the metric system). At 3 footprints, it can be hard to find something you know is within 300 meters of you, but not sure where. Once you get it down to two, the hunt grows much easier. When you finally get it to one, your search area is very small and you should find it quickly. It it very important is to note where you are whenever it changes the number of footprints. That will give you a "border" of whether you're getting hotter or colder and you can adjust your search. Having multiple people going in multiple directions makes this process a whole lot easier. Don't waste too much time, though – rare Pokémon are only there for a little while before leaving!

5. Support Local Business.

If you sit in a business or restaurant to catch Pokémon at a Pokéstop near them, make sure you buy something from them, even if it's small. If too many people come in and don't buy anything, they may stop letting you come in to do it.

6. Use Those Incubators, But Use Them Wisely.

Some of the best Pokémon can come from 10km eggs, with some good ones being in the 5km eggs as well. The 2km tend to contain very common Pokémon, but they still take up room, so you need to clear them out. Use your infinite incubator on the 2km eggs and save any other incubators for eggs of 5km or 10km. Since you only get 3 uses, would you want to only get 6km out of it, or would you rather get 15km up to 30km out of it? Maximize your efficiency and you'll need incubators less often. Either way, keep them going all the time, and don't waste time putting a 10km egg in an incubator – those are exciting and can be great. My first 10km was a Scyther and I was so happy.

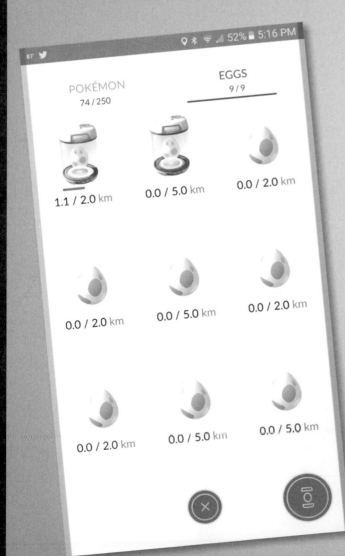

7. Don't Be In A Hurry To Evolve And Power Up Your Pokémon Too Far.

You go through levels pretty quick until you are level 20. I hit level 21 in the first 5 days. From there, it starts to become more of a grind. Don't waste too much dust and candy leveling Pokémon who will be underpowered soon. Maybe get one up pretty good, then hold the rest until about level 20. You'll be able to level up a few awesome guys then! Before you evolve, though, always level your Pokémon as much as possible first! The more you do, the more potential they have!

8. Catch Everything You Can!

Every Pokémon caught, no matter who it is, gives you candy and very important stardust. Don't think "Oh, I have enough of these". You can transfer the ones you don't need later, plus those lower ones are an important part of a strategy I cover in my next point.

9. LUCKY EGGS CAN BE A HUGE BOOST WHEN USED RIGHT.

Don't just crack an egg randomly. Use it when you're going to be in a spot, like a Pokéstop, where you're going to be catching lots of Pokémon to maximize that XP! Also, use all those Pidgeys, Weedles, and Caterpies to get a lot of XP fast. Some of those smaller double evolution Pokémon only cost 12 candy to evolve. Get a bunch to evolve at once. Some other Pokémon, like Rattata, tend to be everywhere. Even costing 25 candy each, I was able to evolve about 16 all at once. I saved up candies, then went on my Twitch stream, cracked a Lucky Egg, and started evolving all at once. Since you get 500XP for evolving (1000 if it's new for you), when doubled is 1,000XP each! I went from Level 18 to Level 21 in less than 1 hour using only 2 eggs!

10, MOVE!

You can't be a real Pokémon Hunter standing still. The better shape you're in, the longer you can hunt. Don't drive - the Incubators know when you're in a car and it won't count. Plus, you miss a lot of Pokéstops and good Pokémon driving or riding in a car because you're moving too fast. Never drive and play at the same time! Only drive if you need to go somewhere far away to look for Pokémon, which does lead to my next point:

PojoDotCom

11. FIND POKÉMON IN THEIR NATURAL ENVIRONMENT!

Water Pokémon tend to be near water, so look for oceans, rivers, lakes, creeks, streams and more. Electric Pokémon can often be found near power generators. Rock Pokémon are plentiful near mountains. Some of the ghost Pokémon will only come out at night, so prepare to hunt during the day and after the sun goes down.

12. BE SAFE AT ALL TIMES!

This means a lot of things. Always be aware of where you are so you don't run into people or things - and so they don't run into you. Also, if it's hot, wear sunscreen – I learned that lesson the hard way my first day. Have snacks and water or some replenishing drink. You can get dehydrated and tired going for long walks in the sun, so make sure you have something to eat and drink with you at all times. I have a Pokémon hunting bag that has sunscreen, a drink, a couple of snacks, and a phone charger. The best hunter is the prepared one! Sometimes you may need to take a break. Don't feel bad about sitting down for a few minutes if you need to rest – your health is more important!

15. HIT THE GYMS!

Battling is one of the best parts, so find a gym and try it. You need practice to get better, so get in there and try. The worst thing that happens is you lose and need to use a revive and potions. Remember the same Pokémon can have different attacks, so find the one with the attacks you like best! Holding gyms is the only way to earn Pokécoins without spending money, so getting good at battling can really help and it's a good source of XP.

13. MANAGE YOUR ITEMS!

Your item bag will fill quickly – don't be scared to get rid of stuff. Things like Revives and Razz Berries are useful, but you usually get too many. Keep a few and get rid of the rest. You want a lot of Pokéballs in your inventory, so make sure you always have room for more!

14. DON'T FEEL BAD ABOUT EXPANDING YOUR POKÉMON BAG SPACE.

The Pokémon Company gives you enough room for playing the game early, but as you go along your space will fill up quickly. You will want to hold more than your initial space will allow. If you can get a little money, expand your bags some, anywhere from 50-200 depending on how you play. It's very frustrating trying to catch Pokémon when you're out hunting and your bags are full. You have to stop and take care of other Pokémon to clear new ones. Don't miss a rare one because your bags are full. Something else that helps with bag space is cleaning your bags at least once a day. Transfer lower Pokémon you don't need to the Professor Willow before you go out hunting, and get some candy. This will make sure you have as much room as possible, but be careful - you don't want to accidentally transfer one you need!

16. GET A SUPPLY ROUTE.

Find a good Pokéstop "supply route" in your area – somewhere you can go to hit a number of Pokéstops and just gather supplies. Depending on how often you can get there, you might want to run the route several times. You can always keep catching while on route, but this will allow you to stock up. Stops replenish about every 5 minutes, so make sure your route takes at least that long to walk.

17. IT'S OKAY TO HAVE DUPLICATE POKÉMON.

Having more than one will let you put a powerful one in a gym and still have one or more to battle with. Plus, they should let us trade later (if they haven't already when you read this). You will want extra powerful Pokémon to trade with friends for ones you need. Even Pokémon more common for you might not be common for a friend who lives farther away, so keeping an extra could help get something you need.

18. USE INCENSE WISELY.

Incense is a mysterious fragrance that attracts Pokemon to your location. Some people use Incense when they're stuck at home. Usually a Pokemon will spawn about every 5 minutes or so. But recently, some computer nerds have discovered in the Pokemon Go coding that the spawn rate will increase to about 1 Pokemon per minute if you travel about 200 meters between spawns! So use your Incense, and get walking!

19. THE AR (AUGMENTED REALITY) IS A FUNNY THING.

It allows for you to take these really cool "real-world" pictures, but then it also subjects you to having to catch the Pokemon in real space. I personally like the AR "On" when I can get neat pictures with it. Turning the AR "Off" makes it easier to judge distance. The times I turn it off is when the server is jammed (this seems to help keep a solid connection, but I can't verify that) or when you can't take good pictures anyway, like at night. For Gym battles, I always turn it off. The first time I tried with it on I got nauseous from the camera moving around. (AR is turned on and off via the toggle on the top right of your screen.)

20. ATTACK IN PACKS!

For Gym Battles, it helps a lot if you can attack it as a team. Get 2-3 of your team together and attack it simultaneously, especially once it's level 1. You'll each get XP, plus swing the gym reputation 2000 in your direction, all at the same time. Enough people attacking simultaneously could lead to being able to put 2, 3, or even 4 Pokemon from your team in right away.

This game is a lot of fun and a great way to get outside and get in shape. Good luck and always remember to trust your instincts! Until next time, keep playing everyone!

Scott streams tips and game-play on TheGamersDome on Twitch. Pay him a visit!